Pentecostal Manifestos

James K. A. Smith and Amos Yong, *Editors*

PENTECOSTAL MANIFESTOS will provide a forum for exhibiting the next generation of Pentecostal scholarship. Having exploded across the globe in the twentieth century, Pentecostalism now enters its second century. For the past fifty years, Pentecostal and charismatic theologians (and scholars in other disciplines) have been working "internally," as it were, to articulate a distinctly Pentecostal theology and vision. The next generation of Pentecostal scholarship is poised to move beyond a merely internal conversation to an outward-looking agenda, in a twofold sense: first, Pentecostal scholars are increasingly gaining the attention of those outside Pentecostal/charismatic circles *as* Pentecostal voices in mainstream discussions; second, Pentecostal scholars are moving beyond simply reflecting on their own tradition and instead are engaging in theological and cultural analysis of a variety of issues from a Pentecostal perspective. In short, Pentecostal scholars are poised with a new boldness:

- Whereas the first generation of Pentecostal scholars was careful to learn the methods of the academy and then "apply" those to the Pentecostal tradition, the next generation is beginning to interrogate the reigning methodologies and paradigms of inquiry from the perspective of a unique Pentecostal worldview.
- Whereas the first generation of Pentecostal scholars was faithful in applying the tools of their respective trades to the work of illuminating the phenomena of modern Pentecostalism, the charismatic movements, and (now) the global renewal movements, the second generation is expanding its focus to bring a Pentecostal perspective to bear on important questions and issues that are concerns not only for Pentecostals and charismatics but also for the whole church.
- Whereas the first generation of Pentecostal/charismatic scholars was engaged in transforming the anti-intellectualism of the tradition, the second generation is engaged in contributing to and even impacting the conversations of the wider theological academy.

PENTECOSTAL MANIFESTOS will bring together both high-profile scholars and newly emerging scholars to address issues at the intersection of Pentecostalism, the global church, the theological academy, and even broader cultural concerns. Authors in PENTECOSTAL MANIFESTOS will be writing to and addressing not only their own movements but also those outside of Pentecostal/charismatic circles, offering a manifesto for a uniquely Pentecostal perspective on various themes. These will be "manifestos" in the sense that they will be bold statements of a distinctly Pentecostal interjection into contemporary discussions and debates, undergirded by rigorous scholarship.

Under this general rubric of bold, programmatic "manifestos," the series will include both shorter, crisply argued volumes that articulate a bold vision within a field as well as longer scholarly monographs, more fully developed and meticulously documented, with the same goal of engaging wider conversations. Such PENTECOSTAL MANIFESTOS are offered as intrepid contributions with the hope of serving the global church and advancing wider conversations.

PUBLISHED

Frank D. Macchia, *Justified in the Spirit: Creation, Redemption, and the Triune God* (2010)

James K. A. Smith, *Thinking in Tongues: Pentecostal Contributions to Christian Philosophy* (2010)

Wolfgang Vondey, *Beyond Pentecostalism: The Crisis of Global Christianity and the Renewal of the Theological Agenda* (2010)

Thinking in Tongues

Pentecostal Contributions
to Christian Philosophy

James K. A. Smith

WILLIAM B. EERDMANS PUBLISHING COMPANY

GRAND RAPIDS, MICHIGAN / CAMBRIDGE, U.K.

Published 2010 by

Wm. B. Eerdmans Publishing Co.

2140 Oak Industrial Drive N.E., Grand Rapids, Michigan 49505 /

P.O. Box 163, Cambridge CB3 9PU U.K.

Printed in the United States of America

16 15 14 13 12 11 10   7 6 5 4 3 2 1

Library of Congress Cataloging-in-Publication Data

Smith, James K. A., 1970-

    Thinking in tongues: pentecostal contributions to Christian philosophy /
James K. A. Smith.

        p.   cm.   — (Pentecostal manifestos)

    Includes bibliographical references and index.

    ISBN 978-0-8028-6184-9 (pbk.: alk. paper)

    1. Pentecostalism.   2. Philosophical theology.   I. Title.

BR1644.S545   2010

230'.994 — dc22

                                       2010005260

www.eerdmans.com

For Rev. Charles Swartwood,
Patrick & Dorothy St. Pierre,
and the saints at Bethel Pentecostal Tabernacle, Stratford, Ontario
for welcoming us to Pentecost;

for Rev. Ron Billings,
David & Stephanie Burton,
and our brothers & sisters at Cornerstone Christian Fellowship,
Abington, PA
for encouraging us to keep the Feast;

and

for Amos Yong,
fellow pilgrim, wise guide, and faithful friend all along the way.

Contents

Acknowledgments

When I once tried to explain this book to a friend who was not a Christian, I realized it sounded like the plot of a David Lodge farce. Indeed, the very idea of "a pentecostal philosopher" has the quirky, whimsical makings of a Wes Anderson film or a Dave Eggers story (you know the sort of plot: "When a one-armed Jewish fashion designer is put in charge of a hog production plant in Pender, Nebraska . . ."). It's easy enough to imagine a wizened Bill Murray or naive Jason Schwartzman in the lead role.

But I have been sustained by a circle of friends and colleagues who have provided the plausibility structures needed for this project to make sense and (hopefully!) resist spiraling into a vaudeville production. More importantly, they have provided support, encouragement, and opportunities for this book to become a reality. I think all the way back, for instance, to my correspondence with Ron Kydd, the first pentecostal scholar I'd ever come in contact with. His letter meant more than he could know. When I was just beginning to imagine myself as a pentecostal philosopher, I was inspired by the crew I thought of as "the Cleveland gang": Chris Thomas, Steve Land, and Rickie Moore, the first editors of the *Journal of Pentecostal Theology*. Only later was I nourished firsthand by conversations at the Society for Pentecostal Studies where, somehow, Don Dayton, Dale Irvin, Ralph Del Colle, and Frank Macchia always ended up back in the hotel room I shared with Amos Yong. Those late-night conversations have been treasured opportunities for me.

I first started to imagine this book when Blaine Charette invited me to give the Pentecostal Lectures at Northwest University in 2006. His kind-

viii

ness and hospitality were matched by Jack Wisemore and others at Northwest, for which I'm grateful. My colleague at Calvin College, Del Ratzsch, very kindly passed on to me his personal library of books, tracts, and newspapers on Pentecostalism that now constitutes the "Del Ratzsch Pentecostal Library" in my office. I'm grateful for his gift, but even more so for his encouragement. Dean Zimmerman provided critical, constructive feedback on an early draft of the book (and shouldn't be blamed for the problems that remain). Ryan Weberling provided help getting the manuscript into some semblance of a book and assisted with the index.

A grant from the John Templeton Foundation funded research on chapter 5 and, coupled with a summer research fellowship from Calvin College, enabled me to finish the manuscript. I'm grateful to Jon Pott and all the good folks at Eerdmans for their patience, and for taking a risk on this little pentecostal manifesto.

Finally I'm grateful to the gracious Spirit who sent me to the friends and communities to whom I dedicate this book. Pastor Charlie Swartwood remains a hero and treasured friend for me, and has journeyed long with our family. Patrick and Dorothy St. Pierre have long supported and prayed for me, which I value more than they know. And Bethel Pentecostal Tabernacle will always be our "home church." But we're also grateful for the saints at Cornerstone Christian Fellowship who received us when we made the pilgrimage to Philadelphia. Pastor Ron Billings holds a special place in our imagination as a generous shepherd, and Dave and Stephanie Burton will always be kindred spirits in the Spirit. Not surprisingly, Amos Yong's fingerprints are all over this book because my own pentecostal imagination has been so shaped by his friendship. It is a joy to have good work to do; it is untold joy to be able to do so with friends like Amos.

Finally, of course, my thanks to Deanna, whose pentecostal heart taught this Calvinist to dance.

*   *   *

Part of chapter 1 originally appeared as "Advice to Pentecostal Philosophers," *Journal of Pentecostal Theology* 11, no. 2 (2003): 235-47. Chapter 4 incorporates my essay "Is the Universe Open for Surprise? Pentecostal Ontology and the Spirit of Naturalism," *Zygon: Journal of Religion and Science* 43 (2008): 879-96. Material in chapter 5 is adapted from "Philosophy of Religion Takes Practice: Liturgy as Source and Method in Philosophy of Religion," in *Contemporary Practice and Method in the Philosophy of Religion:*

New Essays, ed. David Cheetham and Rolfe King (London: Continuum, 2008), pp. 133-47, and "Epistemology for the Rest of Us: Hints of a Paradigm Shift in Abraham's *Crossing the Threshold,*" *Philosophia Christi* 10 (2008): 353-61. And an earlier version of chapter 6 was published as "Tongues as Resistant Discourse: A Philosophical Perspective," in *Speaking in Tongues: Multi-Disciplinary Perspectives,* ed. Mark Cartledge (Carlisle, U.K.: Paternoster, 2006), pp. 81-110. I'm grateful to the editors and publishers of these publications for permission to include this material here.

INTRODUCTION

What Hath Athens
to Do with Azusa Street?

The oak-paneled walls of the McGill Faculty Club glistened with privilege and prestige; the room felt like it incarnated the university's global influence and vaunted heritage. The space was abuzz with the quiet, sometimes affected, chatter and conversation of scholars and fawning graduate students, awash in dark jackets, khaki trousers, and an inordinate number of bowties, it seemed to me. My first foray into the environs of the Canadian "Ivy League," I felt like an early anthropological explorer making first contact with an "exotic" world. This was a long way from Bethel Pentecostal Tabernacle, perched on the edge of Stratford, Ontario — five hundred miles east but a world away. My discomfort, tinged with just a hint of a thrill, was a product of that cultural distance — as if the trip from Bethel to McGill had stretched taut a rubber band now full of energy, but also prone to snap.

I found myself here due to the hospitality of the Canadian Theological Society (CTS). Each year, CTS sponsored a graduate student essay competition and the winner enjoyed travel and accommodations to present the winning paper at the annual meeting. In 1994 this had given me the opportunity to attend my first CTS meeting in Calgary, Alberta; having won the competition a second time, I now found myself at McGill.[1] The smaller academic world in Canada yields a kind of professional life that seems more

1. A version of that 1994 paper in Calgary later appeared as James K. A. Smith, "How to Avoid Not Speaking: Attestations," in *Knowing* Other-*wise: Philosophy on the Threshold of Spirituality,* ed. James H. Olthuis, Perspectives in Continental Philosophy Series (Bronx, NY: Fordham University Press, 1997), pp. 217-34; the 1995 paper presented at McGill later appeared as Smith, "Fire from Heaven: The Hermeneutics of Heresy," *Journal of TAK* 20 (1996): 13-31.

familiar and intimate, more widely suffused with friendship and collegiality, and so the annual banquet of CTS was a charming, lively, chatty affair. It was at this banquet that my award was announced, and upon returning to my seat a distinguished Canadian theologian sitting next to me graciously struck up a conversation. So where are you studying? Who is your adviser? What are you working on? Slowly these questions, in response to my answers, migrated to matters of faith and ecclesial identity. Since I was studying at the Institute for Christian Studies in Toronto, my interlocutor naturally asked: "And so, are you from the Dutch Reformed tradition?"

"Oh, no," I replied. "I'm a Pentecostal."

It's amazing how much human emotion and communication can be crammed into a nanosecond. By the time the word had come to the end of my tongue, I knew I had said something wrong. And before I had even finished the word, a strange brew of academic alarm and snobbery flickered across the face of my conversation partner. I can't remember if he actually coughed and choked on his dinner at that point, or whether that detail is a creation of memory, a pictorial placeholder that captures the response conveyed more covertly. In any case, the good professor could not mask his surprise and bewilderment. "You mean you grew up Pentecostal?" he further inquired. This was clearly a strategy that would allay his cognitive dissonance, as if saying to himself: "A graduate student in philosophical theology, engaging Heidegger and Derrida and Moltmann, can't possibly *be* a Pentecostal. He must have meant he *was* a Pentecostal."

"No," I replied. "I mean I worship in a Pentecostal church every Sunday. I even preach a little bit."

His strategy for resolving the cognitive dissonance denied, the conversation quickly devolved into awkward pleasantries and a final "Would you excuse me?" Left at the table to process what had just happened, I felt farther away than ever from Bethel Pentecostal Tabernacle. And yet, it was in that experience that the seeds for this book were planted.

This is not, however, an exercise in Pentecostal apologetics. I'm not out to mount a defense of Pentecostal scholarship and the perhaps scandalous idea that Pentecostals can be thinkers — though perhaps this book, as a performative apologetic, might counter the lingering assumptions of those unable to imagine something like a "Pentecostal philosophy."[2] Granted, I suppose that, in some fashion, I can't help but implicitly

2. I've already done something like this "apologetic" work in James K. A. Smith, "Scandalizing Theology: A Pentecostal Response to Noll's *Scandal*," *Pneuma: Journal of the Society*

write to my surprised interlocutor in the McGill Faculty Club. He's been with me my whole career: that astonished look of puzzlement, that submerged sneer, that masked incredulity at the very notion of a Pentecostal scholar. But I think the existence of a growing Pentecostal theological and scholarly literature is its own "defense" in this regard, and in footnotes throughout this book I will "display" this Pentecostal scholarship lest there be lingering concerns, thus informing non-Pentecostal scholars who may be unaware of Pentecostal scholarship.[3] But I am not primarily interested in demonstrating that Pentecostals can be just as smart as evangelicals or Catholics are — or more specifically, that Pentecostals can learn to do theology just as evangelicals or Catholics or Reformed folk can.[4]

Rather than an apologetic defense of Pentecostal theology, this book is meant to be an *un*apologetic articulation of the elements of a distinctly Pentecostal philosophy. In chapter 1 below, I'll pursue this further in terms of what Alvin Plantinga describes as the "integrity" of a Christian philosophy. Along these lines, there have already been clarion calls for a distinct and "indigenous" Pentecostal theology. For instance, D. Lyle Dabney has

---

for Pentecostal Studies 19 (1997): 225-38, and more recently in "Thinking in Tongues: The Past and Future of Pentecostal Theology," *First Things,* April 2008, pp. 27-31.

3. Those unaware of Pentecostal scholarship will find that a lively conversation has developed over the past forty years, beginning with the founding of the Society for Pentecostal Studies, which now includes "tracks" in biblical studies, theology, history, ecumenism, missions, practical theology, religion and culture, and (since 2002) philosophy. Similar societies have been formed in Asia, Europe, Africa, and Latin America, and there is a Pentecostal and Charismatic Movements unit within the American Academy of Religion. Scholarship is published in a global network of scholarly journals that includes *Pneuma: Journal of the Society for Pentecostal Studies,* the *Journal of Pentecostal Theology,* the *Asian Journal of Pentecostal Studies,* the *Journal of the European Pentecostal Theological Association, Australasian Pentecostal Studies,* and others. Ph.D. programs in Pentecostal studies can be found at the University of Birmingham, the Free University of Amsterdam, and the Regent University School of Divinity.

4. Unfortunately this seems to be the thrust of Rick M. Nañez, *Full Gospel, Fractured Minds? A Call to Use God's Gift of Intellect* (Grand Rapids: Zondervan, 2005), which seems to lament that Pentecostals aren't evangelicals in the mold of Mark Noll. While I have the utmost respect for Noll and the cadre of evangelical scholars of which he is the doyen, here I'm suggesting that Pentecostal scholarship is not just "evangelical" scholarship + a pneumatology, but that there is a unique "genius" implicit in Pentecostal spirituality that should yield a distinct and integral philosophy. As Terry Cross helpfully and illustratively puts it, Pentecostals are not just providing the "relish" for the evangelical "main course." See Cross, "The Rich Feast of Theology: Can Pentecostals Bring the Main Course or Only the Relish?" *Journal of Pentecostal Theology* 16 (2000): 27-47.

diagnosed "the problem and the promise of Pentecostal theology today" as akin to David's challenge with Saul's armor (1 Sam. 17):

> The problem consists in the fact that the Pentecostal theologians in [the Catholic-Pentecostal] dialogue are clearly immobilized by a set of cultural and theological assumptions that render them virtually helpless before the theological task that now faces them: they, like David of old, are clothed in "Saul's armor." But the promise shines through this dialogue in brief, enticing flashes, hinting at something that is yet just out of reach: the possibility that Pentecostal theologians might yet throw off the dead weight of the "might" and "power" of that armor and discover their own theological voice in a genuine theology of the Holy Spirit — a theological Pentecost indeed.[5]

To paraphrase Gustavo Gutiérrez, this is an attempt to show that we can "drink from our own wells."[6] Animating this is a twofold conviction: first, that implicit within Pentecostal spirituality and practice is a unique theological "genius" that — when articulated — has a distinct apostolate to the church catholic and has unique contributions to make to the broader Christian academy. Second, because of that, it is inadequate and inauthentic for Pentecostals to simply adopt "off-the-shelf" options in current theological and philosophical discussion. While I think important wisdom is to be gained in dialogue, and inescapable debts to be recognized, I also believe that Pentecostals should and can work out the implications of Pentecostal spirituality for how we think about God, ourselves, and the world, even within the discipline of philosophy. In short, my goal is not to encourage Pentecostals to drink from the wells of wider Christian philosophy in order to become "mature"[7] thinkers; rather, my goal is to

5. See especially D. Lyle Dabney, "Saul's Armor: The Problem and Promise of Pentecostal Theology Today," *Pneuma: Journal of the Society for Pentecostal Studies* 23 (2001): 115-46, at pp. 116-17. For a similar methodological manifesto, see Kenneth J. Archer, "A Pentecostal Way of Doing Theology: Method and Manner," *International Journal of Systematic Theology* (2007): 1-14. Below we will have to return to cognate issues of catholicity — how a uniquely Pentecostal theology relates to Christian theology more generally; or, in other words, how this vision for a "Pentecostal philosophy" could be nonsectarian.

6. Gustavo Gutiérrez, *We Drink from Our Own Wells: The Spiritual Journey of a People* (Maryknoll, NY: Orbis, 1984). For a more direct and explicit engagement with Gutiérrez from a Pentecostal perspective, see Eldin Villafañe, *The Liberating Spirit: Toward an Hispanic American Pentecostal Social Ethic* (Grand Rapids: Eerdmans, 1993), especially pp. 165ff.

7. The theme of "maturity" seems to emerge in a number of discussions about Pente-

sketch how we might articulate a uniquely Pentecostal philosophy, and what that Pentecostal philosophy has to offer broader conversations.

At this point, a word of definition and clarification is in order: Just what is meant by "Pentecostal" in this project of articulating a "Pentecostal philosophy"? To clarify, we need to first appreciate something of the history of Pentecostal and charismatic movements across the twentieth century. Pentecostalism is often traced to the Azusa Street revival of 1906-1913 — though there were similar but independent revivals happening before and after this around the world.[8] With deep roots in the Wesleyan-Holiness tradition and African spirituality, the Azusa Street revival engendered what came to be described as "classical" Pentecostalism associated with denominations such as the Assemblies of God, the Church of God in Christ, and the Church of God (Cleveland, Tenn.).[9] "Classical" Pentecostalism was also usually distinguished by a distinct emphasis on speaking in

---

costal theology and scholarship. The latent assumption is that Pentecostalism is inherently immature and childish, an emotional form of Christianity that needs to "grow up" and be rational — which seems to be equated with adopting the regnant paradigms in other Christian traditions, particularly evangelical models. Below I will suggest that Pentecostal thought can undergo a "maturation" process without having to become something else.

8. This is an important point made by Allan Anderson, *Spreading Fires: The Missionary Nature of Early Pentecostalism* (Maryknoll, NY: Orbis, 2007), p. 4: "Pentecostalism is not a movement that had a distinct beginning in the USA or anywhere else, or a movement that is based on a particular doctrine — it is a movement or rather a series of movements that took several years and several different formative events to emerge. Pentecostalism then as now is a polynucleated and variegated phenomenon." Cornelis van der Laan recounts a story with a similar exhortation: "When the Pentecostal assembly of Amsterdam in 1981 commemorated its seventy-fifth anniversary, an American missionary recalled how the Pentecostal message started in the United States and from there came to Europe. The next speaker was Emmanuel Schuurman, the oldest Dutch Pentecostal pioneer still alive. The aged warrior corrected his American colleague by stating that Pentecost did not come from America, but from heaven." Cornelis van der Laan, *Sectarian against His Will: Gerrit Roelof Polman and the Birth of Pentecostalism in the Netherlands* (Metuchen, NJ: Scarecrow Press, 1991), p. 1.

9. For theological backgrounds, see classic studies by Donald W. Dayton, *Theological Roots of Pentecostalism* (Peabody, MA: Hendrickson, 1987), and Walter J. Hollenweger, *The Pentecostals* (London: SCM, 1972). On Azusa Street and its aftermath, see Grant Wacker, *Heaven Below: Early Pentecostals and American Culture* (Cambridge, MA: Harvard University Press, 2001), and Cecil M. Robeck, *The Azusa Street Mission and Revival: The Birth of the Global Pentecostal Movement* (Nashville: Nelson, 2006), though one should note Anderson's concern about "Azusacentrism." For a classic account of the emergence of a "classical" Pentecostal denomination, the Assemblies of God, see Edith L. Blumhofer, *Restoring the Faith: The Assemblies of God, Pentecostalism, and American Culture* (Urbana: University of Illinois Press, 1993).

tongues as "the initial physical evidence of baptism of the Holy Spirit." Taking up "second work" theologies from their Wesleyan heritage, which emphasized an experience of grace and sanctification subsequent to and distinct from salvation, "classical" Pentecostal theology identified this as baptism in the Holy Spirit "evidenced" by speaking in tongues — though they also emphasized the continued manifestation of *all* the gifts of the Spirit. And all this energizing of the Spirit was directed toward empowerment for mission.[10]

In the 1960s and 1970s, Pentecostal-like phenomena and experiences began to be seen in more mainline denominations and traditional churches. This was identified as the "charismatic renewal" and signaled a spillover of Pentecostal spirituality into traditional communions; it included the Catholic charismatic renewal (first begun at Duquesne) as well as renewal movements in Anglican, Lutheran, and Presbyterian traditions.[11] While the spirituality and practices shared certain similarities, especially an emphasis on the Spirit's surprise and the continued operation of even the "miraculous" gifts, the charismatic movement did not adopt the classical Pentecostal notion of "initial evidence." So capital-P Pentecostalism is usually taken to refer to classical Pentecostalism; "charismatic" identifies those traditions and theologians who also emphasize a central role for the Spirit's gifts, but within existing liturgical and theological frameworks. These were later followed by what is often called the "third wave" or "neopentecostal" movement associated with Peter Wagner. This refers to the growth of nondenominational charismatic churches such as Vineyard Fellowship. Like the charismatic renewal, third wave charismatics do not affirm initial evidence, but neither do they identify with traditional denominations or communions (such as the Roman Catholic Church or the Anglican Communion).

While there are important differences between classical Pentecostals, charismatics, and "third wavers," important similarities are also shared across these movements, particularly regarding the centrality of the Spirit, the gifts, and the shape of Pentecostal/charismatic spirituality. Thus some,

10. Robert P. Menzies, *Empowered for Witness: The Spirit in Luke-Acts* (Sheffield: Sheffield Academic Press, 1991), and Frank D. Macchia, *Baptized in the Spirit: A Global Pentecostal Theology* (Grand Rapids: Zondervan, 2006), pp. 75-85.

11. For a synopsis, see Peter D. Hocken, "Charismatic Movement," in *The New International Dictionary of Pentecostal and Charismatic Movements,* ed. Stanley Burgess (Grand Rapids: Zondervan, 2002), pp. 477-519. See also Michael P. Hamilton, ed., *The Charismatic Movement* (Grand Rapids: Eerdmans, 1975).

like Douglas Jacobsen, have adopted the nomenclature of "small-*p*" pentecostalism as a way of honoring the diversity of pentecostal/charismatic theolog*ies* while at the same time recognizing important family resemblances and shared sensibilities.[12] Indeed, the charismatic movement has been a crucial factor in the development of ecumenical dialogue. Protestant Pentecostals and Catholic charismatics found that a shared experience was an important start to honest and open conversations about what they shared in common and where they disagreed.[13]

So, by "pentecostal" I mean to refer not to a classical or denominational definition, but rather to an understanding of Christian faith that is radically open to the continued operations of the Spirit. Thus I use "Pentecostal" in an older, generous sense, which would now include "charismatic" traditions (and I myself identify as charismatic, not Pentecostal). But since the convention Pentecostal/charismatic is so burdensome, henceforth I will employ the convention of small-*p* "pentecostalism" to refer to the broader "renewal" or Pentecostal/charismatic traditions.[14] Thus when I advocate a pentecostal philosophy, "pentecostal" is meant to be a gathering term, indicating a shared set of practices and theological intuitions that are shared by Pentecostals, charismatics, and "third wavers." I would hope, for instance, that Catholic and Anglican charismatics would see and hear their own faith practices informing what I'm calling a "pentecostal" philosophy.

Granted, we will need to unpack just what constitutes the shared constellation of spiritual practices and theological intuitions I'm calling "pentecostal." That will be the task of chapters 1 and 2 below. Here let me just indicate that I will *not* define "pentecostal" *theologically;* that is, I do not locate the center or defining traits of pentecostalism in a set of doctrines. Instead, I will unpack the elements that make up what I'll describe as a

12. See Douglas Jacobsen, *Thinking in the Spirit: Theologies of the Early Pentecostal Movement* (Bloomington: Indiana University Press, 2003), pp. 8-12.

13. See Kilian McDonnell, "Improbable Conversations: The International Classical Pentecostal/Roman Catholic Dialogue," *Pneuma: The Journal of the Society for Pentecostal Studies* 17 (1995): 163-88.

14. In this sense, I'm using the term "pentecostal" in a way that is similar to Mark Cartledge's use of the term "charismatic" in *Encountering the Spirit: The Charismatic Tradition* (Maryknoll, NY: Orbis, 2006), p. 18 and passim. Cartledge reserves "Pentecostal" and "Pentecostalism" for specific denominations. I have opted to not simply use the term "charismatic" since the lexical range of the term seems just a bit too expansive such that a "charismatic philosophy" might simply be taken to be an "enthusiastic" philosophy; in this respect, I think "pentecostal philosophy" is more immediately descriptive.

pentecostal "worldview" or, following Charles Taylor, a pentecostal "social imaginary." I do so to honor the lived nature of pentecostalism as a *spirituality*, an embodied set of practices and disciplines that implicitly "carry" a worldview or social imaginary.[15] One of the tasks of a pentecostal philosophy, I'll suggest, is to work at articulating the worldview that is implicit in pentecostal spirituality. On the other hand, I will also suggest that a philosophy can be "pentecostal" only insofar as it is nourished and fueled by the intuitions that are implicit in pentecostal spirituality.[16]

While I hope such a project will serve pentecostal philosophers, theologians, and scholars, I'm primarily interested in articulating a pentecostal philosophy in order to join conversations beyond the environs of Pentecostal and charismatic Christianity. So I don't aim to articulate a sectarian pentecostal philosophy for pentecostals; rather, I'm interested in making a pentecostal contribution to Christian philosophy. My conviction is that there are elements of a pentecostal worldview that are, one might say, "simply Christian"; that is, I don't see these aspects of pentecostal spirituality as optional add-ons to Christian faith. Pentecost is in the DNA of the holy, catholic, apostolic church. Insofar as the pentecostal and charismatic renewal has reminded the church of her pentecostal heritage, pentecostal spirituality is a catholic spirituality. In addition, I believe there are aspects of pentecostal spirituality and practice that uniquely stretch and challenge some of our settled philosophical frameworks. In this respect, I see the fledgling project of a pentecostal philosophy as analogous to the philosophical program that came to be described as "Re-

15. Cp. Hollenweger's final chapter of *The Pentecostals*: "Practice as a Theological Statement," pp. 497-511. More recently, Steven J. Land has sought to honor pentecostalism as a *spirituality* and to see that spirituality and its practices *as* theology (see Land, *Pentecostal Spirituality: A Passion for the Kingdom,* Journal of Pentecostal Theology Supplement 1 [Sheffield: Sheffield Academic Press, 1993], pp. 15-57). Cartledge also describes a charismatic "spirituality" as something "akin to a 'worldview'" (*Encountering the Spirit,* p. 27).

16. I grant that the prospect for a distinctly pentecostal philosophy assumes, and is indebted to, wider projects that have articulated the possibility of *Christian* philosophy. I can float the rather outlandish idea of a pentecostal philosophy only because philosophers such as Alvin Plantinga, Nicholas Wolterstorff, Eleonore Stump, and C. Stephen Evans have already laid the groundwork by articulating and defending the shape of a Christian philosophy more generally. In this respect, I should also note that, for the most part, the renaissance in "Christian philosophy" has largely amounted to a renaissance in merely "theistic" philosophy. Insofar as the more specific aspects of a distinctly *Christian* philosophy remain underdeveloped, the more specific notion of a *pentecostal* philosophy will seem proportionately outlandish. (My thanks to Del Ratzsch for a helpful conversation on this point.)

formed epistemology."[17] Reformed epistemology, drawing on theological intuitions in John Calvin and the Reformed tradition, articulated an epistemological framework whose cachet was not limited to philosophers working within Reformed confessional frameworks; in other words, while the impetus for this epistemological revolution unabashedly drew upon the particularity of the Reformed tradition, the model was articulated *for* a much wider audience. And given the broad reception of the program, one might surmise that this particular tradition had something to offer to the wider philosophical community and Christian academy. My hope is that the articulation of a pentecostal philosophy might have the same wide purchase — that it might offer philosophical insights and frameworks that can be productively received beyond those philosophers who could identify as pentecostal or charismatic. However, this is a first shot across the bow — more of a (perhaps indecent) proposal that sketches the outlines of such a program rather than accomplishing it. I hope it might be received as an impetus for others to join in the work.

How shall we go about this task? Before diving into the project itself, let me note three methodological procedures that will be operating throughout the book. First, as already suggested, and as will be unpacked in chapter 2, my goal is to make explicit what is implicit in pentecostal spirituality and worship; in other words, one of the tasks of a pentecostal philosophy is to articulate the worldview that is latent within pentecostal practice.[18] Because pentecostalism is primarily a *spirituality* — what Land describes as an "integration of beliefs and practices in the affections which are themselves evoked and expressed by those beliefs"[19] — a pentecostal worldview is not a set of doctrines or dogmas. Instead, latent, implicit theological and philosophical intuitions are embedded within, and enacted by, pentecostal rituals and practices.[20] In talking about a "pentecostal philosophy," I don't want

17. On Reformed epistemology, see Alvin Plantinga and Nicholas Wolterstorff, eds., *Faith and Rationality: Reason and Belief and God* (Notre Dame, IN: University of Notre Dame Press, 1983), and Kelly James Clark, *Return to Reason: A Critique of Enlightenment Evidentialism, and a Defense of Reason and Belief in God* (Grand Rapids: Eerdmans, 1990). I don't mean to suggest overlapping intuitions between pentecostal philosophy and Reformed epistemology, though one should note the important role of the Spirit in Plantinga's *Warranted Christian Belief* (New York: Oxford University Press, 2000), chapter 8.

18. In chapter 2 I will distinguish this from the task of pentecostal *theology*, though I'm not concerned with neat and tidy boundaries between the two.

19. Land, *Pentecostal Spirituality*, p. 13. Cartledge describes charismatic spirituality as a framework of narrative, symbols, and praxis (*Encountering the Spirit*, pp. 28-30).

20. Granted, classic Pentecostals will not be entirely comfortable with "ritual" lan-

to intellectualize pentecostalism; I'm not out to disclose the propositional core of pentecostalism. Rather, I'm interested in mining and "reading" pentecostal spirituality in order to discern the "understanding" of the world that is implicit in these practices.[21] Of course, that means one will best be able to appreciate and understand this project only if one also has some familiarity with the practices that make up the lived religious experience that is pentecostal spirituality. I cannot hope to introduce or summarize pentecostalism by drawing up a list of doctrinal claims or dogmatic propositions. Pentecostalism is not first and foremost a doctrinal or intellectual tradition; it is an affective constellation of practices and embodied "rituals." In Wittgensteinian terms, we could say that pentecostal spirituality is "a form of life."[22] Thus, in articulating the intuitions implicit in this spirituality, I will be reading practices, not texts, though limited space means that I cannot reproduce rich ethnographic descriptions. Those readers unfamiliar with pentecostal spirituality will find helpful descriptions in the explosion of social scientific literature on pentecostalism, particularly work in anthropology and other ethnographic fields.[23]

Second, I will philosophically grapple with pentecostal spirituality and practice as a *limit case*. The marginality — one might say "liminality"[24] —

---

guage, but for an analysis of pentecostal spirituality through the lens of ritual studies, from a pentecostal perspective, see Daniel Albrecht, *Rites in the Spirit: A Ritual Approach to Pentecostal/Charismatic Spirituality* (Sheffield: Sheffield Academic Press, 1999). For an analysis of Catholic charismatic spirituality, see Thomas J. Csordas, *The Sacred Self: A Cultural Phenomenology of Charismatic Healing* (Berkeley: University of California Press, 1994), and Csordas, *Language, Charisma, and Creativity: The Ritual Life of a Religious Movement* (Berkeley: University of California Press, 1997).

21. In chapter 2 it will become clear that I am indebted to Charles Taylor and Robert Brandom for this way of formulating the project.

22. Ludwig Wittgenstein, *Philosophical Investigations*, 3rd ed., trans. G. E. M. Anscombe (New York: Macmillan, 1958), §23. So perhaps, paradoxically, I am offering a "cultural-linguistic" account of pentecostal spirituality despite the fact that it seems to be a quintessential example of what George Lindbeck would describe as an "experiential-expressive" religious framework (Lindbeck, *The Nature of Doctrine: Religion and Theology in a Postliberal Age* [Philadelphia: Westminster, 1984], p. 16).

23. On this score, see the work of Csordas noted above and Donald Miller, *Global Pentecostalism: The New Face of Christian Social Engagement* (Berkeley: University of California Press, 2007), which also includes a DVD of pentecostal worship and ministry.

24. As employed by Victor Turner, *The Ritual Process: Structure and Anti-Structure* (Ithaca, NY: Cornell University Press, 1977). For a development of this notion with respect to pentecostalism, see Albrecht, *Rites in the Spirit;* Craig Scandrett-Leatherman, "Can Social Scientists Dance? Participating in Science, Spirit, and Social Reconstruction as an Anthro-

of pentecostal spirituality vis-à-vis the dominant practices of the Christian tradition(s) makes it a kind of theoretical provocateur.[25] For instance, as I'll explore in chapter 6 below, the pentecostal practice of glossolalia ("speaking in tongues") presents a unique case and challenge to the received paradigms in philosophy of language. The phenomenon eludes existing reified categories and contests the dominant, settled frameworks for thinking about language. Because it is such a marginal, and therefore largely unknown, practice, the reality of glossolalia rarely (if ever) makes it onto the theoretical radar of philosophers of language, even Christian philosophers. But I will suggest that confronting philosophy of language with the lived reality of glossolalia is philosophically productive insofar as it pushes us to interrogate the staid categories with which we have become philosophically comfortable.[26] I think this is true across a range of philosophical questions in metaphysics, epistemology, and philosophy of religion. Our philosophical categories are calibrated to a certain range of phenomena and experience; when we encounter phenomena outside that range, the experience stretches and contests those categories and frameworks, forcing us to retool and reconfigure our assumptions, categories, and methodologies.[27] For instance, an overly rationalist conception of human persons and the nature of the belief will not be primed to appreciate the nature of a spirituality that is more affective and embodied (as I'll sug-

---

pologist and Afropentecostal," in *Science and the Spirit: A Pentecostal Engagement with the Sciences*, ed. James K. A. Smith and Amos Yong (Bloomington: Indiana University Press, 2010); and Margaret Poloma, "Glossolalia, Liminality, and Empowered Kingdom Building: A Sociological Perspective," in *Speaking in Tongues: Multi-Disciplinary Perspectives*, ed. Mark Cartledge (Milton Keynes, U.K.: Paternoster, 2006), pp. 169-73.

25. Perhaps the marginality of pentecostal spirituality is most intensely seen in the serpent-handling tradition in the Appalachians, which takes seriously the pentecostal epilogue to Mark's Gospel: "And these signs shall follow them that believe; In my name shall they cast out devils; they shall speak with new tongues; They shall take up serpents; and if they drink any deadly thing, it shall not hurt them; they shall lay hands on the sick, and they shall recover" (Mark 16:17-18 KJV). For a comprehensive discussion, see Ralph W. Hood, Jr., and W. Paul Williamson, *Them That Believe: The Power and Meaning of the Christian Serpent-Handling Tradition* (Berkeley: University of California Press, 2008).

26. I think this encounter is also mutually beneficial insofar as grappling with philosophy of language becomes an occasion for pentecostals to critically reflect upon their experience as well as the institutional frameworks in which such a practice is embedded.

27. One can see a similar challenge for social scientific accounts of pentecostal spirituality. See Hood and Williamson's delineation of the problem with "empiricist-analytic psychology" and their proposal for a hermeneutic and phenomenological approach in *Them That Believe*, appendix 3, pp. 247-56.

gest in chapter 5, I think this is precisely the case with the regnant paradigms in philosophy of religion). In that case, an encounter with pentecostal spirituality will point up the narrowness and insufficiency of current
paradigms. More broadly, I will argue that implicit in pentecostal spirituality and the experience of pentecostal worship are philosophical and
theological "intuitions" (I use the word loosely) that, when made explicit,
offer challenges to received wisdom and the status quo.[28] Far from being a
seething bed of emotionalist anti-intellectualism, then, pentecostal spirituality can be a source for philosophical *critique*.

     In concert with this emphasis on pentecostal spirituality as lived prac-
tice, a third methodological strategy will be operative throughout the
book: a constructive role for testimony, witness, and story. Upon first discovering the *Journal of Pentecostal Theology,* I can still recall reading the
opening editorial that described testimony as "the poetry of Pentecostal
experience."[29] This resonated deeply with my own experience of pentecostal worship and spirituality wherein testimony played a central role in the
shape of gathered worship and in the narration of one's identity in Christ.
In worship at Bethel Pentecostal Tabernacle, Pastor Swartwood would regularly make room for "God sightings" — an open time for the saints to
share the story of God's work in their lives, to share testimonies of the
Spirit's surprises in the past week, to give God praise and glory for healing
or the return of a prodigal child, to attest to the love and compassion of a
God who knew the number of hairs on our head and who knew we needed
rent money by Friday. Testimony is central to pentecostal spirituality because it captures the dynamic sense that God is active and present in our
world and in our personal experience while also emphasizing the
narrativity of pentecostal spirituality.[30] This is also bound up with what
Hollenweger has called the "orality" of pentecostal spirituality. As he
acerbically comments, "the Pentecostal poor are oral, nonconceptual peo-

---

28. At the conclusion of chapter 6 I'll explore this "liminality" of pentecostal experi-
ence as a mode of what David Bromley describes as "spiritual edgework" in Bromley, "On
Spiritual Edgework: The Logic of Extreme Ritual Performances," *Journal for the Scientific
Study of Religion* 46 (2007): 287-303.

29. Steven J. Land, Rick D. Moore, and John Christopher Thomas, "Editorial," *Journal
of Pentecostal Theology* 1 (1992): 5.

30. I will attend to the dynamics of pentecostal narrative epistemology in chapter 3 below. For a Christian philosophical reflection on the importance of narrative, see Kelly James
Clark, "Story-Shaped Lives in *Big Fish,*" in *Faith, Film, and Philosophy,* ed. R. Douglas Geivett
and James S. Spiegel (Downers Grove, IL: InterVarsity, 2007), pp. 37-51.

ples who are often masters of story. Their religion resembles more of the early disciples than religion taught in our schools and universities."[31] And there is something *irreducible* about this mode of testimony — it cannot be simply reduced to a mere pool for extracting philosophical propositions, nor can it be simply translated into theological dogmas.[32]

Thus one might suggest that *memoir* is the consummate pentecostal theological genre. Or at the very least, something like testimony is integral to even pentecostal theorizing, even if this is not properly "academic."[33] In fact, this is just one performative way that pentecostal theoretical practice evinces an aspect implicit in pentecostal spirituality: against the Enlightenment ideal of the impersonal, impartial, abstract "knower," pentecostalism affirms an affective, involved, confessing knower who "knows that she knows that she knows" *because of* her story, *because of* a narrative, she can tell about a relationship with God. Thus I have appreciated that pentecostal theologians such as Amos Yong and Frank Macchia have eschewed academic decorum and instead embraced the centrality of testimony in their pentecostal theorizing, seeing such narratives as central to the theological

31. Walter Hollenweger, "The Pentecostal Elites and the Pentecostal Poor: A Missed Dialogue?" in *Charismatic Christianity as a Global Culture,* ed. Karla Poewe (Columbia: University of South Carolina Press, 1994), p. 213.

32. This has been the burden of Kenneth Archer's work on story as the central "hermeneutic" for pentecostal spirituality and, hence, for pentecostal theology. See Kenneth J. Archer, "Pentecostal Story: The Hermeneutical Filter for the Making of Meaning," *Pneuma: Journal of the Society for Pentecostal Studies* 26 (2004): 36-59. Thus he later cautions against Pentecostal theologians abandoning such narrative intuitions in their theologizing, cautioning that, even if their task might be to "explain" the story, it is important to appreciate the irreducibility *of* story. In short, we need a pentecostal theological methodology that resonates with the narrative character of pentecostal spirituality. Thus Archer cautions, "In explaining, Pentecostals may opt for modernistic epistemological modes that are inherently hostile to Pentecostal practices of story-telling and testimony" (Archer, "A Pentecostal Way," p. 6). I'm trying to heed the same admonition in developing a pentecostal philosophy.

33. On this point, I think a pentecostal philosophy resonates with a critique of philosophical methodology that has been articulated by feminist philosophers who have argued for the significance of narrative and taking seriously our "standpoint." In their critique of the methodological status quo, these feminist critiques make room for autobiography and narrative testimony. For related discussion, see Lorraine Code, *What Can She Know? Feminist Theory and the Construction of Knowledge* (Ithaca, NY: Cornell University Press, 1991); Hilde Lindemann Nelson, *Damaged Identities, Narrative Repair* (Ithaca, NY: Cornell University Press, 2001); Susan Sherwin, "Philosophical Methodology and Feminist Methodology: Are They Compatible?" in *Feminist Perspectives: Philosophical Essays on Method and Morals,* ed. Lorraine Code et al. (Toronto: University of Toronto Press, 1988); and most winsomely, Christine Overall, "Writing What Comes Naturally?" *Hypatia* 23 (2008): 227-35.

task.[34] In a similar way, I see the testimonies and narratives included here as integral to the sensibility that characterizes a pentecostal philosophy.

With these three methodological procedures in play, my goal is to articulate and make explicit the philosophical intuitions that are implicit in pentecostal spirituality and practice, with a view to sketching the shape of a distinctly "pentecostal philosophy." Chapter 1, echoing Alvin Plantinga's "Advice to Christian Philosophers," is something of a manifesto for the very idea of a pentecostal philosophy, laying the ground for the articulation of that in chapters 2–4. In chapter 2 I unpack the elements of a pentecostal "worldview" and then explore the philosophical implications for that in terms of epistemology (chapter 3) and ontology (chapter 4). Chapter 4 also functions as a sort of transitional chapter, taking up a more specific "case" of philosophical engagement from a pentecostal perspective — namely, questions about naturalism in relation to science. This is followed by two more "case studies" that are meant to function as examples of a pentecostal philosophy "at work," so to speak, while also addressing core issues of pentecostal spirituality. Chapter 5 argues that the very nature of pentecostal spirituality, worship, and practice poses a liminal challenge to the regnant paradigms in philosophy of religion, which are largely primed for the "heady" religion of more mainstream Protestantism. I'll argue for a certain revolution in the methodology in philosophy of religion as the only way to properly honor the lived reality of pentecostal experience. Chapter 6 considers a hallmark of pentecostal identity — glossolalia, or "speaking in tongues" — as a liminal challenge to the regnant paradigms in philosophy of language while also suggesting that implicit in tongues-speech is a sociopolitical critique of the status quo. In short, it suggests that philosophy of language and ethics are intertwined in important ways and that such an intuition is implicit in pentecostal experience.

In the end, I don't want to promise too much for this little book. It makes no claim to being exhaustive or even comprehensive. It is offered in the mode of both a manifesto and a sketch and is thus programmatic in two senses. On the one hand, my goal is to articulate a (rather scandalous) call for a distinctly pentecostal philosophy, but not just for pentecostals. Rather, the wager is that a distinctly pentecostal philosophy has something

---

34. In Amos Yong, *Discerning the Spirit(s): A Pentecostal-Charismatic Contribution to Christian Theology of Religions* (Sheffield: Sheffield Academic Press, 2000), and Yong, *Theology and Down Syndrome: Reimagining Disability in Late Modernity* (Waco, TX: Baylor University Press, 2007), each chapter opens with a narrative testimony. Similarly, Macchia's *Baptized in the Spirit* opens with and intersperses testimony throughout.

unique to contribute to wider conversations in Christian philosophy and has gifts to offer that can be received by those not necessarily identified with the pentecostal or charismatic traditions. On the other hand, I'm trying to sketch the outlines and elements of such a philosophy, hopefully modeling a certain philosophical procedure while also laying out a program for further research to be taken up by others. The studies here are exploratory forays, a first report from early reconnaissance, not the final statement on the matter. At times I worry that the "sketch" or "outline" amounts to little more than a cartoon. But if it can function as a cartoon in its older sense — a preparatory outline for a fuller painting or tapestry — then this little manifesto will have done its work. Edward Burne-Jones and William Morris, Pre-Raphaelite collaborators on tapestries and stained glass, created a host of such "cartoons" that would then be executed by a team of artisans, transforming the outlines of angels into the sumptuous, prismatic colors of stained-glass narratives. The hope for this "outline" of pentecostal philosophy is that other artisans will join me in filling in the colors.

1 Thinking in Tongues

Advice to Pentecostal Philosophers

I must begin with a confession: my vision for a pentecostal philosophy owes an original debt to Calvinists. In fact, the chapter subtitle hearkens back to my junior year in college: sitting in chapel, I excitedly opened a letter from the University of Notre Dame. Several weeks earlier I had the audacity to write a personal letter to one of the leading figures in philosophy of religion: Alvin Plantinga, then recently appointed as John A. O'Brien Professor of Philosophy at Notre Dame and a key figure in a Christian renewal in philosophy both at Notre Dame and across the profession. Just before that I had come across Plantinga's 1983 inaugural address given on the occasion of this appointment and later published as "Advice to Christian Philosophers."[1] Plantinga's manifesto was my *tolle lege*[2] moment, my wake-up call to a vocation. Having heard what I believed was God's call to become a Christian philosopher — through my concurrent reading of

---

1. Alvin Plantinga, "Advice to Christian Philosophers," *Faith and Philosophy* 1 (1984): 253-71. (Subsequent references will be included in parentheses in the text.) One should note that this also appears in the inaugural volume of *Faith and Philosophy*, the journal of the Society of Christian Philosophers that has now grown into the leading society in its field and is an important model for Christian academics. In some ways this spawned more specific societies such as the Evangelical Philosophical Society (publisher of *Philosophia Christi*), the Wesleyan Philosophical Society, and the Philosophy Interest Group of the Society for Pentecostal Studies. (An earlier draft of this chapter was presented in the inaugural year of the latter.)

2. Augustine, *Confessions*, trans. H. Chadwick (Oxford: Oxford University Press, 1998), 8.12.28.

other Calvinists, like W. G. T. Shedd's *Dogmatic Theology* and Francis Schaeffer's *Trilogy* — I began to contemplate graduate study in philosophy and turned to the obvious place: Plantinga and Notre Dame. The letter I opened was Professor Plantinga's gracious reply that encouraged me in my pursuits. And while my training would take place at another Catholic university — and in quite a different philosophical tradition — I am happy in this chapter, which sketches a vision for a distinctly pentecostal philosophy, to repay something of a debt to Plantinga's influential vision for an integrally Christian philosophy and his personal encouragement to an aspiring Christian philosopher.

Plantinga's "Advice" quickly became something of a manifesto for a movement of Christian, and largely evangelical,[3] philosophers — a call to them to exercise "Christian courage" and "display more faith, more trust in the Lord" in their development of an "integral" Christian philosophy. "We must," he urges, "put on the whole armor of God" (p. 254). I want to issue a similar call to the community of pentecostal scholars to have the same courage — maybe even "Holy Ghost boldness" — in the development of a distinctly and integrally pentecostal philosophy. I will do so by engaging Plantinga's program for Christian philosophy, then considering how a pentecostal philosophy should further develop this program.

Excursus: Why a Pentecostal Philosophy?

But before doing so, I need to first answer some questions. I can anticipate — and have heard — several initial reactions and objections to the notion of a "pentecostal philosophy." The first comes from my brothers and sisters in the Pentecostal and charismatic communities who, quoting Colossians 2:8, have grave concerns about philosophy per se and are concerned that a "pentecostal philosophy" would be akin to "pentecostal transcendental meditation." Since they do not constitute my audience here, however, I will limit my comments to one point of reply: Paul's concern in the letter to Christians in Colossae is not philosophy per se but a specific philosophy that undermined Christian faith and was founded "according to human

3. However, the renaissance in Christian philosophy spawned by Plantinga, Nicholas Wolterstorff, Bill Alston, and the Society of Christian Philosophers has also been a catalyst for a renewal in Catholic philosophical circles and the American Catholic Philosophical Association (see the work of Linda Zagzebski, John Zeis, John Haldane, and others).

tradition" rather than revelation. Paul speaks of "*the* philosophy," indicating a particular philosophical school that would have been known by the Colossian Christians. The point is illustrated by how he qualifies this philosophy: it is "according to the tradition of men, according to the elementary principles of the world, *rather than* according to Christ" (Col. 2:8). This final apposition points to the possibility of a philosophy that *would be* "according to Christ."[4] In addition, Paul himself employs philosophical reasoning in his proclamation of the gospel (e.g., Acts 17), and other NT authors, particularly in the Johannine tradition, take up philosophical concepts (such as *logos*) to communicate the Christian faith.

The second set of reservations would be expressed by scholars from within the pentecostal community and has two aspects: First, do we really need a "philosophy"? Are not the questions that such a philosophy pursues already broached by our theologians? Doesn't the development of a pentecostal philosophy run the risk of treading upon pentecostal theology's turf? Second, if we do need a philosophy, shouldn't it be enough that it be a *Christian* philosophy? Can we not simply adopt the conclusions of other Christian and evangelical philosophers?

In response to the first aspect of this concern, it is important to distinguish between the different tasks of a philosophy and a theology and the corresponding distinction between their "fields" of concern. First, we might distinguish between "religion" (or "spirituality"), on the one hand, and theology and philosophy on the other: both theology and philosophy are modes of second-order reflection on our lived faith or religion, which indicates our pretheoretical, fundamental commitments implicit and embedded in practices and disciplines of the faith.[5] As Wittgenstein's aphoristic interjection suggests, theology is akin to grammar, whereas lived religion or spirituality — the lived practices of faith — are akin to "speaking

---

4. For a helpful commentary on the Greek text, see F. F. Bruce, *The Epistles to the Colossians, to Philemon, and to the Ephesians,* New International Commentary on the New Testament (Grand Rapids: Eerdmans, 1984), pp. 97-99.

5. I develop this distinction in more detail in James K. A. Smith, *Introducing Radical Orthodoxy: Mapping a Post-secular Theology* (Grand Rapids: Baker Academic, 2004), pp. 166-79. According to the rubric there, what I'm here calling "theology" would be equivalent to "theology$_2$." In this respect, I completely concur with Kenneth Archer's claim that "[w]orship is our [i.e., pentecostal] primary way of doing theology" (Kenneth J. Archer, "A Pentecostal Way of Doing Theology: Method and Manner," *International Journal of Systematic Theology* [2007]: 9). This is why I described worship as "theology$_1$" in *Introducing Radical Orthodoxy.*

the language."[6] A grammar is a second-order articulation of the norms and rules that are implicit when competent users speak the language — and one can be a competent user of the language without necessarily being able to articulate the grammar. One might operate with a competent but implicit understanding of such grammatical norms and rules. In a similar way, theology and philosophy are articulations of what is implicit in a religion or spirituality (understood as a constellation of practices and rituals that embody the faith). Theology and philosophy, as theoretical modes of reflection, bubble up from pretheoretical faith. Thus pentecostal spirituality or "religion" is not first and foremost a "theology" (which is theoretical) but, more fundamentally, a kind of "worldview" (which is pretheoretical). Such a pentecostal worldview — the constellation of practices and beliefs that constitute pentecostal spirituality — should then undergird both a pentecostal theology *and* a pentecostal philosophy. What distinguishes the theology from the philosophy is not its *faith basis* (as though philosophy were somehow neutral or autonomous)[7] but rather its *field* or *topic.* Theology might be described as a "special science" that investigates and explicates our being-toward-God and God's revelation of himself in the Scriptures. As such, theology ought to be done in the church, by the church, and for the church;[8] in addition, it ought to be always a *biblical* theology rooted in revelation and investigating the narrative of Scripture and the dogmas of the church that arise from that (classical loci such as incarnation, sin, grace, and eschatological hope). Philosophy, on the other hand, also undergirded by (pentecostal) faith, investigates fundamental questions of ontology and epistemology: the nature of reality and knowl-

---

6. Ludwig Wittgenstein, *Philosophical Investigations,* 3rd ed., trans. G. E. M. Anscombe (Oxford: Blackwell, 1952), §373: "(Theology as grammar)."

7. For my critique of this notion of an "autonomous, neutral" philosophy that operates on the basis of "pure, unaided human reason" (including a critique of Plantinga's version), see James K. A. Smith, "The Art of Christian Atheism: Faith and Philosophy in Early Heidegger," *Faith and Philosophy* 14 (1997): 71-81.

8. One of the laudatory elements of Plantinga's "Advice" is to remind us that Christian philosophers also do their work for the sake of the church. This is reemphasized by Merold Westphal in his "Taking Plantinga Seriously," *Faith and Philosophy* 16 (1999): 173-81, where he calls on Christian philosophers to "close the gap between metaphysics and spirituality" (p. 180) and develop "a different way of doing metaphysics, one in which metaphysical reflection grows . . . directly out of practices of prayer and public action" (p. 181). While Plantinga's work provides a seminal model, I would recommend Westphal's work in Christian philosophy as another important resource and example of integral Christian philosophy.

edge.[9] If the theologian asks, "How can we know God?" the philosopher asks, "How can we know?" The latter is not a neutral question — and no answer to that question will be religiously neutral. So it's *not* the case that the philosopher is "objective" and "rational" whereas the theologian is biased and committed. Our philosophical reflection is also always already informed by pretheoretical faith commitments. But the philosopher is asking questions that are more *formal*. Because of this, the philosopher has a different methodological formation (with a specific focus of argumentation and analysis) as well as a different set of conversation partners across time.[10] While these aspects of philosophy are historically contingent, they do mean that philosophy today constitutes a different universe of discourse from theology.

There is a further complication of this relationship between faith, philosophy, and theology: historically, philosophy has often provided the basic concepts *(Grundbegriffe)* that theology employs.[11] Thus theology has to be suspicious of what's "loaded" into the philosophical concepts it employs. If no philosophy is religiously neutral, then the Christian theologian must be critically aware of the *religious* assumptions that are implicit in philosophical concepts and frameworks. Ideally, Christian theology should find its basic concepts in an integrally *Christian* philosophy — which should itself be nourished by a Christian spirituality or "worldview." In a similar but more specific manner, pentecostal theology should utilize basic concepts forged in a *pentecostal* philosophy.[12] And just as an integral pen-

9. I have provided a more detailed account of the relationship between theology and philosophy in my "Scandalizing Theology: A Pentecostal Response to Noll's *Scandal*," *Pneuma: Journal of the Society for Pentecostal Studies* 19 (1997): 225-38.

10. I'm passing over significant differences of methodological orientation within "philosophy" itself (e.g., the difference between "analytic" and "continental" philosophy). In some ways, the distinction between theology and philosophy might be as fuzzy (or as difficult to delineate) as the distinction between analytic and continental philosophy. They are both the sort of distinction that almost anyone can see but almost no one can articulate well.

11. For further discussion of this point, see Martin Heidegger, *Phänomenologie und Theologie* (Frankfurt: Klostermann, 1970) / "Phenomenology and Theology," trans. James G. Hart and John C. Maraldo, in *Pathmarks*, ed. William McNeill (Cambridge, 1998), pp. 39-62. For a fuller discussion of Heidegger's understanding of theology, see my *Speech and Theology: Language and the Logic of Incarnation*, Radical Orthodoxy Series (New York: Routledge, 2002), chapter 3.

12. For a helpful analysis of the relationship between theology and philosophy as sketched here, see Herman Dooyeweerd, *In the Twilight of Western Thought: Studies in the Pretended Autonomy of Philosophical Thought*, Collected Works B4, ed. James K. A. Smith (Lewiston, NY: Edwin Mellen Press, 1999), pp. 91-106.

tecostal theology cannot simply adopt the theological frameworks of evangelical theology (as Archer and Dabney have admonished above), so a pentecostal philosophy should integrally develop from the resources and implicit intuitions that are "carried" in pentecostal spirituality and worship.[13] In this respect, just as pentecostal theology ought to be wary of adapting off-the-shelf theological paradigms from, say, evangelical theology, so too must a pentecostal philosophy exhibit a prophetic suspicion of the regnant paradigms in Christian philosophy and its evangelical permutations.[14] Outlining just what such an "integral" pentecostal philosophy could look like is the task of this book.

A third concern about the very idea of a "pentecostal philosophy" — skeptical in tone — might come from the broader community of Christian philosophers who, after an initial surprise (and perhaps chuckle), will question what pentecostals could possibly bring to the philosophical

13. This sentiment expresses what I think of as the "Cleveland school" in pentecostal theology. As I see it, the questions I'm raising here are parallel to the broader historical and theological question of how pentecostalism relates to evangelicalism (or, to cite an even more specific case, how one views the inclusion of a Pentecostal denomination like the Assemblies of God in the National Association of Evangelicals [NAE]). One school of thought (the "Springfield school?") has viewed pentecostalism as something like evangelicalism with a special accent on pneumatology. This school views the assimilation of Pentecostals into the NAE, and evangelicalism more generally, as a positive development consistent with the "evangelical" nature of Pentecostalism. As Pentecostals were thus absorbed into an evangelical "mainstream," Cheryl Bridges Johns notes, "the enemies of the Evangelical peer group became the enemies of the Pentecostal movement. Evangelical battles became Pentecostal battles" (Johns, "The Adolescence of Pentecostalism: In Search of a Legitimate Sectarian Identity," *Pneuma: Journal of the Society for Pentecostal Studies* 17 [1995]: 7). However, there is another school of thought, which I'm calling the "Cleveland school" since I see its catalytic epicenter located at the Church of God Theological Seminary in Cleveland, Tennessee — though one could argue that this is developing an emphasis seen in the work of Walter Hollenweger (see Johns, p. 4 n. 4). According to the Cleveland school, the assimilation of Pentecostals into evangelicalism represents a selling of their birthright and a compromising of the distinctives of pentecostal spirituality. While I'm not a card-carrying member, so to speak, my project here has deep sympathies with the Cleveland school.

14. I think one can see something like this sort of "synthesis" in the recent work of J. P. Moreland (see his *Kingdom Triangle: Recover the Christian Mind, Renovate the Soul, Restore the Spirit's Power* [Grand Rapids: Zondervan, 2007]). While I applaud Moreland's newfound appreciation for the supernatural, and his abandonment of cessationism, I don't think he has let this charismatic openness impinge upon the rationalist models of "knowledge" appropriated from evangelicalism. In short, I would suggest that if Moreland followed through the implications of his openness to the Spirit's power, he should also revisit his epistemological and ontological commitments.

table.[15] Will there now be altar calls at meetings of the Society of Christian Philosophers? Would papers be delivered in tongues? These, of course, are caricatures; but they are intended to indicate that the broader Christian philosophical community is only acquainted, secondhand, with caricatures of pentecostal worship and lacks an understanding of pentecostal distinctives that would make a difference in the philosophical community. One of the goals of this "outline" of pentecostal philosophy will be to indicate those distinctive pentecostal commitments that should impact epistemological and ontological reflection. In doing so, I hope to lay out the task of the ensuing chapters as well as sketch a program for an emerging generation of pentecostal philosophers.

Plantinga's Program for Christian Philosophy

A model for the development of a distinctly pentecostal philosophy can be found in Plantinga's "Advice" to those developing a Christian philosophy. In this seminal article Plantinga consistently emphasizes three key themes: (1) an apologetic movement defending the "rights" of Christian philosophers to philosophize from out of their Christian commitments; (2) a related call to Christian philosophers to demonstrate more "autonomy" vis-à-vis the philosophical establishment and more "integrity" or "integrality" (p. 254) in their philosophizing; and (3) the need for Christian philosophy to display more Christian boldness or self-confidence. Let me briefly unpack each of these before considering their implications for the development of a distinctly pentecostal philosophy.

First, Plantinga's address is dominated by what we could describe, following Mary Ann Glendon, as "rights talk." Here, in response to the (secular and antitheistic) philosophical establishment's dogma regarding the "objectivity" or "neutrality" of philosophy, Plantinga clears space for the viability of a Christian philosophy by pointing out that even these supposedly "secular" philosophers begin from fundamental prephilosophical commitments and assumptions (pp. 255-56). So if the neutrality thesis of the philosophical establishment is a myth, and "secular" philosophers have

15. Of course, there would be an even more incredulous response from the broader philosophical community, who are generally skeptical about Christian philosophy and whose criticisms would be intensified when faced with the proposal for a pentecostal philosophy. My response to the broader philosophical community would follow the same lines as Plantinga's apologia and need not be taken up here.

a "right" to their prephilosophical assumptions, then by the same rules Christian philosophers cannot be denied their corresponding "right" (an "epistemic right" [p. 261])[16] to philosophize from their *Christian* prephilosophical assumptions. Plantinga functions here as a kind of civil rights advocate for Christian philosophers, standing on the steps of the Lincoln Memorial (or, in fact, under the shadow of the Golden Dome and Touchdown Jesus)[17] demanding, not "special" rights for Christian philosophers, but simply *equal* rights with respect to the role of prephilosophical assumptions in philosophizing. If W. V. O. Quine can begin from his philosophical assumptions, then "the Christian philosopher has a perfect right to the point of view and pre-philosophical assumptions that he brings to philosophic work" (p. 256).

But while this is a persistent apologetic element of his article, it is interesting to note that the point is precisely to free Christian philosophers from the self-imposed burden of *only* engaging in apologetics. In asserting that "the Christian philosophical community quite properly starts, in philosophy, from what it believes," Plantinga then notes that "this means that the Christian philosophical community need not devote all of its efforts to attempting to refute opposing claims and/or to arguing for its own claims" (p. 268).

By thus outlining the "rights" of Christian philosophers to begin from their fundamental Christian commitments, Plantinga is led to the second key emphasis of his "Advice": the need for the Christian philosophical community to demonstrate more independence and *autonomy* from the guild of philosophy at large (which is dominated by assumptions antithetical to Christian faith). By this he means that the agenda of investigation for the Christian philosopher should not be determined by trends in the philosophical establishment, but rather by questions that arise out of the Christian community and the Christian faith of the philosopher. "My plea," he emphasizes, "is for the Christian philosopher, the Christian philosophical community, to display, first, more independence and autonomy: we needn't take as our research projects just those projects that currently enjoy widespread popularity; we have our own questions to think about"

16. This is related to Plantinga's later work on the concept of "warrant." See his trilogy from Oxford University Press: *Warrant: The Current Debate* (1993), *Warrant and Proper Function* (1993), and *Warranted Christian Belief* (2000). A broader version of this sort of argument can be found in George Marsden, *The Outrageous Idea of Christian Scholarship* (New York: Oxford University Press, 1998).

17. Plantinga's "Advice" was originally delivered at Notre Dame.

(p. 268).[18] Note that this alternative agenda stems from the fact that the Christian philosopher serves the Christian community, the church: "The Christian philosopher does indeed have a responsibility to the philosophical world at large; but his fundamental responsibility is to the Christian community, and finally to God" (p. 262). Plantinga also warns, however, that this does *not* mean that Christian philosophers should withdraw from the wider philosophical community into a kind of Christian ghetto: "Nor do I mean to suggest that Christian philosophers should retreat into their own isolated conclave, having as little as possible to do with non-theistic philosophers. . . . Christian philosophers must be intimately involved in the professional life of the philosophical community at large both because of what they can learn and because of what they can contribute" (p. 270). In other words, one of the responsibilities of the Christian philosopher will be to function as a *witness* to the broader philosophical community — but not in the narrow sense of evangelism. Rather, such philosophical work witnesses to creational wisdom and unveils the structures of a good creation. Indeed, it gives witness to the creational goodness of engaging in the cultural task of philosophizing. This leads to what Merold Westphal describes as the "two hats thesis": the Christian philosopher has two audiences (the church and the academy) and even two allegiances (first to the church and secondarily to the academy, based on the notion of "integrity" below).[19] As such, we also have two vocations: to serve the Christian community but also to be a witness and testimony to the academy.

Christian philosophers, then, will demonstrate more autonomy by establishing an agenda that arises from their own faith commitments and their service to their own (distinctive) faith communities. This demands what Plantinga calls "integrity" or "integrality": our philosophy and philosophizing must begin from our Christian commitments, not assumptions laid down by the antitheistic philosophical establishment. "The Christian philosopher who looks exclusively to the philosophical world at large," he warns, "who thinks of himself as belonging primarily to *that* world, runs a two-fold risk. He may neglect an essential part of his task as a Christian philosopher; and he may find himself adopting principles and procedures that don't comport well with his belief as a Christian" (p. 264). While we may

18. In this light, I was impressed by John Christopher Thomas's testimony, in the preface to his *The Devil, Disease, and Deliverance: Origins of Illness in New Testament Thought*, Journal of Pentecostal Theology Supplement 13 (Sheffield: Sheffield Academic Press, 1998), p. 7, where he shared that he determines his research projects by *prayer*.

19. Westphal, "Taking Plantinga Seriously," pp. 174-75.

display autonomy by choosing philosophical questions that are unique to the Christian community, we must also think about those questions in a way that does not unwittingly adopt frameworks that are foreign to, and likely antithetical to, our fundamental Christian commitments. Now, to display this autonomy the Christian philosopher — as part of the Christian philosophical community — will need to be reflective and critically consider just what those "fundamental Christian commitments" are and what they entail. Then she or he will be in a place to critically evaluate trends in the broader philosophical community. As a result, the Christian philosopher who demonstrates such integrity "may have to reject certain currently fashionable assumptions about the philosophic enterprise — he may have to reject widely accepted assumptions as to what are the proper starting points and procedures for philosophical endeavor" (p. 256).

This is why Plantinga also argues that the development of an autonomous, integral Christian philosophy will demand Christian boldness or "Christian self-confidence" (p. 254). The integrity and autonomy of a Christian philosophy will require Christian philosophers to display "less readiness to trim their sails to the prevailing philosophical winds of doctrine and more Christian self-confidence" (p. 258). Why, he asks, "should we be intimidated by what the rest of the philosophical world thinks plausible or implausible" (p. 269)? Plantinga's own work is a testament to such courage.

A Program for Pentecostal Philosophy

Plantinga's clarion call and program for a Christian philosophy provide a model for the development of a distinctly pentecostal philosophy.[20] My only major criticism of Plantinga, voiced elsewhere, is a too easy identification of "Christian philosophy" with a merely "theistic" philosophy (see, e.g., pp. 254, 264, 267, 270). I think this compromises the distinctiveness of

---

20. As noted above, by a "pentecostal" philosophy I do not mean, of course, some kind of official "denominational" philosophy, but rather a philosophy that begins from pentecostal or charismatic prephilosophical commitments. In "Advice," Plantinga employs only the broad term "Christian" (and even broader "theistic"). Elsewhere, however, Plantinga speaks of a distinctly "Reformed epistemology." So it seems to me that the more specific project of a "pentecostal" philosophy is not excluded by his program for a Christian philosophy. Indeed, we might ask whether a philosophy could ever be simply "Christian." Would it not always already be "Reformed" or "Wesleyan" or "Catholic," etc.?

a *Christian* philosophy that begins, not with the simple affirmation of "the existence of God" (p. 261), but with a relationship with the triune God who has revealed himself — *uniquely* — in Christ, and more specifically God in Christ as he gave himself on the cross. Thus a Christian philosophy must be fundamentally incarnational and cruciform, rooted not simply in theism but in the revelation of the incarnation, the scandal of the cross, and the confession of the resurrection. And it should be just this incarnational starting point that distinguishes Christian philosophy from merely "theistic" philosophy. But with that proviso in mind, let me sketch how Plantinga's program might be further specified for the development of a pentecostal philosophy.

First, we should recognize our "right" to philosophize not only from out of our broadly Christian prephilosophical commitments, but also from our distinctly *pentecostal* assumptions; indeed, it would be difficult — and ill advised — to separate the two. But this raises the question of just what these "fundamental pentecostal commitments" would be and how they would differ from those of the broader Christian or evangelical philosophical community. As I will suggest in chapter 2, I think this constellation of commitments must be located as implicit within the *practices* of pentecostal spirituality. So instead of identifying certain key doctrines or dogmas, I will tease out the prephilosophical commitments latent within pentecostal spirituality. The articulated form of the implicit assumptions will be described as a pentecostal "worldview" or, following Charles Taylor, a pentecostal "social imaginary."[21] Whether one considers the small congregation gathering for a revival in the Appalachians, or Nigerian pentecostals worshiping in Brooklyn, or Catholic charismatics engaged in prayer in the Philippines, or Indian Anglicans testifying to miracles in Bangalore, my wager is that there are five key aspects of a pentecostal worldview that are shared across this range of global contexts and denominational traditions.[22]

---

21. This is somewhat akin to what Donald Dayton describes as the "gestalt" of early pentecostal theology (Dayton, *Theological Roots of Pentecostalism* [Peabody, MA: Hendrickson, 1987], pp. 16-17). However, Dayton's account is still quite narrowly focused on specifically doctrinal or theological aspects of pentecostalism. We'll return to these issues in chapter 2.

22. I first articulated something like this outline of a pentecostal worldview in James K. A. Smith, "What Hath Cambridge to Do with Azusa Street? Radical Orthodoxy and Pentecostal Theology in Conversation," *Pneuma: Journal of the Society for Pentecostal Studies* 25 (2003): 97-114. I have since slightly revised the formulation.

1. A position of **radical openness to God**, and in particular, God doing
   something *differently* or *new*.[23] In terms adopted from continental discourse, we might describe this as a fundamental openness to alterity or
   otherness.[24] More traditionally, we might simply describe it as an
   openness to the continuing (and sometimes surprising) operations of
   the Spirit in church and world, particularly the continued ministry of
   the Spirit, including continuing revelation, prophecy, and the centrality of charismatic giftings in the ecclesial community.

2. An **"enchanted" theology of creation and culture** that perceives the
   material creation as "charged" with the presence of the Spirit, but also
   with other spirits (including demons and "principalities and powers"), with entailed expectations regarding both miracles and spiritual
   warfare.

3. A **nondualistic affirmation of embodiment and materiality** expressed in an emphasis on physical healing (and perhaps also in gospels of "prosperity").[25]

4. Because of an emphasis on the role of experience, and in contrast to
   rationalistic evangelical theology, Pentecostal theology is rooted in an
   affective, narrative epistemology.

5. An **eschatological orientation to mission and justice**, both expressed
   in terms of empowerment, with a certain "preferential option for the
   marginalized."

A complete exegesis of this pentecostal worldview will have to wait
until chapter 2. And I would be very happy to see this articulation of a pen-

23. As I'll unpack in chapter 2, I take the central point of the narrative of Acts 2 to be
Peter's courage and willingness to recognize in these "strange" phenomena the operation of
the Spirit and declare it to be a work of God. To declare "this is that" (Acts 2:16) was to be
open to God working in unexpected ways. There will be some ironic tension, I concede, between this reading of Pentecost as openness to God doing something "new" and the Pentecostal primitivism that takes itself to be recovering the spiritual practices of the first century.
(Such primitivism seems to be shared by classical Pentecostals and third wave charismatics,
not Catholic or mainline charismatics.)

24. In Emmanuel Levinas's ethical phenomenology, to be open to the Other is precisely
to be open to *novelty*, to something *new*.

25. As will become clear below, by "nondualistic" I mean an ontological model that
does not denigrate materiality as evil. Pentecostal spirituality is clearly predicated on a dual-
ity between material and immaterial ("spiritual") entities (the latter including angels and
demons). I will generally reserve the term "dualism" for positions that not only make this
distinction but also devalue and denigrate the material.

tecostal worldview challenged, revised, and supplemented — indeed, the task of identifying and reflecting upon pentecostal philosophical commitments should be part of the agenda of a pentecostal philosophy. In any event, I believe that if we engage in reflection we will be able to see, and then demonstrate, that these distinctively pentecostal assumptions have significant implications for classical philosophical questions. And, *pace* Plantinga's program, we will be well within our "rights" to pursue such questions out of these prephilosophical commitments. For example (to name just a few), in epistemology, the pentecostal emphasis on experience and affectivity would be the ground for a critique of dominant rationalisms (particularly in evangelical philosophical and theological circles)[26] and provide a fund for unique developments in phenomenology and our accounts of knowledge. In addition, given the centrality of testimony and witness in pentecostal experience, one might expect pentecostal philosophers to grapple with epistemological questions surrounding testimony with a unique urgency and interest.[27] In ontology, the pentecostal belief in a *continually* "open" universe, evidenced in the central belief in the miraculous and God's continued activity in the world, should make a fundamental difference in the way we construct our metaphysics. And pentecostal beliefs in the holistic nature of the gospel, healing both soul and body, should contribute to a unique philosophical anthropology and theory about the nature of the human person. Chapters 4–6 below are intended as studies that carry out just this sort of work.

Further, pentecostals (or at least, philosophers with a pentecostal sen-

---

26. Here again I think J. P. Moreland's project is an interesting case in point. I suggest that while he has come to embrace something like a pentecostal worldview, he has not yet appreciated how aspects of that spirituality might impinge upon the philosophical commitments he has adopted over the course of his (precharismatic) work.

27. Such a line of research would do well to return to Paul Ricoeur, "The Hermeneutics of Testimony," in *Essays on Biblical Interpretation*, ed. Lewis S. Mudge (Philadelphia: Fortress, 1980), pp. 119-54. Ricoeur opens by asking (and answering) a question of relevance to pentecostal spirituality: "What sort of philosophy makes a problem of testimony? I answer: A philosophy for which the question of the absolute is a proper question, a philosophy which seeks to join an *experience* of the absolute to the *idea* of the absolute" (p. 119). Epistemological (and political) questions around "testimony" could also facilitate a pentecostal philosophical engagement with the history of philosophy (e.g., with Hume, for whom the question of testimony is at the heart of his critique of miracles). Furthermore, this line of inquiry would be another point of contact with feminist scholarship, particularly the work of Julia Kristeva. For a relevant discussion, see Kelly Oliver, *Witnessing: Beyond Recognition* (Minneapolis: University of Minnesota Press, 2001).

sibility) might approach the history of philosophy with a different set of commitments and questions that could open up historical figures and texts in new ways. I am thinking, for instance, of the unique readings and new insights that might result from a pentecostal engagement with Pascal or Augustine — the way in which unique sympathies might open new interpretive trajectories that could be instructive for the philosophical community as a whole.[28] I also think that pentecostal research in the history of philosophy would raise interesting questions about the philosophical "canon," insofar as pentecostals might be positioned to find resources in more marginal sources in the history of philosophy, or at least be prone to be attentive to important figures who are less read today.[29] Indeed, it seems to me that a pentecostal history of philosophy would work from the margins, so to speak, seeking to give voice to voices that were ignored or silenced by the dominant Western (and rationalist) tradition.[30] So when I advocate the development of a pentecostal philosophy, I am also advocating a pentecostal *history* of philosophy — not as exhaustive or comprehensive (seeking to debunk "mainstream" history of philosophy), but as a unique contribution to be made by pentecostal scholars.[31]

Second, following Plantinga's program for Christian philosophy more generally, pentecostal philosophers will need to display autonomy and integrity, pursuing philosophical questions and a research agenda that grows out of their pentecostal commitments and the pentecostal communities of which they are a part. In this way they will display autonomy not only vis-

28. Consider, for instance, Amos Yong's engagement with Charles Sanders Peirce's unique rendition of pragmatism in Yong, *Spirit-Word-Community: Theological Hermeneutics in Trinitarian Perspective* (Aldershot: Ashgate, 2002), pp. 151-65.

29. For instance, if there are important resonances between German pietism and pentecostalism (see Frank D. Macchia, *Spirituality and Social Liberation: The Message of the Blumhardts in the Light of Wuerttemberg Pietism* [Metuchen, NJ: Scarecrow Press, 1993]), then pentecostals should be interested in the voices of countermodernity in the work of Hamann and Jacobi. Or, given the affective epistemology implicit in pentecostal spirituality, we should expect pentecostals to be engaging an alternative Augustinian tradition in epistemology that runs through Pascal up to Heidegger. (Cp., for instance, James R. Peters, *The Logic of the Heart: Augustine, Pascal, and the Rationality of Faith* [Grand Rapids: Baker Academic, 2009].)

30. I think a pentecostal history of philosophy would have some sympathy with Michel Foucault's method of historical investigation that participates in an "insurrection of subjugated knowledges." See Foucault, "Two Lectures," in *Critique and Power: Recasting the Foucault/Habermas Debate,* ed. Michael Kelly (Cambridge, MA: MIT Press, 1994), pp. 17-46.

31. Consider, for instance, the role Reformed epistemology played in retrieving the importance of Thomas Reid for contemporary epistemology. See Nicholas Wolterstorff, *Thomas Reid and the Story of Epistemology* (Cambridge: Cambridge University Press, 2004).

à-vis the broader philosophical establishment, but even with respect to the broader Christian or evangelical philosophical community. For instance, we would expect pentecostal philosophers to engage the classical question of miracles in a way that poses the issue not merely as a matter of historical possibility,[32] but rather as a question of contemporary possibility, given our belief in the continued miraculous work of the Spirit in the church. Or pentecostal reflections on philosophy of language and the possibility of God-talk might develop uniquely, given the core practice of glossolalia. Our philosophical "curiosity" should grow out of our pentecostal commitments — and we must be alert to the risk of adopting even "Christian" philosophical commitments and methods that run counter to our pentecostal beliefs. One of Plantinga's concerns was the number of Christians who were trained in philosophy but never trained to *integrate* their faith with their philosophy; in the same way, we want to avoid having pentecostals develop a philosophy that is unconnected to their distinctly pentecostal faith. In this way we will display "integrity" as pentecostal philosophers who have *integrated* our philosophical projects and methods with our pentecostal beliefs and practices.

Finally, given the fact that we are within our "epistemic rights" to pursue our own agenda, we need to exhibit confidence and boldness — "Holy Ghost boldness" — in the development and pursuit of such a philosophic program. Indeed, if pentecostal philosophy is to be rooted in the *practice* of pentecostal spirituality (and not just working with the ideas of a pentecostal theology), then such a philosophy must be pursued from within a web of worship practices that inform and inculcate a pentecostal worldview. The work of the pentecostal philosopher will not be a compartmentalized, merely "academic" operation carried out upon charismatic "topics." Rather, refusing an anti-intellectual pietism, we need to ask for grace and perhaps an "anointing" to undertake such a task with courage found in humility and dependence. With Paul, we need to pray that we "may not be bold with the confidence with which I propose to be courageous to some, who regard us as if we walked according to the flesh" (2 Cor. 10:2). Paul continues, "For though we walk in the flesh, we do not war according to the flesh, for the weapons of our warfare are not of the flesh, but divinely powerful for the destruction of fortresses. We are destroying speculations and every lofty thing raised up against the knowledge of God, and we are

---

32. As seen, for instance, in Norman Geisler, *Miracles and the Modern Mind* (Grand Rapids: Baker, 1992).

taking every thought captive to the obedience of Christ" (2 Cor. 10:3-5). The mission and task of the pentecostal philosopher will be unapologetically informed by the practices of a pentecostal spirituality. This is just to say that a pentecostal philosophy is not merely a matter of topic, but of method and approach. A pentecostal philosophy will not simply be a detached philosophical reflection on charismatic phenomena; it will be a charismatic reflection on philosophical questions. The moment that pentecostal phenomena are reified and abstracted from the "form of life" that is pentecostal spirituality, the resulting philosophy will fail to be pentecostal in a radical, integral sense — possessing a form of pentecostal spirituality but denying the power thereof.[33]

---

33. This is not meant to be a way of insulating pentecostal experience from critical analysis. However, any critique must also honor the unique nature of pentecostal spirituality *as a spirituality* and not simply castigate it for not being a form of piety that is more "intellectual" or "evangelical." In general, I am not engaging in an apologetic defense of pentecostal spirituality in this book.

2 God's Surprise

Elements of a Pentecostal Worldview

Pentecostal Worship: A Vignette

A rather flat light glances off stucco houses and strip malls as we make our way down Inglewood Avenue into the northern environs of Hawthorne, California. Once ravaged by the Los Angeles riots of 1992, the area has been restored to its prior mediocrity: low-slung tract housing interspersed with cash-advance stores and fast-food restaurants. We make our way past the remnants of a mall long abandoned on our way to one of the many nondescript strip malls that is home to Resurrection Life Assembly.

The tiny parking lot is already full so we find space on a side street. We see other pilgrims making their way up the sidewalk from the nearby apartment complex, while also noting the stream of folks already leaving the storefront sanctuary, having just participated in a Spanish service. It's curious to see parents who are leaving the church greeting their teenage children just arriving, making their way to the English service.

There is much laughter and conversation happening on the sidewalk and in the parking lot. Young children are dashing around the lot oblivious to any vehicular threats, hiding between the skirts of their grandmothers or behind the trash bin, giggling all the while. The atmosphere is one of relaxed jocularity coupled with spiritual earnestness seen in an array of eager and interested conversations, expressions of concern on worried faces in conversation, and a demonstrative prayer huddle with hands laid on a young mother. No one seems too eager to move inside, though music is already thumping through the large plate glass windows on the front of the storefront space, under a temporary vinyl banner proclaiming this as the home of Resurrection Life. As we make our way to the door, we are greeted with smiles and nods. When the glass door opens, the music spills out and the rhythmic thud of the bass and drums begins to hit us in the chest.

After our eyes adjust from the external sun to the interior fluorescent lighting, we survey the space — the "sanctuary." The tiled, ten-foot-high ceiling feels as if it's pressing down on the group and compressing the sound of the band within a narrow depth. About twenty-five feet wide, the worship space is narrow and deep, with what are probably stairs to a basement just visible in the back. The walls are draped with a rainbow of flags (which we later learn represent the nations of birth of members of the congregation). The remnant of a cashier's counter now functions as a welcome center, and we are warmly greeted with a two-fisted handshake from an elderly African American woman who seems to carry herself with matriarchal concern and motherly welcome. We are given a black-and-white photocopied brochure with information for visitors and invited to make ourselves comfortable in the sanctuary. But before we move to the chairs the woman gets down on both knees to introduce herself to our children, ask them their names, and invite them to join the other children at "kids' church" in the basement after the singing is finished. Promises of candy seem to trump their anxiety about unfamiliar surroundings.

We turn back to the interior to find seats amongst the folding chairs lined up in two sections with a central aisle. There are about 100 seats available, and currently no one is sitting in any of them, though folks are congregated amongst them. Instead, a musical team at the front seems to be providing a sound track for their conversations. Stopped along the way by several folks who introduce themselves and welcome us to Resurrection Life, we find several chairs near the back just as a change in the music signals parishioners to make their way inside and find their seats — but not to sit down. Instead, a worship leader — a young Latino man — comes to the microphone. He immediately begins to pray, and the congregation joins him in their posture: eyes are closed, hands are outstretched or arms are raised, some are swaying and also praying quietly as the worship leader invokes the "King of Heaven": "King of Heaven," he prays, "we gather today to worship you, to exalt your name, to see you high and lifted up. We long for your coming. Maranatha! Even so, come now, Lord Jesus! But until you come, we long to meet you here, in this place. Father in Heaven, send your Spirit so that our eyes and hearts are open to meeting Jesus. . . ." His prayers are met with shouts of "Amen!" and "Yes, Lord!" A woman surrounded by young children tugging on her pants has begun to weep, but almost immediately a middle-aged woman has moved beside her and wrapped her arms around the young mother, praying quietly but fervently with her other hand raised, sometimes clenched like a clam, at other times opened and pleading. As the opening chorus is sung, the women embrace and the young woman "enters in" to worship.

No one has been seated since the service began, and only an elderly couple are seated during forty-five minutes of sung worship — interrupted only by another prayer of adoration from the worship leader that washes over the congregation until almost everyone, simultaneously, is engaged in prayers of exaltation and praise, many singing extemporaneous prayers, some singing in tongues. But far from the cacophony one might expect, there is an almost surreal symphonic character to the prayer. This leads into a quieter, more meditative song service, which seems aimed at introspection as parishioners seem to retreat into themselves a little more. Some are now kneeling, rocking in supplication; others have abandoned their inhibitions in bodies splayed on the floor; while still others remain standing, arms outstretched as if asking heaven to come down. Some of the children watch their parents curiously but quietly, puzzled and perhaps not a little perplexed by tears from their father.

Quietly the lyrics end, but an electronic piano continues to play as the pastor, also quite a young, burly man with tattoos on his neck and left hand and a suit that doesn't quite fit, comes to the front of the sanctuary (there's no podium or rostrum), invites people to be seated, and begins to pray. It begins as a prayer of intercession for parishioners who are beset by illness, unemployment, financial difficulties, and prodigal children, but he also prays for the public school system and about recent gang violence in the neighborhood. He prays against the work of the devil and all the ways the enemy threatens — that the name of Jesus would give victory over the evil one, and that the Spirit of God would enable them to resist the wiles of the devil. The prayer then concludes with thanksgiving for the offering that is about to be received. At the conclusion of the prayer, the music becomes a little louder and once again the congregation stands, so we join them. We sing songs of adoration and thanksgiving as deacons stand at the front of the church with baskets. During the singing, parishioners randomly make their way forward to leave their offering.

We are once again seated as the pastor comes to the front with his Bible in hand and invites us to read along (in the Bibles we should have brought with us!) in Mark 9. We note that this is the first that the Word has been read, and yet find that the cadences and rhythms of the prayers have been so suffused with Scripture that we didn't notice earlier. The sermon focuses on the call to discipleship — to take up our cross and follow Christ. The preacher courses across the front of the sanctuary, even making his way halfway down the center aisle — referring to parishioners by name, laughing with them, sometimes weeping, almost always quite loud. The sermon is more aesthetic than didactic, an exhortation not a lecture, and draws on metaphors and illustrations of mainly working-class life and football. Having a general (and perhaps mistaken) impression that many of the folks here endure daily struggles with which we are unfamiliar, we are somewhat surprised that the preacher seems to add to their burden by exhorting them to take up their crosses. But our middle-class expectations are chastised when the pastor brings the service to its culmination: the altar call.

As he leads us in a concluding prayer of confession, the musicians once again play softly in the background. The pastor then speaks again: "I sense that the Spirit of God has work to do here today. That some of us need to take up our crosses again, that we've traded them for our own comfort and pleasure. The Spirit is inviting us to recrucify our passions and pleasures and selfishness. To come to this altar with a broken and contrite heart — and find *healing*. Find *restoration*. Find *hope*."

In the space of his pause for breath, a voice calls out from the middle of the chairs: "Thus saith the Lord!" A middle-aged woman has mustered the courage to be obedient in sharing a prophetic word, a sort of targeted encouragement from God for this congregation, in this place, at this time. Its cadences and language find their provenance in the canon of Scripture. Rather than bringing some "new" or secret knowledge, this word is prophetic because it is targeted. "I am Jehovah Rothah," she begins, "the Lord your healer. I am able to restore what the locusts have eaten. I alone can bring good from evil. I want to redeem your life from the pit. Why do you resist my invitation? Why would you stay mired in sadness? Cast off those things that so easily entangle you! Come to me you who are weary and heavy-laden. I'm here to give you rest." Her voice trails off and the word is received somberly but gladly. The pastor chants quietly, "Hallelujah, hallelujah, hallelujah, thank you, Lord," while shouts of "Amen!" and "Praise the Lord!" resound from around the sanctuary along with the sniffles and muffles of weeping.

The pastor explains that this has been a prophetic word from the Lord, directed to the saints at Resurrection Life — that God is calling them to come. Almost immediately people begin to stream from their chairs toward the front of the sanctuary. Chairs at the front are shuffled back unceremoniously to make room for those who have come to pray. They are shortly surrounded by others from the congregation who lay hands on their shoulders and heads. A young couple has timidly come to the front, hand in hand, and they are now surrounded by an elderly gentleman, an older couple, and another young couple who have all laid their hands gently on their shoulders. The younger woman asks what they can pray for, and the shoulders of the man who came forward begin to heave as sobs rack his body. His wife falls into his chest in an embrace, and all the "prayer warriors" huddle close, tenderly embracing them. They each continue to take the lead in prayer, then fade into quiet prayer, some in tongues, asking for redemption, restoration, forgiveness, and healing. While the altar has invited brokenness, its end is healing.

The pastor walks prayerfully between the clusters of people kneeling for prayer and being "prayed over" by others, carefully stepping over legs and bodies. He stops at each group and adds to the chorus of prayer, gently touching each one. An older gentleman has made his way to the pastor and whispers briefly in his ear. The pastor listens carefully and then explains to the praying congregation: "Jack has received a word of knowledge from the Spirit and has been obedient in sharing that," turning the microphone over to this elderly man, who takes it awkwardly. "The Spirit has told me," he timidly begins, "that there is a woman here who is suffering as Sarai did. You have been unable to have a child; you've had much trouble getting pregnant. You and your husband have been quietly suffering because of this. You haven't even told your family. But the Lord knows your suffering; he knows that you have been crying in private. He has heard your prayers! He has healing in his wings. He wants to give you hope and a future. He wants to make you a Hannah." A gasp of sobbing erupts from behind us, as if this word has birthed from her a sadness that has been incubating within her for months. A woman has nearly collapsed, supported and sustained by her husband, who now carefully leads her to the front for prayer as the congregation breaks into spontaneous applause, its own hopeful prayer. The matriarchal woman who met us at the door has met her at the front of the sanctuary, and has carefully placed her hands upon the young woman's belly, fervently interceding, claiming the promise of God's prophetic word.

A glance around the space takes in what could seem like a chaotic scene with all sorts of different activities bustling in different corners of the room. The staid, orderly rows of chairs are now sprawled askew, as if swirled by a whirlwind. Perhaps they have been. As this "work" of prayer continues, the pastor briefly informs those few of us still in our seats that the Spirit still has work to do today; we are to feel free to leave with the Lord's blessing, but if we would like to stay, the church is having a potluck lunch immediately following the service.

Hermeneutical Courage and Unapologetic Pentecostalism

In the chaos and confusion that must have been the Pentecostal feast narrated in Acts 2, I reserve a special admiration for Peter. And my interest in Peter stems directly from my work as a scholar and academic; indeed, I see Peter as providing a model and exemplar of some virtues that I, as a scholar — and particularly as a *pentecostal* scholar — ought to emulate. The two integrated virtues that I would highlight are embedded in Acts 2:14-16 (NASB): "But Peter, taking his stand with the eleven, raised his voice and declared to them: 'Men of Judea, and all you who live in Jerusalem, let this be known to you, and give heed to my words. For these men are not drunk, as you suppose, for it is only the third hour of the day; but this is what was spoken of through the prophet Joel.'" In this prefatory narrative to Peter's Pentecostal proclamation, what I find exemplary is what we might describe as Peter's *hermeneutical courage* or interpretive boldness. You will notice Peter's boldness in verse 14: Peter took a stand; he "stood up" (NIV) and so stood out from the crowd — and he did so precisely in the face of many who were mocking (v. 13) and disparaging him and his associates ("Aren't these people uneducated Galileans?" [v. 7]). But then, notice to what end this courage and boldness are enacted. What does Peter do when he takes a stand? He offers an *interpretation*. In other words, he marshals courage to articulate an interpretation of the events that are unfolding — a construal of the world in which they find themselves. When Peter raises his voice, it is to offer an explanation — an account of the phenomena that are swirling around them. His bold interpretation is actually a *counter*interpretation. The mockers had already offered an interpretation: these phenomena (speaking in other tongues) were attributed to drunkenness. But Peter courageously offers a different interpretation. An outlandish and surprising one, to be sure — which only heightens the boldness that such an interpretive stand required. Peter's interpretation hinges on verse 16: "this is that";[1]

---

1. This terse phrase, laden with pronouns, was the title of a famous tract by Pentecostal evangelist Aimee Semple McPherson: *This Is That: Personal Experiences, Sermons, and Writings* (Los Angeles: Echo Park Evangelistic Association, 1923). See an excerpt in Douglas

in other words, what you're seeing is actually the fulfillment of a promise spoken by Joel — that a day would come when God's Spirit would be poured out so lavishly and with such extravagance that it would erase old distinctions of class and gender. This Spirit would wash over both men and women, both young and old, with indiscriminate abandon. It would signal the inauguration of a new economy of abundance rather than the miserly administration of an old order. It would indicate a new creation that entailed even cosmic transformation. It would signal the last days — which is to say, a new day. And that day, Peter proclaimed, is *today*.

And so right there at Pentecost we already see something we have come to associate with postmodernity: a conflict of interpretations.[2] The complexity of the world and events gives rise to the question, "What does this mean?" (v. 12),[3] and in response we can offer only interpretations. The mockers offer their own rendering of phenomena (the "wine theory"); Peter courageously offers an alternative (the "Spirit theory"). And the bold proclamation of the interpretation does not guarantee that others will see the world in this way (not all "received his word" [v. 41]).[4] Nevertheless, the interpretation Peter offers revolutionizes how many see the world. What marks Pentecost, then, is Peter's interpretive courage that offers a new hermeneutical framework. Pentecost, we might say, is a hermeneutic.[5]

Jacobsen, ed., *A Reader in Pentecostal Theology: Voices from the First Generation* (Bloomington: Indiana University Press, 2006), pp. 185-96.

2. For a classic discussion, see Paul Ricoeur, *The Conflict of Interpretations: Essays in Hermeneutics,* ed. Don Ihde (Evanston, IL: Northwestern University Press, 1974). The fact that there is a plurality of interpretations going on here — a state of affairs that seems quite undeniable — does not mean that all interpretations are equal, or that Peter is offering just "one more" interpretation. Peter takes his interpretation to be the *right* interpretation, the true interpretation (and I agree with him). Recognizing the hermeneutic nature of Peter's claim does not deflate it as a *truth* claim. For relevant discussion about the hermeneutical issues here, see James K. A. Smith, *The Fall of Interpretation: Philosophical Foundations for a Creational Hermeneutic* (Downers Grove, IL: InterVarsity, 2000), especially pp. 159-84.

3. Somewhat akin to Aimee Semple McPherson's *This Is That,* a classic Pentecostal work on tongues took up this later question: Carl Brumback, *What Meaneth This? A Pentecostal Answer to a Pentecostal Question* (Springfield, MO: Gospel Publishing House, 1947).

4. The conflict of interpretations could be a helpful lens through which to read the narrative of Acts, as a series of episodes in which phenomena are accounted for differently — and in response to which we see different "receptions" (e.g., at Mars Hill [Acts 17:32]; Festus in Acts 25).

5. On charismatic spirituality *as* (and not just "having") a unique hermeneutic, see Mark Cartledge, *Encountering the Spirit: The Charismatic Tradition* (Maryknoll, NY: Orbis, 2006), pp. 125-31.

And this interpretive stance is what marks pentecostal spirituality that functions as nothing short of a revolutionary interpretation of the world unapologetically proclaimed as a *counter*interpretation of the world — one that counters the regnant interpretations ("wine theories")[6] of our world and events that unfold within it.

Drawing on Walter Brueggemann's account of Israel's "legitimate sectarian hermeneutic," Cheryl Bridges Johns captures this hermeneutic nature of pentecostalism. In his reading of 2 Kings 18–19 (the Assyrian siege of Jerusalem under Hezekiah's reign), Brueggemann notes two different universes of discourse at work in the narrative: the narrative of empire "on the wall" versus Israel's language "behind the wall." "Both conversations construct reality. On the wall, the empire constructs reality utilizing the agenda of the imperial system. In this conversation, no prophet speaks and Yahweh is silent. The conversation behind the wall constructs reality based on the decisive prior claim of covenant with Yahweh. Here we have the voice of the prophet. Here the imperial voice is silent. Here only Hebrew is spoken. It is the language of the covenant."[7] Each functions as a hermeneutic, "a proposal for reading reality through a certain lens." But Israel's constitutes a "counter-perception of reality" that challenges the hegemony of the dominant, imperial hermeneutic.[8] "It serves as a basis for ordering a community in such a way that puts a distance between it and the dominant order."[9] On the basis of this Hebrew precedent, Johns admonishes pentecostals toward maturity by embracing the legitimacy of a sectarian hermeneutic, thus exhorting pentecostals to exhibit the sort of hermeneutic courage we see in Peter's Pentecost sermon: "They [should] have the courage to pose the question, 'Will the real sectarian stand up?' By raising this question, a challenge is made to the old scientific paradigm which assumed that there was the possibility of a nonsectarian, noninterested, nonpartial hermeneutic. By raising this question Pentecostals could feel free to bring to the Christian table their own imaginative proposal for or-

---

6. Indeed, we might say that the wine theory of Acts 2:13 was the first naturalistic account of religious phenomena — a proto–Daniel Dennett.

7. Cheryl Bridges Johns, "The Adolescence of Pentecostalism: In Search of a Legitimate Sectarian Identity," *Pneuma: Journal of the Society for Pentecostal Studies* 17 (1995): 3-17, at p. 12, summarizing Walter Brueggemann, "The Legitimacy of a Sectarian Hermeneutic," *Horizons in Biblical Theology* 7 (1985): 1-42.

8. One of the burdens of Brueggemann's argument is to show that the imperial hermeneutic is no less sectarian (Brueggemann, "Legitimacy," p. 22).

9. Johns, "Adolescence," p. 13.

dering the Christian household without bringing with it a pervading sense of shame."[10]

Pentecostal spirituality is a construal of the world, an implicit understanding that constitutes a "take" on things. And this pentecostal construal of the world has something to say not only on the steps of the temple in Jerusalem (Acts 2), but also in the Areopagus of Athens (Acts 17). One of my claims in this book is that pentecostal spirituality is relevant and important not only for "religious" edification, but also that a pentecostal "worldview" has something unique, powerful, and viable to say to the academy precisely because implicit within pentecostal practice is a take on our being-in-the-world. Pentecostal spirituality is not just a compartmentalized way of being "religious"; the practices of pentecostal spirituality carry within them an understanding of the world that spills over any sacred/secular divides.[11] Thus I want to offer an interpretation of pentecostal faith that involves not only *speaking* in tongues, but also — to stretch the metaphor — *thinking* in tongues.[12] Pentecostalism offers not only a distinct way of worshiping, but also a distinct way of *thinking;* embedded in pentecostal practice is not only a spirituality (in the narrow sense), but also something like a "worldview." If, as I suggested in chapter 1, there is to be something like a "pentecostal philosophy," then we need to discern the shape of the prephilosophical assumptions that constitute this constellation of pentecostal commitments. To appreciate the ranging implications of this, I don't want to narrowly describe this as a pentecostal "theology"[13] — unless by a

10. Johns, "Adolescence," pp. 16-17. One might suggest that Plantinga's project also calls into question the sectarian/nonsectarian distinction. A Christian philosophy is legitimate precisely because *every* philosophy is, in a sense, "sectarian."

11. Edith Blumhofer summarizes early Pentecostal experience as an experience of "divine encounter" that "infused the present with cosmic significance, offered tangible solutions for every pressing problem, provided a community of likeminded believers, and introduced meaning, certainty, and mission into even the most humble existence." Edith L. Blumhofer, *"Pentecost in My Soul": Explorations in the Meaning of Pentecostal Experience in the Early Assemblies of God* (Springfield, MO: Gospel Publishing House, 1989), p. 16.

12. As will become clear below, I'm also stretching the notion of "thinking" with this already-stretched metaphor. Cp. Stathis Gourgouris, *Does Literature Think?* (Stanford, CA: Stanford University Press, 2003).

13. However, Douglas Jacobsen is surely right to emphasize that, contrary to the popular myth of pentecostals as emotivists lacking any theology, in fact theology is central to pentecostal practice. As he summarizes, "There is no question that spiritual affections are hugely important within pentecostalism, but that emphasis on experiential faith does not require a concomitant diminution of the intellect or a rejection of theology. In fact, one might argue that, apart from theology, pentecostalism would not exist. It is not necessarily

"theology" we just mean the nexus of practices that make up pentecostal spirituality (which might be described as an "implicit theology" or perhaps even a "folk theology").[14] But usually "theology" is associated with the more narrow, propositional aspect of faith — doctrines, dogma, and theoretical reflection. Following Steve Land, I want to emphasize that what defines pentecostalism — and what is shared across the range of Pentecostal and charismatic traditions — is a *spirituality*. To describe this as a spirituality is not to retreat into mushy emotivism; that would be the case only if we assumed the modern dichotomy between "reason" and "emotion."[15] By a "spirituality," Land means "the integration of beliefs and practices in the affections which are themselves evoked and expressed by those beliefs and practices."[16] Such a spirituality, then, has its own kind of knowledge

---

the uniqueness of their experiences that set pentecostals apart; it is the way those experiences are theologically categorized and defined" (Jacobsen, introduction to *Reader in Pentecostal Theology,* p. 5).

14. Thus Jacobsen's *Reader in Pentecostal Theology* finds its resource mainly in sermons. One might suggest that, in this sense, pentecostal theology is a liturgical theology par excellence. Jacobsen's anthology of early Pentecostal theology well conveys its kerygmatic matrix. This is theology forged at the pulpit and in prayer, in the heat of revival and swelter of the camp meeting. One might say that it is a theology that bears the stamp of its liturgical origins (Pentecostals might be a tad skittish about the "liturgical" bit, though that's changing). In this *Reader* we find a collection of pastor-theologians who, though they lacked the imprimatur of the German academy, were nonetheless engaged in serious theological reflection on the work of the Spirit. It is non-Pentecostals who impose such caricatures and false dichotomies on Pentecostal and charismatic traditions. While early Pentecostal theology could not marshal the categories of *academic* theology, it was not therefore essentially atheological or anti-intellectual (though, admittedly, anti-intellectualism — so common to the American psyche in general — also manifests itself within Pentecostalism).

15. As Land rightly comments, "in a postmodern era perhaps the dichotomy of reason and emotion, which has characterized much of American historiography, can be transcended, and new, more wholistic, integrative categories devised. Pentecostals, perhaps more than any other group, came to recognize the dangers of mere emotionalism very early in the movement" (Steven J. Land, *Pentecostal Spirituality: A Passion for the Kingdom,* Journal of Pentecostal Theology Supplement 1 [Sheffield: Sheffield Academic Press, 1993], pp. 122-23). Reflection on emotion would be another appropriate and important line of research for pentecostal philosophy. Such a trajectory would do well to begin with the work of Christian philosopher Robert C. Roberts, *Emotions: An Essay in Aid of Moral Psychology* (Cambridge: Cambridge University Press, 2003), but will also find an important dialogue partner in feminist thought. See, for example, Alison Jagger, "Love and Knowledge: Emotion in Feminist Epistemology," in *Gender/Body/Knowledge: Feminist Reconstructions of Being and Knowing,* ed. Alison Jagger and Susan Bordo (Brunswick, NJ: Rutgers University Press, 1989), pp. 145-71.

16. Land, *Pentecostal Spirituality,* p. 13.

— what Land describes as "an affective understanding."[17] In the milieu of pentecostal worship (as described in the opening vignette of this chapter), we see a panoply of embodied (we might say "liturgical") practices that "carry" within them a tacit understanding, a latent sort of knowledge. Implicit in these practices are not only "beliefs," but also an unarticulated, affective understanding that, when articulated, we will describe as a pentecostal "worldview." However, it should be noted that being able to articulate this is *not* a requirement for absorbing the understanding; rather, this affective understanding can be transformatively absorbed, shaping our passions and dispositions, even if we might not have the theoretical ability to articulate what we "know." While the pentecostal believer might not be able to elucidate this tacit understanding in theologemes, she's nonetheless right when she emphasizes, "I know that I know that I know." This is a knowledge, an "affective understanding," that is on a register prior to propositional articulation.

A pentecostal philosophy will be a philosophy informed and nourished by a pentecostal spirituality. But this is possible only because implicit within pentecostal spirituality is a tacit, unique understanding of the world. I'm suggesting that, rather than describing this tacit understanding as a pentecostal "theology," we might describe it as a pentecostal "worldview."[18] By referring to this as a worldview, I don't mean to suggest that this is a system of doctrines (as the term has sometimes been used); rather, a worldview is a passional orientation that governs how one sees, inhabits, and engages the world.[19] In outlining the elements of a pentecostal worldview, then, I would like to work with a definition of "worldviews" offered by James Olthuis: "A worldview (or vision of life) is a framework or set of fundamental beliefs through which we view the world and our calling and future in it."[20] Note several elements of this account of worldview:

17. Land, *Pentecostal Spirituality*, p. 133.

18. Cartledge also deploys this term to get at something of the "essence" of charismatic spirituality; for pentecostals and charismatics, he observes, "God is encountered in the preaching of Scripture, in the community of the Church as people have fellowship together and in many events within the life of the worshipping and witnessing church because the Spirit can and does 'enliven' all things within the kingdom of God. The ways in which all these features can be located within a framework are akin to a 'worldview' and provide a set of lenses through which the world is viewed and by which reality makes sense" (*Encountering the Spirit*, p. 27).

19. I develop these themes in more detail in James K. A. Smith, *Desiring the Kingdom: Worship, Worldview, and Cultural Formation* (Grand Rapids: Baker Academic, 2009), pp. 27-34.

20. James H. Olthuis, "On Worldviews," *Christian Scholar's Review* 14 (1985): 155.

1. It is a *framework* of fundamental beliefs: a worldview provides the grid
   or framework through which we "make sense" of our world — the "set
   of hinges" on which our thinking and doing turn.

2. It is a framework of *fundamental* beliefs: as fundamental, we could say
   that these beliefs are *pretheoretical*. They are often not beliefs that we
   consciously, rationally reflect upon. They are the "control beliefs"[21]
   that operate subterraneously. Thus, I would suggest that we think
   about a worldview operating at the level of *imagination*, not thinking.
   (We'll return to this below.)

3. It is a framework of fundamental *beliefs:* as "ultimate beliefs,"
   worldviews are fundamentally *religious* in character, shaping the root
   commitments of individuals and communities. It is in this sense that
   Abraham Kuyper can describe all of life as *religious* in some fundamental sense, even for the naturalistic atheist.

4. It provides a view of the *world:* as such, worldviews are *comprehensive,*
   giving us an account of how the big picture hangs together. In this way,
   they help us make sense of the totality of our experience, not just our
   "religious" experience.

5. A worldview tells us something about our *calling:* how we understand
   our world then determines how we understand our roles *in* it. By determining our calling, worldviews shape our *identity* by constituting
   the telos of our being-in-the-world. It defines what matters.

Olthuis emphasizes that, in a way, a worldview provides answers to
questions that "elude our intellectual grasp": they are ultimately confessions
of faith.[22] To put this otherwise: there is no such thing as a "secular" perspective, if by "secular" one means neutral and objective — as if operating without some faith commitments.[23] The crucial implication here is a certain lev-
eling of the playing field: if everyone operates on the basis of a worldview,
and all worldviews have a basically confessional status, then a specifically

21. See Nicholas Wolterstorff, *Reason within the Bounds of Religion* (Grand Rapids:
Eerdmans, 1984).

22. For further discussion of this notion of faith, not as assent to propositions, but as a
pretheoretical trust and commitment, see James H. Olthuis, "Dooyeweerd on Religion and
Faith," in *The Legacy of Herman Dooyeweerd,* ed. C. T. McIntire (Lanham, MD: University
Press of America, 1985), pp. 21-40.

23. I explore this in much more detail in James K. A. Smith, *Introducing Radical Orthodoxy: Mapping a Post-secular Theology* (Grand Rapids: Baker Academic, 2004).

Christian or pentecostal worldview has as much right to come to the scholarly table as any other.[24]

So, to speak of a worldview is to speak about our most fundamental orientation to the world; a framework that operates even prior to thought; a passional orientation of our imagination that filters and explains our experience of the world. It operates unconsciously at the very core of our identity. But precisely because a worldview is not just a rational system or set of cognitive beliefs, we might also consider a couple of related terms as near synonyms, and try to hear this in our use of the term "worldview." In particular, I find Charles Taylor's notion of a "social imaginary" and Amos Yong's account of the "pneumatological imagination" to be rich ways of naming what I'm trying to get at here.

Taylor develops his notion of the "social imaginary" along lines adopted from Heidegger. In *Being and Time,* Heidegger distinguished between "knowledge" *(Wissen)* and "understanding" *(Verstehen).* "Knowledge" referred to the sort of standard picture of knowledge we usually assume — knowledge as justified true belief that traffics in objectified, propositional content. However, Heidegger distinguishes this sort of intellectual, cognitive knowledge from a precognitive "understanding" — a more primordial, affective "attunement" to the world that constitutes the matrix for knowledge. "Thinking" is thus a derivative of "understanding."[25] Drawing on this distinction between knowledge and understanding, Taylor emphasizes that human action and understanding are embedded not, first and foremost, in frameworks of "knowledge" but rather in "social imaginaries" that are "much broader and deeper than . . . intellectual schemes."[26] The social imaginary is a tacit, affective understanding of the world that constitutes the "background" of our being and doing: "It is in fact that largely unstructured and inarticulate understanding of our whole situation, within which particular features of our world show up for us in the sense they have."[27] Very similar to what we've described above as a worldview,

24. Making this case was the burden of Plantinga's "Advice to Christian Philosophers" and, more expansively, *Warranted Christian Belief* (New York: Oxford University Press, 2000).

25. For the classic discussion, see Martin Heidegger, *Being and Time,* trans. John Macquarrie and Edward Robinson (New York: Harper and Row, 1966), §§31-32. I discuss this in more detail in *Desiring the Kingdom,* pp. 63-71.

26. Charles Taylor, *Modern Social Imaginaries* (Durham, NC: Duke University Press, 2004), p. 23.

27. Taylor, *Modern Social Imaginaries,* p. 25.

Taylor emphasizes the "imaginary" descriptor because it captures the sense that this understanding is affective, even aesthetic. This understanding is not an implicit set of propositions; it is more like a story we know by heart. So it is "not expressed in theoretical terms, but is carried in images, stories, and legends."[28] The social imaginary traffics in the currency of the imagination and, Taylor emphasizes, is "carried" in practices. This understanding is not something that is transferred and absorbed by trading propositions; it is a disposition and attunement to the world that seep into our imagination through the practices that "carry" it. As Taylor puts it, such an understanding is "implicit in practice."[29] The ritual *is* its own kind of understanding. So when I argue that pentecostal spirituality has latent within it a pentecostal worldview, we might say that carried in the practices of pentecostal worship is a precognitive understanding that constitutes a "pentecostal social imaginary."

This resonates with Amos Yong's description of the "pneumatological imagination."[30] This locates the imagination at the orchestral center of our experience — receiving, synthesizing, and constructing in a "holistic connection between the mind . . . and the heart: the human center which coordinates the affections, the will, and the spirit."[31] In this framework, Yong continues, "thinking itself is a selectively valuational enterprise, beginning with the imagination and proceeding toward interpretation, theory, and the pursuit of responsibility."[32] Thus the pneumatological imagination "drives both discernment and engagement."[33] In short, pentecostal spirituality is a nexus of practices that dispose us to imagine the world in a certain way, to "make" the world under a Spirit-charged construal.[34] The praxis of pentecostal spirituality affectively forms both our dispositions and our understanding *(Verstehen)*. A pentecostal social imaginary takes practice; it *is* practice. In other words, a pentecostal worldview is *first* em-

---

28. Taylor, *Modern Social Imaginaries*, p. 23.

29. Taylor, *Modern Social Imaginaries*, p. 26.

30. Amos Yong, *Spirit-Word-Community: Theological Hermeneutics in Trinitarian Perspective* (Aldershot: Ashgate, 2002), pp. 119-49.

31. Yong, *Spirit-Word-Community*, p. 129.

32. Yong, *Spirit-Word-Community*, p. 131.

33. Yong, *Spirit-Word-Community*, p. 149.

34. This is consistent with Yong's later account of the relationship between Christian beliefs and practices — and how doctrine emerges from practices. See Amos Yong, *Hospitality and the Other: Pentecost, Christian Practices, and the Neighbor* (Maryknoll, NY: Orbis, 2008), pp. 38-64.

bedded in a constellation of spiritual practices that carry within them an implicit understanding.[35] Pentecostal worship performs the faith.

Elements of a Pentecostal Worldview

I have been arguing that pentecostalism has distinctive elements of its own worldview that offer a unique interpretation of and orientation to the world that, in turn, would inform a distinctly pentecostal philosophy. By a "pentecostal worldview" I don't mean to suggest that pentecostalism has its own catalogue of propositional truths sitting on a shelf that deductively tell us how to think differently about the world. Rather, I mean that embedded in the embodied practices and spirituality of pentecostalism are the elements of a latent but distinctive *understanding* of the world, an affective "take" on the world that constitutes more of a social imaginary than a cognitive framework.[36] My goal in this section is to make explicit what is implicit in pentecostal spirituality — to articulate what is unarticulated in

35. In putting it this way, I slightly disagree with Michael Wilkinson's account of the relation between Pentecostal theology and practice. As he puts it, "Despite some of the vast differences among Pentecostal and charismatic Christians, there is an underlying narrative, a shared spirituality, a set of beliefs about a 'normative social order.' This conception of 'how life ought to be' has given rise to a set of practices and social institutions that constitutes and directs social life for these Pentecostal charismatic Christians." See Michael Wilkinson, "Pentecostalism in Canada: An Introduction," in *Canadian Pentecostalism: Transition and Transformation,* ed. Michael Wilkinson (Montreal and Kingston: McGill-Queen's University Press, 2009), p. 7, citing Christian Smith, *Moral, Believing Animals* (New York: Oxford University Press, 2003). I completely concur that there is a shared narrative and spirituality we can describe globally as "pentecostal." Where I differ is in the relation of beliefs and practices. While Wilkinson sees the beliefs "giving rise to" practices, I'm suggesting that, in some significant sense, it is the practices that give rise to (articulated) beliefs.

36. As noted in chapter 1, it is my hope that what I delineate as the elements of a pentecostal worldview will have a *global* validity about them; that is, I believe these aspects of pentecostal spirituality would be tacitly affirmed by pentecostal and charismatic practices throughout world Christianity. In this sense, "pentecostalism" is a kind of "global culture." That said, I also appreciate Michael Wilkinson's caution: "It is often thought that Pentecostalism is a global culture. Yet that means different things to different people. It is usually claimed that Pentecostals share a common culture characterized by Spirit baptism and speaking in tongues, healing, dreams and visions, and prophecy. It is often thought that Pentecostalism is experiential, biblical, egalitarian, and motivated by mission. While this may be true, it cannot be assumed that these characteristics look the same in all cultures. Specifically, these cultural qualities of Pentecostalism also intermingle with the local cultures in which they take root." Wilkinson, "Pentecostalism in Canada," p. 6.

the practices of pentecostal worship. Thus we're interrogating not pentecostal doctrine as much as pentecostal practice. In effect, I'm asking: What understanding of the world is implicit in the pentecostal worship sketched in the opening vignette of this chapter? What tacit construal of the world is operative in the practices that constitute pentecostal spirituality? My goal is to "read" these practices in order to discern the pentecostal social imaginary that is implicit in them.[37] Once we have articulated the elements of a pentecostal worldview, we'll then consider their philosophical import in the following chapters.

But first a brief word about how I understand the relation between a distinctively pentecostal worldview and the shape of a broader Christian worldview. On this point I am unapologetic: I think the key elements of pentecostal/charismatic spirituality represent the way to be authentically Christian. In other words, I think the birth of the body of Christ at Pentecost represents that the church is properly — and therefore should be — pentecostal. To be Christian is to be charismatic.[38] Authentic, radical, catholic Christianity is properly charismatic or pentecostal. Therefore, I would suggest that the elements of what I'm calling a distinctively "pentecostal worldview" ought to be the elements of a (catholic) Christian worldview. However, insofar as the broader Christian — and especially evangelical — imagination has been captivated by a cessationist assumption, a pentecostal worldview *in practice* is not synonymous with a more generally Christian worldview.[39] But I think the fullest, most authentic expression of radical discipleship is a Christian faith that is both catholic and charismatic.

With that in mind, as already outlined briefly in chapter 1, I suggest we can identify five key elements of a distinctively pentecostal worldview:[40] (1) a position of *radical openness to God,* and in particular, God doing something *differently* or *new;* (2) an *"enchanted" theology of creation and culture;*

37. I have done a similar exegesis of the practices of historic Christian worship in *Desiring the Kingdom,* chapter 5.

38. This, of course, does not at all translate into some kind of primacy for "Pentecostal" denominations. In fact, I would argue that classical Pentecostal denominations compromise the catholicity of charismatic Christianity; however, I'll not make that argument here.

39. On cessationism and the evangelical tradition, see Jon Ruthven, *On the Cessation of the Charismata: The Protestant Polemic on Postbiblical Miracles* (Sheffield: Sheffield Academic Press, 1993).

40. Or, to put this otherwise, there are five pentecostal distinctives of an authentically Christian worldview. So I don't take these five elements to be exhaustive of a "Christian" worldview. For an exposition of the elements of a Christian worldview implicit in Christian worship more broadly, see my *Desiring the Kingdom,* chapter 5.

(3) a *nondualistic affirmation of embodiment and materiality;* (4) an *affective, narrative epistemology;* and (5) an *eschatological orientation to mission and justice.* With this formulation I am trying to articulate the "understanding" implicit in pentecostal spirituality in its most "catholic" (i.e., universal) form. It is my hope that charismatic Christians around the globe would find in these five elements what they consider to be core aspects of their spirituality, whether in Angola or Alabama, Zion or Zambia.[41]

1. Radical Openness to God

At the heart of pentecostal spirituality, as glimpsed in our opening vignette, is a deep sense of expectation and an openness to surprise. One of the reasons pentecostal spirituality is so often linked to spontaneity is that pentecostal worship makes room for the unexpected. Indeed, we might say that, for pentecostals, the unexpected is expected. The surprising comes as no surprise. While I don't mean to propose a ranking of these five elements of a pentecostal worldview, I do think the first is the condition for all the others: a position of radical openness to God, and in particular, openness to God doing something *differently* or *new.* I take the central point of the narrative of Acts 2 to be Peter's courage and willingness to recognize in these strange phenomena the operation of the Spirit and declare it to be a work of God. To declare "this is that" (Acts 2:16) was to be open to God working in unexpected ways. In other words, the crux of the Pentecost story is not the spectacular events of Acts 2:1-4, but rather later, in 2:16, where Peter, with characteristic hermeneutical boldness, asserts: "This is from God!"

We need to appreciate the context here: the disciples have gathered in Jerusalem to await the promised Holy Spirit, as the Lord commanded (Acts 1:8). Ten days later, on the Sabbath, everyone is together and "suddenly" very strange things begin happening: a loud noise like wind and a startling phenomenon that looks like fire. And then the cacophony of voices as 120 people begin speaking in other languages. I don't think this is what the apostles expected! In other words, this inbreaking of the Spirit was not something that was anticipated or predelineated. To use the language of Gadamer's hermeneutics, this was not anticipated by their "hori-

---

41. See Ogbu U. Kalu, "Preserving a Worldview: Pentecostalism in the African Maps of the Universe," *Pneuma: Journal of the Society for Pentecostal Studies* 24 (2002): 110-37.

zons of expectation."[42] In fact, they likely expected God to move quite differently, in ways that their past experience could imagine and anticipate.

But despite all the strangeness and chaos; despite the fact that this is not what they had expected; despite the fact that God had never done this before, Peter stood up and boldly proclaimed: "*This is* God! *This is* what the prophets spoke about! *This is* what we've been waiting for! *This is* the Spirit!"[43] Such a claim required a unique hermeneutic able to nimbly respond to the advent of surprise, as well as a kind of hermeneutical courage to make such a claim. In short, it required forsaking existing, status quo ideas and expectations of how God works. That is why I think Pentecost is really about radical openness to God — especially an openness to a God who exceeds our horizons of expectation and comes unexpectedly.[44] This comes up time and time again in the Spirit-filled narrative of Acts (continuing, I think, the unexpected advent of the incarnation); as, for example, when God begins to move amongst the Gentiles (Acts 10:9-16). The church, of course, does not "kiss its brains good-bye" (hence the meeting, Acts 11:18; 15), but it was open to having its idea and expectations of God changed by God himself. It is this openness that I think lies at the heart of Pentecost, at the heart of being pentecostal, and so at the root of a pentecostal worldview.

It must be admitted that, in our late modern world, increasingly governed by the naturalisms of technology and the market (indeed, the tech-

---

42. See Hans-Georg Gadamer, *Truth and Method,* trans. Joel Weinsheimer and Donald G. Marshall, 2nd rev. ed. (New York: Continuum, 1993), pp. 300-307. One could also describe this openness to surprise in terms of Jacques Derrida's account of the "invention of the other" in "Psyche: Inventions of the Other," trans. Catherine Porter, in *Reading de Man Reading,* ed. Lindsay Waters and Wlad Godzich (Minneapolis: University of Minnesota Press, 1989), pp. 25-65. This particular case, admittedly, is complicated. On one level this mode of the Spirit's advent was not "expected" by the disciples gathered in that upper room. So it came as a surprise. On the other hand, the narrative and story of the people of Israel, including Joel's prophecy, enabled them to narrate this surprising advent in terms of a particular significance. Indeed, the surprising descent of the Spirit had a retroactive effect, making ancient Scriptures come to life in a new way.

43. This is not meant to provide a blanket affirmation of all such claims. Certainly this aspect of pentecostal spirituality is open to abuse. For a novelistic account of this, see Tim Parks, *Tongues of Flame* (London: Heinemann, 1985).

44. Such openness, of course, has its risks and dangers. For a philosophical analysis, see Richard Kearney, *Strangers, Gods, and Monsters: Interpreting Otherness* (London: Routledge, 2002). For a theological caution about charismatic experience in particular, see *We Believe in the Holy Spirit: A Report of the Doctrine Commission of the General Synod of the Church of England* (London: Church House Publishing, 1991).

nology *of* the market), such an openness to divine surprise is easily disdained — looked down upon by the secularly enlightened as parochial, provincial, and primitive.[45] Indeed, such a worldview seems to be a fossil of traditional societies, or a parasitic reaction to the threats of modernity. Pentecostalism clings to the plausibility structures of a mythical world, and these habits of mind are, at best, quaint and, at worst, dangerous. If it's not demonized as a backward retreat from progress, it's patronizingly dismissed as a "simple" faith. But in describing this as a *worldview,* we're also trying to level the playing field a bit — which will require (in chapter 4) that we point up the ways in which the confident secular naturalism that dismisses the "simplicity" of pentecostalism is *also* a worldview, a constellation of commitments that narrates the world on the basis of a kind of faith. And if we can level the playing field, perhaps we can also turn the tables and suggest that this "simple" faith has a kind of complexity about it that has a certain beauty — that the practices and plausibility structures that sustain pentecostal spirituality have their own sort of "logic." And that these plausibility structures have an enduring significance that has been sustained, and will be sustained, longer than the tenuous naturalism that has captured the hearts and minds of a secular elite.

In this respect, I find myself contemplating Félicité, the "simple soul" featured in Flaubert's *Three Tales* — a character whose sensibility we might describe as "pentecostal."[46] Granted, there is an ambiguity in the narrative voice: it might be that Flaubert embodies the gaze of just this naturalized elite, looking down his nose at the "bliss" *(félicité)* of such a simple soul whose bliss is, no doubt, the fruit of her proverbial ignorance. On the other hand, his tale functions as a beautiful encomium to Félicité, a moving portrait of one who, despite her class and circumstances, in a life marked by piety and charity, has secured a joy (a *félicité*) that eludes her aristocratic masters. Perhaps piety has a secret that has eluded the enlightened.[47]

Like so many of Flaubert's characters, Félicité inhabits the lower spec-

45. Peter Berger suggests that a secularized world is an essentially "surprise-free" world. See Berger, *A Rumour of Angels: Modern Society and the Rediscovery of the Supernatural* (Harmondsworth: Penguin, 1969), p. 30.

46. Gustave Flaubert, "A Simple Heart," in *Three Tales,* trans. Robert Baldick (London: Penguin, 1961), pp. 17-56.

47. Jean Morris comments that, with the "newfound sense of plenitude and unity" at the end of the story, "the ironic charge that the name *Félicité* appeared to carry is dissipated." Morris, "Félicité," in *A Gustave Flaubert Encyclopedia,* ed. Laurence M. Porter (Westport, CT: Greenwood Press, 2001), p. 124.

trum of provincial life in France. She moves in a stratum of the world not
so far from the majority of pentecostal believers. Rather than defined by
wealth (of which she has none) or intellect (apart from attending catechism with her charge, she has received no education), she *is* her affections. "Like everyone else," Flaubert alerts us, "she had her love story."[48]
But her story is not a tale of just one courtship gone awry but rather of a
life marked by charity on all fronts; Félicité is shaped by her loves. And this
love is nourished by a tactile spirituality, a faith that traffics not in the abstract realm of dogma and concepts but in a sort of gritty religion of practices and materiality. Each day she would arise at dawn "so as not to miss
Mass," and she would go to sleep each night "with her rosary in her
hands."[49] When she takes young Virginie to catechism, it is Félicité's imagination that is activated by the imagery of the faith. It is the stained-glass
depictions of a story that capture this simple heart, and when the priest
begins to outline the sweeping narrative of redemption, "Félicité saw in
imagination" the scenes unfolding. The story of the Passion moved her to
tears, and the Gospels' imagery of lambs and sowers and doves and stables
took her to a familiar world, but also transformed how she inhabited her
own world.[50] "She found it difficult, however, to imagine what the Holy
Ghost looked like, for it was not just a bird but a fire as well, and sometimes a breath." This turns Félicité to consider her familiar environment as
perhaps enchanted by this Spirit: "She wondered whether that was its light
she had seen flitting about the edge of the marshes at night, whether that
was its breath she had felt driving the clouds across the sky, whether that
was its voice she had heard in the sweet music of the bells."[51] Her devotion
is not a Gnostic desire for escape or a Manichean denigration of materiality; quite to the contrary, for Félicité, Spirit and matter intermingle in
messy but natural ways. Thus her piety is material: her devotion finds its
most elaborate expression in her zealous commitment to the Corpus
Christi feast, but it is also seen in her mundane attachment to relics. Her
room, "to which few people were ever admitted, contained such a quantity
of religious bric-à-brac and miscellaneous oddments that it looked like a

48. Flaubert, "A Simple Heart," p. 19.
49. Flaubert, "A Simple Heart," p. 18.
50. "The sowing of the seed, the reaping of the harvest, the pressing of the grapes — all
those familiar things of which the Gospels speak had their place in her life. God had sanctified them in passing, so that she loved the lambs more tenderly for love of the Lamb of God,
and the doves for the sake of the Holy Ghost." Flaubert, "A Simple Heart," pp. 29-30.
51. Flaubert, "A Simple Heart," p. 30.

cross between a chapel and a bazaar."[52] Her veneration on both counts is testament to a sacramental faith that finds the Spirit in and through the material. For a "simple heart," the so-called natural world is more than it seems; in other words, this "simple" soul has an understanding of the world that complexifies it (in contrast to the reductionistic naturalisms of those who would disdain her simplicity).

This sacramental devotion finds its apogee when Félicité is finally given an image to help her picture the Holy Spirit. While she had difficulty picturing the Holy Ghost, something (someone) enters her life that will change this. A departing aristocrat leaves with the house a parrot, Loulou, to whom Félicité becomes immediately devoted. At one point, she sees something anew: "In church she was forever gazing at the Holy Ghost, and one day she noticed that it had something of the parrot about it. This resemblance struck her as even more obvious in a colour-print depicting the baptism of Our Lord. With its red wings and its emerald-green body, it was the very image of Loulou."[53] To the official, doctrinaire religion of the elite, to even suggest this is not only gauche but almost sacrilegious.[54] But for Félicité, this brought new significance to both: "They were linked together in her mind, the parrot being sanctified by this connexion with the Holy Ghost, which itself acquired new life and meaning in her eyes." This mutual illumination deepens her faith and devotion and finds expression in practice: "although Félicité used to say her prayers with her eyes on the picture, from time to time she would turn slightly towards the bird."[55] The connection was a tactile gift for this simple soul. And it becomes the occa-

52. Flaubert, "A Simple Heart," p. 49. I'm reminded here of Jean-Luc Marion's evaluation of the "kitschy" expressions of devotion associated with Saint-Sulpice parish in Paris, site of a bazaar of religious merchandise. As Marion notes, such "Sulpician" art "practices, more than 'great art,' the impoverishment of the image and the transfer of veneration from the image to the original. Its unintentional *arte povera* assures that less than ever does it seize veneration for the sake of the image, thus protecting it against every tyranny of the image." Marion, *The Crossing of the Visible*, trans. James K. A. Smith (Stanford, CA: Stanford University Press, 2004), pp. 63-64.

53. Flaubert, "A Simple Heart," p. 50.

54. But in a beautiful scene of pastoral care near the end of the story, when Félicité wants to donate something for the altar at the Corpus Christi feast, it is the priest — representative of "official religion" — who allows her to place Loulou's stuffed body on the display. "The neighbors protested that it would not be seemly, but the curé gave his permission" (Flaubert, "A Simple Heart," p. 53). This brings to mind the church's hospitality shown to Lars and his artificial companion (a sex doll) in *Lars and the Real Girl*.

55. Flaubert, "A Simple Heart," p. 53.

sion for a final, saintlike ecstasy in her dying breaths: "A blue cloud of incense was wafted up into Félicité's room. She opened her nostrils wide and breathed it in with a mystical, sensuous fervour. Then she closed her eyes. Her lips smiled. Her heart-beats grew slower and slower, each a little fainter and gentler, like a fountain running dry, an echo fading away. And as she breathed her last, she thought she could see, in the opening heavens, a gigantic parrot hovering above her head."[56]

Like the practices of pentecostal spirituality, such strange devotion is scandalous to the staid rhythms of a disenchanted Christianity. But the awkward messiness and even sensual devotion that characterize pentecostalism are informed by a simple sacramentality like Félicité's coupled with a sense of enchanted expectation and craving for God's surprise. Indeed, Flaubert notes that it is this same expectation that marks "simple hearts" like Félicité: "to minds like hers," he notes, "the supernatural is a simple matter."[57] It is that "natural" expectation of the so-called supernatural that marks pentecostalism's radical openness to divine surprise.

It is because pentecostal faith constitutes a community characterized by a radical openness to God that pentecostal communities emphasize the continued ministry of the Spirit, including continuing revelation, prophecy, and the centrality of charismatic giftings in the ecclesial community.[58] In short, pentecostal spirituality takes the book of Acts as a picture of "normal" and "normative" Christianity. As Jack Deere succinctly puts it, "The book of Acts is the *best* source that we have to demonstrate what normal church life is supposed to look like when the Holy Spirit is present and working in the church. Here we find a church that has passion for God, is willing to sacrifice — even to the point of martyrdom — and is a miracle-working church."[59]

---

56. Flaubert, "A Simple Heart," p. 56.

57. Flaubert, "A Simple Heart," p. 39.

58. See Thomas W. Gillespie's sketch of the dynamism of the early ecclesial community, drawing on Paul's epistles and the *Didache*, in *The First Theologians: A Study in Early Christian Prophecy* (Grand Rapids: Eerdmans, 1994).

59. Jack Deere, *Surprised by the Power of the Spirit* (Grand Rapids: Zondervan, 1993), p. 114. On the centrality of Luke-Acts to specifically Pentecostal narrative identity, see Robert P. Menzies, *Empowered for Witness: The Spirit in Luke-Acts* (Sheffield: Sheffield Academic Press, 1991), especially part II. Granted, this retrieval of Luke's pneumatology is, in many Pentecostal denominations, accompanied by an ecclesiological primitivism and a penchant to recover "New Testament Christianity." However, I don't see this ecclesiological primitivism as endemic to a pentecostal worldview since the dynamics of a Lukan pneumatology are clearly affirmed by Roman Catholic and Anglican charismatics whose ecclesiological sensibility would be opposed to any naive primitivism or restorationism.

This translates into a dynamic ecclesiology *in practice* — where worship is shaped by a persistent openness to surprise and an expectation of the miraculous.[60] The "miraculous" gifts are affirmed as operative, and thus pentecostal spirituality is shaped by a fundamental mode of *reception;* while it is crucial that the gifts be exercised, even their exercise is a matter of reception. Gift, for pentecostal spirituality, goes all the way down. Thus in our opening vignette, at the heart of pentecostal worship is an "altar service" that both makes room for God to be heard (in prophecy, in tongues, in "words of wisdom") and makes room for God to work (to heal, to convict, to transform, to grab hold of the body in all sorts of ways). The pentecostal emphasis on "signs and wonders," along with the continued operations of all the spiritual gifts, grows out of this fundamental conviction: that God's Spirit is a spirit of surprise.

2. An "Enchanted" Theology of Creation and Culture

However, in addition to producing a more dynamic ecclesiology — the sense that the Spirit remains dynamically active *in the church* — implicit in pentecostal spirituality is also a unique theology of creation and culture.[61] Endemic to a pentecostal worldview is the implicit affirmation of the dynamic, active presence of the Spirit not only in the church, but also in creation. And not only the Spirit, but also other spirits. Thus central to a pentecostal construal of the world is a sense of "enchantment."[62]

---

60. Here I think pentecostal theology is poised to make unique contributions to broader discussions. Indeed, the Catholic charismatic movement has already impacted ecclesiology in liturgical renewal within the Catholic tradition. For development of this claim, see the forthcoming manifesto along these lines by Wolfgang Vondey, *Beyond Pentecostalism,* Pentecostal Manifesto Series (Grand Rapids: Eerdmans, forthcoming). Primarily what I have in mind here is a picture of the church operating "in the Spirit" — functioning dynamically as recipient of God's continued gifts and activity within the body of Christ. For a more popular but rich discussion of this, see Deere, *Surprised by the Power of the Spirit.* I should "testify" that this book was crucial in my own pilgrimage and pentecostal formation.

61. I take "culture" (the work of human "making" that elucidates the potentialities folded into creation) to be itself part of "creation." In distinguishing "creation" and "culture" this way, I only mean to distinguish between "nature" and "culture."

62. For a discussion of wider, nonpentecostal attempts to "reenchant" the world, see James K. A. Smith, "Secularity, Globalization, and the Re-enchantment of the World," in *After Modernity? Secularity, Globalization, and the Re-enchantment of the World,* ed. James K. A. Smith (Waco, TX: Baylor University Press, 2008), pp. 3-13.

Pentecostal spirituality, we've noted, is bound up with an expectation that the Spirit operates *within* the created order. In other words, pentecostal spirituality is marked by a deep sense of the Spirit's immanence. While it might not be articulated as such, implicit in the prayers of pentecostals is a richly pneumatological understanding of creation that affirms the Spirit's continued presence and activity in what we could call the "given" or physical layer of creation — "nature" — as well as the Spirit's operation in the "made" or human layer of creation — "culture."[63] The Spirit is understood to be the Trinitarian person in which creation lives and moves and has its being. So nature, in a sense, is "suspended" in the Spirit of creation; or we might say that creation is "charged" with the Spirit's presence.[64] Nature, then, is always more than "the natural." It is suffused with something more; there is always more than meets the naturalizing eye.[65] But the Spirit's presence in creation is not only found in "nature." As Vincent Bacote has recently suggested, a robust sense of the Spirit's presence and activity in creation as *culture* translates into a more positive approach to the Spirit's work in the realm of human culture-making, including the spheres of politics, commerce, and the arts.[66] This sense that all of creation

63. For a rich articulation of just such a pneumatological theology of creation, see Amos Yong, *The Spirit Poured Out on All Flesh: Pentecostalism and the Possibility of Global Theology* (Grand Rapids: Baker Academic, 2005), pp. 267-302.

64. I unpack this in more detail in James K. A. Smith, "The Spirit, Religions, and the World as Sacrament: A Response to Amos Yong's Pneumatological Assist," *Journal of Pentecostal Theology* 15 (2007): 251-61.

65. Harvey Cox, commenting on a leading scientist's account of the mysteries of quantum order, confessed the following: "as I read these words it seemed a little humorous to me that even though many western Christians and certainly most academic theologians would find the primal cosmos of the African indigenous churches 'primitive' or even 'superstitious,' the real situation is very different. We may be the ones who are behind the times. Perhaps modern, liberal western theology — the kind I learned as a graduate student — has been vainly striving to reconcile religion to an allegedly scientific worldview which is actually becoming more outdated every day. Paradoxically, the traditional African cosmology, which the indigenous Christian churches incorporate so inventively, may be more in tune with the 'quantum world' than western theology is." Cox, *Fire from Heaven: The Rise of Pentecostal Spirituality and the Reshaping of Religion in the Twenty-first Century* (Reading, MA: Addison-Wesley, 1995), pp. 257-58. For a scientific account of "the natural" that sees room for the emergence of spirit, see Philip Clayton, *Mind and Emergence: From Quantum to Consciousness* (New York: Oxford University Press, 2004). We will return to these issues in more detail in chapter 4.

66. Vincent Bacote, *The Spirit in Public Theology* (Grand Rapids: Baker Academic, 2005), pp. 117-48. This would also entail (as Bacote notes, pp. 136-39) a sense of the Spirit's

— nature and culture — is charged with the presence of the Spirit is implicit in the prayers and practices of pentecostal spirituality.

However, there is a flip side to this sense of the Spirit's enchantment of creation: pentecostal spirituality is also deeply attentive to what we might describe as the mis-enchantment of the world by other spirits. And this, too, is present in the prayers and practices of pentecostal spirituality. Pentecostal praxis is sometimes almost overwhelmed by a concern with spiritual warfare and the demonic that finds expression in ministries of "deliverance" and liberation. There is a deep sense that multiple modes of oppression — from illness to poverty — are in some way the work of forces that are not just "natural." Thus the "full gospel" of pentecostal salvation sees Christ's triumph over "the powers" expressed in the Spirit's ministry of deliverance. Prayer and worship are a mode of struggle against "the rulers, against the authorities, against the cosmic powers of this present darkness, against the spiritual forces of evil in heavenly places" (Eph. 6:12). While North American pentecostalism is increasingly "naturalized" on this score, all commentators agree that the implicit cosmology assumed by spiritual warfare is one of the primary factors in the explosion of Christianity in the majority world, particularly where indigenous or "primal" religions emphasize a similarly enchanted cosmology. This clearly has implications for working out a pentecostal ontology, as well as the shape of a pentecostal engagement with the sciences — an increasingly important encounter to stage as both pentecostalism and science represent two very different modes of globalization.

3. A Nondualistic Affirmation of Embodiment and Materiality

Included in this ministry of the Spirit is a distinctive belief in the healing of the body.[67] This once again reflects the fact that the pentecostal under-

---

more general presence and operation in another sphere of human culture, namely, religion — even non-Christian religion. This point, of course, has been the central contribution of Amos Yong's work. See Yong, *Discerning the Spirit(s): A Pentecostal-Charismatic Contribution to Christian Theology of Religions,* Journal of Pentecostal Theology Supplement 20 (Sheffield: Sheffield Academic Press, 2000) and *Beyond the Impasse: Towards a Pneumatological Theology of Religions* (Grand Rapids: Baker Academic, 2003).

67. Some classical Pentecostal denominations see physical healing as an aspect of Christ's work of atonement. See, for example, the Assemblies of God *Statement of Fundamental Truths,* §12: "Divine Healing is an integral part of the gospel. Deliverance from sick-

standing of the gospel tracks closely that of Jesus for whom the message of salvation was primarily a message of *liberation* from sin and its effects, including the material effects of illness and disease, as well as oppression and poverty (Luke 4:18-19). Deliverance and liberation, then, are not just "spiritual"; the gospel is not just a tonic for souls. Implicit in this affirmation of bodily healing is a broader affirmation, namely, a sense that the full gospel values the *whole* person. In other words, inchoately embedded in this central affirmation that God cares about our bodies is a radical affirmation of the goodness of creation that translates (or *should* translate) into a radical affirmation of the goodness of bodies and materiality *as such*. Here, I think, is one of the most underappreciated elements of a pentecostal worldview. Or rather: here is a central element of pentecostal practice, the implications of which have not been completely appreciated by the pentecostal tradition. Indeed, this central belief is an indication of a (potential) pentecostal deconstruction of fundamentalist dualisms — dualisms that pentecostal Christians have too often adopted uncritically.[68] By dualism I mean a basically Manichean (or Platonic) approach to the world that sees material reality — both bodies and material elements associated with bodies (sexuality, the arts) — as fundamentally bad or evil, and therefore something to be avoided, suppressed, and ultimately escaped.[69] This runs counter to God's own affirmation of the goodness of material creation (including bodies, Gen. 1:27), as well as the reaffirmation of the body in the incarnation (John 1:14) and resurrection.

What I'm suggesting is that, even though pentecostals have often accepted such dualistic rejections of "the world," a core element of a pentecostal worldview — the affirmation of bodily healing — actually deconstructs such dualism. One of the concomitant effects of this should be a broader affirmation of the goodness of embodiment and materiality, and therefore an affirmation of the fundamental goodness of spheres of culture related to embodiment, such as the arts. We might note that it is pre-

---

ness is provided for in the atonement, and is the privilege of all believers (Isaiah 53:4-5; Matthew 8:16-17; James 5:14-16)." See also John Christopher Thomas, *The Devil, Disease, and Deliverance: Origins of Illness in New Testament Thought,* Journal of Pentecostal Theology Supplement 13 (Sheffield: Sheffield Academic Press, 1998), especially the concluding chapter.

68. See Doug Petersen, *Not by Might nor by Power: A Pentecostal Theology of Social Concern in Latin America* (Oxford: Regnum, 1996), pp. 35, 97-106.

69. As noted above, pentecostal spirituality remains dualistic in a different sense insofar as it maintains an ontological distinction between spirit and matter, and affirms the existence of immaterial entities.

cisely the *holism* of this aspect of pentecostal spirituality that might also explain why pentecostal spirituality is also often attended by a prosperity gospel. That is, the prosperity gospel (for all its failures) might be an un-witting testimony to the holism of pentecostal spirituality. The prosperity gospel — which often attends pentecostalism whether in Africa, Brazil, or suburban Dallas — is, we must recognize, a testament to the very "worldli-ness" of pentecostal theology. It is one of the most un-Gnostic moments of pentecostal spirituality that refuses to spiritualize the promise that the gos-pel is "good news for the poor." In this sense, we might suggest that the im-plicit theological intuition that informs pentecostal renditions of the pros-perity gospel is not very far from Catholic social teaching or liberation theology. It is evidence of a core affirmation that God cares about our bel-lies and bodies.[70]

4. An Affective, Narrative Epistemology

Keep in mind that we are trying to explicate the elements of a pentecostal worldview from implicit assumptions and affirmations that are embed-ded in pentecostal practice and confession. I want to suggest that implicit in pentecostal experience is a unique understanding of the nature of hu-man persons — what we could call a philosophical anthropology. Because of an emphasis on the role of experience, and in contrast to rationalistic evangelical theology (which reduces worship to a didactic sermon, and conceives of our relation to God as primarily intellectual, yielding only "talking head" Christianity), pentecostal spirituality is rooted in affective, narrative epistemic practice.[71] According to this model, knowledge is rooted in the heart and traffics in the stuff of story. It's not that proposi-

70. Granted, this means something very different in the comfort of an air-conditioned megachurch in suburban Dallas (where "prosperity" signals more consumer accumulation of luxury) as opposed to what "prosperity" promises in famished refugee camps in Uganda. The former deserves our criticism; the latter requires careful listening. I discuss this further in James K. A. Smith, "What's Right with the Prosperity Gospel?" *Calvin Theological Semi-nary Forum* (Fall 2009).

71. The most systematic development of this to date is found in Steven J. Land's *Pente-costal Spirituality,* especially pp. 125-81, where he develops this in dialogue with Jonathan Ed-wards. The same theme is broached in an earlier work by Howard M. Ervin under the rubric of a "Pentecostal epistemology." See Ervin, "Hermeneutics: A Pentecostal Option," *Pneuma: Journal of the Society for Pentecostal Studies* 3 (1981): 11-25.

tional truths can be "packaged" in narrative format for "the simple"; rather, the conviction is that story comes before propositions — imagination precedes intellection. We know *in* stories. As Christian Smith has observed, "we not only continue to be animals who make stories but also animals who are *made by* our stories."[72] Implicit in pentecostal spirituality is the epistemological intuition that we are "narrative animals." And as I hope to demonstrate in the next chapter, it is precisely this affective, narrative epistemology that yields a deep affinity between postmodernism and a pentecostal worldview.

5. An Eschatological Orientation to Mission and Justice

While baptism in the Holy Spirit, or even speaking in tongues, is often considered the hallmark of pentecostal spirituality, a growing cadre of scholars has emphasized that eschatology is *as* or even *more* important in early pentecostal spirituality. The outpouring of the Spirit has meaning and significance precisely because this is a sign of "the last days"; in other words, the baptism of the Holy Spirit functions as a sign only within an overarching narrative that has an eschatological orientation toward the coming kingdom. Thus Steven Land describes pentecostal spirituality as an "apocalyptic vision."[73] Peter Althouse captures this intertwinement of the Spirit, tongues-speech, and eschatology: "The ability to speak in tongues was thought to empower the recipient to proclaim the 'glorious fulfillment' of Jesus' imminent coming to establish his kingdom. At the same time, though, the eschatological message of early Pentecostals envisioned a world that was more equitable and just because it was a foretaste of the rule of Jesus Christ and anticipated the second coming."[74]

So, contrary to common assumptions about the "otherworldliness" of pentecostals — indeed, contrary to some of the habits of pentecostals

---

72. Christian Smith, *Moral, Believing Animals,* p. 64.

73. Land, *Pentecostal Spirituality,* pp. 58-121. The now classic study on early Pentecostal eschatology is D. William Faupel, *The Everlasting Gospel: The Significance of Eschatology in the Development of Pentecostal Thought* (Sheffield: Sheffield Academic Press, 1996). For an analysis of contemporary Pentecostal eschatology, see Peter Althouse, *Spirit of the Last Days: Pentecostal Eschatology in Conversation with Jürgen Moltmann* (London: T. & T. Clark, 2003), especially pp. 61-106.

74. Peter Althouse, "Apocalyptic Discourse and a Pentecostal Vision of Canada," in *Canadian Pentecostalism,* p. 59.

themselves — endemic to a pentecostal worldview is an eschatology that engenders a commitment both to mission and to ministries of empowerment and social justice, with a certain "preferential option for the marginalized" tracing back to its roots in the fishermen at Pentecost. This empowerment of the marginalized was reactivated at Azusa Street as a kind of paradigm of marginalization — a revival in an abandoned stable, led by an African American preacher, William Seymour.[75] This stems, I think, from our first principle: the revolutionary activity of the Spirit always disrupts and subverts the status quo of the powerful. That is why the Corinthian church — the church that was perhaps a little *too* open to the gifts of the Spirit! (1 Cor. 14:39-40) — was a community of *me onta*, those who "are not," the despised and foolish of the world. Amongst this revolutionary community of the Spirit, one does not find "many wise according to the flesh, not many mighty, not many noble" (1 Cor. 1:26). Thus one of the signs of the eschatological inbreaking of the Spirit into the present is the subversion of the powerful by the weak — who, in the Spirit, function as the very power of God. This is why, as Cheryl Sanders comments, Azusa Street preacher William Seymour found more "evidence" in racial reconciliation than glossolalia: "Seymour saw the breaking of the color line as a much surer sign than tongue-speaking of God's blessing and of the Spirit's healing presence."[76] The "latter rain" of the Spirit translates not into a desire to escape from this world but into a desire to embody and model the coming kingdom, and even to foster the transformation of *this* world. As Althouse points out, this is "an eschatology of transformation rather than one of world destruction."[77] So, contrary to expectations of a militant chiliasm as a kind of cosmic death wish, the eschatological orientation of pentecostal spirituality translates into a social program that seeks to embody the kingdom in the midst of a broken creation — a pentecostal rendition of the social gospel. "While the social gospel wanted to make the world a more just place," Althouse remarks, "early Pentecostal

75. For a helpful narrative tracing this connection between the early beginnings of the movement and Pentecostal social theory, see Petersen, *Not by Might*, pp. 1-40.

76. Cheryl J. Sanders, *Empowerment Ethics for a Liberated People: A Path to African American Social Transformation* (Minneapolis: Fortress, 1995), p. 73. Cp. Cox, *Fire from Heaven*, p. 63.

77. Althouse, *Spirit*, p. 22. Crucial here is Gerald Sheppard's account of the tension between a properly pentecostal eschatology and the dispensationalist eschatology that many Pentecostals came to accept. See Gerald T. Sheppard, "Pentecostalism and the Hermeneutics of Dispensationalism," *Pneuma: Journal of the Society for Pentecostal Studies* 2 (1984): 5-34.

belief in tongues and healing as a prolepsis of the Second Coming embodied within it (albeit in embryonic form) material social implications for the transformation of society."[78] Thus pentecostal communities — like the interracial community at Azusa Street, or early pentecostal pacifism[79] — are called to be countercultural witnesses of how culture can and will be otherwise.

Now granted, distilling this eschatological emphasis on cultural transformation as a core element of pentecostal identity might actually be the occasion for critical reflection on contemporary Pentecostal practice. If a Pentecostal denomination can produce the likes of John Ashcroft (emerging from the Assemblies of God, Ashcroft was a functionary of the Religious Right in his role as attorney general in the Bush administration), then there are clearly tensions within pentecostal practice — tensions between what's implicit in pentecostal spirituality and what pentecostals have more explicitly adopted as their cultural stance. In this respect, articulating the elements of a pentecostal worldview can be an occasion for critical reflection on who we are, and who we're called to be — and might thereby be the occasion for a deconstruction of who we've become. In particular, recovering a sense of the prophetic, eschatological edge of a pentecostal worldview should be an occasion for us to call into question the way in which North American pentecostals have been so quick to ally themselves with power and the status quo — with "law and order" and military might, rather than the meek of the earth and "weak things of the world" (1 Cor. 1:27). Thus rather than the convergence we so often witness between Pentecostalism and prosperity — between the "full gospel" and big business — we ought to expect a certain confluence between "Marx and the Holy Ghost."[80]

78. Althouse, "Apocalyptic Discourse," p. 66.

79. As Paul Alexander has demonstrated, early Pentecostals were almost universally pacificist. See Alexander, *Pentecostals and Peacemaking: Heritage, Theology, and the 21st Century* (Eugene, OR: Pickwick, 2009) and *Peace to War: Shifting Allegiances in the Assemblies of God* (Telford, PA: Cascadia/Herald, 2008). See also Joel Shuman, "Pentecost and the End of Patriotism: A Call for Restoration of Pacifism among Pentecostal Christians," *Journal of Pentecostal Theology* 9 (1996): 70-96, and Jay Beaman, *Pentecostal Pacifism: The Origin, Development, and Rejection of Pacific Belief among the Pentecostals* (Hillsboro, KS: Center for Mennonite Brethren Studies, 1989).

80. This is the title of the final section of Mike Davis's essay, "Planet of the Slums: Urban Involution and the Informal Proletariat," *New Left Review* 26 (2004): 5-34. We'll explore this in more detail in chapter 6 below.

Conclusion: Seeing Otherwise

We know and confess the Spirit as the Lord our healer. And included in the Spirit's healing and renewing work is the very way in which we perceive the world — the worldview that governs our perception, the imagination that orients how we inhabit our world. In outlining these key elements of a pentecostal worldview, I mean to highlight the way in which the Spirit invites us to see the world otherwise. In the ensuing chapters I will consider the philosophical implications of this pentecostal "understanding," aiming to outline more concretely the shape of a pentecostal philosophy that begins unapologetically, to paraphrase Plantinga, from "what we 'know' as pentecostals."

3 Storied Experience

A Pentecostal Epistemology

Introduction: "I Know That I Know That I Know"

As she made her way to the altar, Denise carried herself in a way that indicated she already knew her story was "irrational." Her steps were halting and timid, her eyes cast downward in a shaded look of mild embarrassment — as if the criteria for "rationality" were perched on her shoulder like little devils, mocking her and trying to dissuade her from testifying to such nonsense. Indeed, it wasn't just the ethereal taunts of demonic dissuaders she was contending with; she could easily recall the flesh-and-blood skepticism of her father and sister as she had relayed the story to them earlier that week. Through a million little channels Denise had absorbed enough of the wider culture's plausibility structures to "know" that this was crazy. And yet here she was, making her way forward in response to the pastor's invitation for the congregation to share their "God sightings" for the past week — their stories and testimonies about where they saw the Spirit living and active in their day-to-day lives. Granted, this Sunday evening ritual could easily devolve into a parade of tales about divinely secured parking spaces or supernatural deliverance from failing to do one's homework. But the "testimony service" was woven into the very warp and woof of discipleship at Cornerstone Vineyard Fellowship — these stories of faith were as important as any Sunday morning sermon.

Grasping the microphone handed to her by the pastor, Denise has to catch her breath and clear her throat. While a week ago she couldn't imagine standing in front of 300 people and speaking in public, tonight she can't imagine *not* doing it.

"Um, hi. I'm Denise," she says just a little bit too loudly, the mic squealing mildly in response. Jolted, she holds the microphone away from her face and pauses again before continuing — the pastor nodding and smiling in encouragement, a hand on her shoulder.

"Uh, I've never done this before. But when Pastor invited us to share our 'God sightings,' the Spirit wouldn't let me sit on my hands any longer. I just *have* to tell you — I have to tell someone, *every*one." Her words are met with various echoes of "Yes, Lord!" and "Amen!"

"As some of you know, Gary and I have been married for almost eight years. And maybe you noticed that we don't have any children." There is a crackle in her voice but she continues: "I've shared with some of the ladies at Bible study how much trouble we've had getting pregnant. It's been *so* hard, and *so* long." The cacophony of prayers and shouts settles down to a rapt silence as Denise continues her story.

"And I've gotta be honest with you: I've been pretty mad at God. There are all these women in the Bible who couldn't have babies. But it seems like their stories always ended with a miracle. 'Where's my miracle?' I kept asking God." Her voice has fallen off, her face has dropped, and her shoulders are beginning to tremble. The pastor inches closer and wraps her arm around Denise in comfort and encouragement. The congregation's attention is suspended in a bit of a netherworld, not sure where this story is going. Only rarely have "God sightings" been honest laments. But Denise takes a deep breath, wipes the mascara from her cheeks, and resumes her story. Gary has joined her at her side.

"A few weeks ago at Bible study I had . . . well . . . a complete meltdown!" she announces in a tearful laugh. Others join in her mirth and some of the older ladies smile at one another knowingly. "I was just so frustrated and hopeless — and angry, to be honest. I was just so sad and so tired. But then sister Rose stopped everything and said, 'We've gotta pray.' And so all the ladies gathered round me, and laid their hands on me, and they prayed and prayed and prayed. It was as if they were lifting me on a blanket in their prayers and I fell back into them in the strangest feeling I've ever had. I heard sisters praying the names of Sarah and Hannah and Elizabeth and I *so* wanted their story to be my story. But I was too tired to believe it anymore — but I was also kinda too tired to *not* believe it. So I just let myself fall back into their prayers. I think I might have even fallen asleep!" Denise testifies with a sheepish grin. Gary smiles with her, his eyes fixed on the carpet, his hand trembling around her waist.

"When I woke up, I didn't feel any different. A little embarrassed maybe. In fact, that's why I didn't come to church last Sunday. I was too embarrassed to see all those ladies again." The ladies respond with puckered chins and frowns meant to be encouraging. "Anyway, I pretty much forgot about the whole thing. Or at least I tried to forget about the whole thing. It's just so tiring to keep thinking about it."

"But . . . ," Denise begins, but her breath seems taken away. She resumes her story in a rapid, breathy falsetto, trying her best to get the words out: "Something was sorta wrong this past week — in a way that could be good, or really, really bad. Gary encouraged me to go to the doctor, so I had an appointment on Friday." She's now doubled over, shaking her head in disbelief, but then explodes up like a Jack-in-a-box and loudly proclaims, "I'm pregnant!" The words roll out of her in an ecstasy that tilts between joy and sorrow; she is overwhelmed and exhausted by the tale. Pastor and Gary have now enfolded her in an embrace, supporting her as the congregation erupts in shouts of praise and thanksgiving. But Denise has more to say.

"Some people didn't believe me. When the doctor told me, I just had to tell him about the prayer meeting. He talked to me about hormone levels and stress. Even when I told my father and sister, they looked at me like I was a freak — like I didn't know what I was talking about. But like Brother Jack always says: 'I know that I know that I know!' I know that I know that I know that God was working my belly! And I don't care what others think," she adds, now falling back into the King James English of her upbringing. "I am not ashamed, for I know whom I have believed, and am persuaded that he is able!"

Pentecostalism as Countermodernity

"I know that I know that I know" is a common refrain in pentecostal worship services that make room for testimony and witness. And making room for testimony is central to pentecostal spirituality precisely because narrative is central to pentecostal identity. As Grant Wacker observes, "Like countless Christians before them, early pentecostals assumed that their personal faith stories bore normative implications for others. Consequently, they devoted much of the time in their worship services — maybe

a third of the total — to public testimonies about their spiritual jour-
neys."[1] This narrative function of testimony is bound up in the very DNA
of Pentecost where, in Acts 2, we see Peter and the disciples making sense
of their experience by weaving it into a larger received narrative: to be able
to say that "this is that" (Acts 2:16, pointing to Joel 2:28-32) is to frame and
make sense of the phenomenon by situating it within a narrative.[2] In testimony, then, pentecostals enact an identity by writing themselves into the
larger story of God's redemption. "Crucifixion, resurrection, Pentecost,
parousia, all formed one great redemption, one story in which they were
participants with assigned roles to play."[3] Narrative provided a framework
to make sense of their own struggles and victories: "by interpreting their
daily life and worship in terms of the significant events of biblical history,
their own lives and actions were given significance."[4] And this narrative
understanding of God's action yielded a practice that was integral to pentecostal worship: testimony.[5] As Wacker summarizes, "The testimony
forcefully asserted that the believer's passage on this earth formed part of a
magnificent drama in which cosmic good vanquished evil. . . . Each person's private struggles somehow soared above the merely private and reap-
peared in a framework that spanned the millennia."[6]

1. Grant Wacker, *Heaven Below: Early Pentecostals and American Culture* (Cambridge, MA: Harvard University Press, 2001), p. 58.

2. Steven Land reminds us that this narratival hermeneutic is also eschatological: it's not just a matter of filling in a "back story," but also projects a future that is envisioned by the narrative (Land, *Pentecostal Spirituality: A Passion for the Kingdom,* Journal of Pentecostal Theology Supplement 1 [Sheffield: Sheffield Academic Press, 1993], p. 72 n. 1). This same narratival move is then repeated by early pentecostals in the 1900s who, confronted with strange phenomena, make sense of them by framing them in terms of a larger narrative (viz., the biblical story) that is also ultimately eschatological. See, for instance, Aimee Semple McPherson, "This Is That," in *A Reader in Pentecostal Theology: Voices from the First Generation,* ed. Douglas Jacobsen (Bloomington: Indiana University Press, 2006), pp. 186-96.

3. Land, *Pentecostal Spirituality,* p. 72.

4. Land, *Pentecostal Spirituality,* p. 73.

5. Wacker considers the basic structure and substance of early Pentecostal testimony in *Heaven Below,* pp. 58-69. Testimonies (from around the world) also made up a significant part of the material published in the *Apostolic Faith,* the newsletter of the Azusa Street Mission published from 1906 to 1908 (reprinted in *Like as of Fire,* collected by Fred T. Corum [Wilmington, MA, 1981]). Edith L. Blumhofer's *"Pentecost in My Soul": Explorations in the Meaning of Pentecostal Experience in the Early Assemblies of God* (Springfield, MO: Gospel Publishing House, 1989), also collects testimonies of first-generation Pentecostals.

6. Wacker, *Heaven Below,* p. 69.

In chapter 2 I outlined the basic elements of a pentecostal worldview that are implicit in the practices of pentecostal worship and experience. The point of that "articulation project" — making explicit what is implicit in pentecostal practice — is to now consider the philosophical ramifications of this pentecostal "understanding." In this chapter I want to particularly consider the tacit epistemic commitments that are embedded in the pentecostal practice and experience of testimony, to consider the inchoate "understanding of understanding" at work in the pentecostal claim that "I know that I know that I know." In particular, I want to suggest that at work here is a kind of proto-postmodern intuition about knowledge that constitutes a performative critique of modern criteria for knowledge — a pentecostal critique of the rationalism (or cognitivism or "intellectualism")[7] that characterizes modern accounts of knowledge. Pentecostal practice can function as a sort of countermodernity.[8] Thus there are elements of a pentecostal worldview that resonate with a "postmodern" critique of autonomous reason such that we might see Azusa Street as a postmodern revival.[9] In this chapter I want to first explore how pentecostal testimony and experience constitute an implicit critique of rationalism. I'll then consider how the function of story and narrative carries within it fundamental epistemic commitments (exploring how these resonate with a biblical epistemology). Finally, given the centrality of affect and imagination in pentecostal narrative and testimony, the chapter will close with a tentative outline for a pentecostal aesthetics.

When Enoch Adeboye, leader of the Redeemed Christian Church of God in Nigeria, gives his testimony, it has "the usual Augustinian elements:

7. Charles Taylor criticizes "intellectualist" models of the human person in Taylor, "To Follow a Rule . . . ," in *Bourdieu: Critical Perspectives*, ed. Craig Calhoun, Edward LiPuma, and Moishe Postone (Chicago: University of Chicago Press, 1993), pp. 45-60.

8. I use the term advisedly. One of Wacker's aims, it seems, is to show the extent to which Pentecostals, despite their stated opposition to "modernism," nonetheless deeply drunk from its well. I don't necessarily deny that; I would admit that pentecostalism is complex and variegated on this score. In seeing its implicit account of knowledge as "countermodern," I have in mind John Milbank's reading of the "radical pietists" Hamann and Jacobi as modern critics of modernity. See John Milbank, "Knowledge: The Theological Critique of Philosophy in Hamann and Jacobi," in *Radical Orthodoxy: A New Theology*, ed. John Milbank, Catherine Pickstock, and Graham Ward (London: Routledge, 1999), pp. 21-37.

9. Carl Raschke has recently suggested that "Charismatic Christianity is not modern, but instead thoroughly postmodern." See *The Next Reformation: Why Evangelicals Must Embrace Postmodernity* (Grand Rapids: Baker Academic, 2004), p. 157.

prestige, women, booze."[10] But as Andrew Rice goes on to note, Adeboye also confesses a "distinctive weakness": an "idolatrous reliance on reason." As Pastor Adeboye explains, "It begins to give man the impression that man is the almighty, that man can do anything. He can go to the moon, go to Mars, perform operations with a laser beam without spilling blood. The problem, the way I see it, is that because of the advance of technology, science and investing, the Western world began to feel that they didn't need God as much as before. Whereas in Africa, we need him. We know we need him to survive."[11]

Most philosophers would be getting uncomfortable at this point. This critique of an "idolatrous reliance on reason" sounds like license for just the sort of anti-intellectualism that is often associated with pentecostalism, and such an anti-intellectualism would not only be unphilosophical but also antiphilosophical. And, of course, there's no shortage of examples of pentecostal anti-intellectualism.[12] But I'm suggesting that we need a more fine-grained analysis of what's embedded in pentecostal experience and what's being said in such testimonies. While pentecostals (like all sorts of other evangelical Christians) might be prone to fall into anti-intellectualism, I don't think this is endemic to pentecostal spirituality as such. Rather, it attends the populism that characterizes most expressions of pentecostalism. But if we filter our analysis more carefully, and try — at least theoretically — to sort out populist anti-intellectualism from the pentecostal practice of testimony, I think we can discern in pentecostal spirituality a sort of inchoate epistemic grammar, perhaps best described as a hermeneutic — a tacit understanding of what constitutes "knowledge" and the means by which we know. This incipient epistemology is not anti*rational,* but antirational*ist;* it is not a critique or rejection of reason as such but rather a commentary on a particularly reductionistic model of reason and rationality, a limited, stunted version of what counts as "knowledge." If the pentecostal practice of testimony is a kind of critique of our "idolatrous reliance on reason," it's not reason that is the target, but our idolatrous construction of it.

In its critique of idolatrous constructions of reason — rational*isms* of various stripes — pentecostalism amounts to a kind of proto-postmodernism insofar as postmodernism (as a loosely bounded set of ideas)

10. Andrew Rice, "Mission from Africa," *New York Times Magazine,* April 12, 2009 [http://www.nytimes.com/2009/04/12/magazine/12churches-t.html].

11. Rice, "Mission from Africa."

12. This is the primary concern in Rick M. Nañez, *Full Gospel, Fractured Minds? A Call to Use God's Gift of Intellect* (Grand Rapids: Zondervan, 2005), pp. 19-131.

is itself a critique of modern, Western rationalism.[13] As trickle-down from a conglomeration of philosophical sources, we have inherited a particular picture of what constitutes and counts as "knowledge" — a picture bound up with a related picture of human persons as "thinking things," autonomous rational agents, transcendental logical egos, disembodied centers of cognitive perception.[14] For instance, the implications of Descartes's famous delineation of the essence of the human person as a thinking thing, a "mind" only contingently and temporarily housed in a body, are twofold: a valorization of *thinking* as the core of human identity and a devaluation of *embodiment* as a source of deception and distress. Thus we can describe this understanding of the human person as *rationalism* because it privileges reason or thinking as the essence of what it means to be human, and denigrates material embodiment as not only accidental to being human, but even regrettable. Furthermore, it conceives the nature of reason and "thinking" on a narrow register of calculation and deduction — as a kind of "processing" of the world that would provide the metaphors for our increasingly computerized world.[15]

This picture of the human person as a "thinking thing" or essentially rational being has further implications, beyond the general denigration of material, embodied existence. First, if the essence of the human person is thinking, then what really matters is what can be thought — and what can be thought is what can be calculated, inferred, deduced, and articulated in propositions. In other words, there is an attendant cultural privileging of what is *cognitive*, what can be thought and calculated — which finds its culmination in what Lyotard described as the "computerization" of knowledge.[16] What counts as "knowledge" is that which conforms to the calcula-

---

13. For a fuller account of postmodernism as a critique of modern rationalism, see James K. A. Smith, *Who's Afraid of Postmodernism? Taking Derrida, Lyotard, and Foucault to Church* (Grand Rapids: Baker Academic, 2006), pp. 59-80.

14. I expand my critique of this philosophical anthropology in James K. A. Smith, *Desiring the Kingdom: Worship, Worldview, and Cultural Formation* (Grand Rapids: Baker Academic, 2009), chapter 2.

15. Cf. Heidegger's critique of "calculative thinking" in *Discourse on Thinking*, trans. John M. Anderson and E. Hans Freund (New York: Harper and Row, 1966).

16. This theme in Jean-François Lyotard's *The Postmodern Condition: A Report on Knowledge*, trans. Geoff Bennington and Brian Massumi (Minneapolis: University of Minnesota Press, 1984) is not often appreciated. But central to Lyotard's "report" on the state of knowledge is his account of how the "status" of knowledge is altered because it has been commodified. "[O]nly if learning is translated into quantities of information" can it count as "knowledge" (p. 4). Thus, "[a]long with the hegemony of computers comes a certain

ble standards of logical operation. Or even worse, what counts as knowledge is only what can be reduced to "information" or data.[17]

In addition to the priority of the cognitive, modernity's rationalistic picture of the human person has a second important side effect: the emergence of a new focus on the *universality* of reason — or perhaps better, the *neutrality* of reason because of its universality. Beginning with the assumption that reason or thinking is what is essential to the human person — what really *defines* the human person — and having relegated the particularities of embodiment to the realm of the contingent, accidental, and impure (the body as a "taint" on reason), modernity yields a new universalism of a sort. The idea is this: the disembodied minds that really define us as human share in common the universal principles of reason and logic. So what counts as "rational" must be the same for everyone. What make us different are only the particularities and contingencies of our embodied lives: where we live, the cultures we inhabit, the languages we learn, the religions we believe, the traditions we have received, the (gendered) bodies we inhabit, and so on. But, for instance, the Enlightenment mission (as a particular instantiantion of modernity) is to negate all those particularities, precisely because it has already negated the body. Those features of embodied existence that shape and tailor our "perspective" on the world must be suppressed and negated in order to escape to the pure, untainted realm of reason and cognition — the world

---

logic, and therefore a certain set of prescriptions determining which statements are accepted as 'knowledge' statements" (p. 4). Indeed, the reduction of knowledge to what can be "stated" is the first step in this reduction.

17. This priority of the cognitive and rational made a huge impact on the institutions of modernity, and also came to have a major impact on the church and theology, perhaps particularly in evangelical circles (even though the Enlightenment thought it was precisely this rationalism that made religion merely superstition and part of a "tradition" from which reason liberated us). Charles Hodge, for instance, famously declared that the Bible was a "storehouse of facts," indicating a very modern, reductionistic way of understanding the narrative of Scripture. I would suggest that the regnant orthodoxy in evangelical theology and philosophy adopts this rationalistic picture of the human person and thus reduces Christian faith to a set of logical propositions to which we give our cognitive assent. Somewhat ironically, I think it is this rather reductionistic model of rationality that is advocated by Nañez's call for Pentecostals to embrace "the life of the mind" (in *Full Gospel, Fractured Minds?* pp. 135-43 and 163-83), and something similar is extolled as an antidote to "relativism" by J. P. Moreland, *Kingdom Triangle: Recover the Christian Mind, Renovate the Soul, Restore the Spirit's Power* (Grand Rapids: Zondervan, 2007), pp. 111-39. I'm suggesting that the epistemology implicit in pentecostal spirituality would call into question this embrace of rationalist models of knowledge.

of the intellect of which all human beings are citizens.[18] It is this confident assumption about the *universality* and therefore *neutrality* of reason that yields one of modernity's most powerful fruits: the notion of *secularity* and the doctrine of secular*ism* — both of which remain powerful forces today, in Europe especially, but also in the United States. "Secular" becomes code for what is (supposedly) neutral, objective, unbiased, and above all, *not* religious. Religious belief, then, becomes the very antithesis (and nemesis) of reason — and religious *experience* would only be worse. Indeed, the Enlightenment offered universal reason as a cure for the disease of religious belief and "superstition."

It is just this rationalism (or "cognitivism")[19] — along with its attendant denigration of embodiment and promotion of secularism — that is called into question by the postmodern critique of reason. Contrary to caricatures, the postmodern critique is not a rejection of rationality and a celebration of irrational madness; rather, it is a critique of the thinking-thing picture of the human person bequeathed to us by Descartes, Kant, and others. In other words, what postmodernism calls into question is not rationality per se but the particular construal of rationality and knowledge characteristic of modern rational*ism*. And it does so in an interesting way:

18. Well, truth be told, the Enlightenment folks didn't actually think all *Homo sapiens* qualified as rational human beings; in particular, women and Africans were considered less than human in this respect. And so there's a dark underside to modernity's triumphalism that finds expression in institutions such as slavery and patriarchy. I think it is not insignificant, then, that early Pentecostalism contested both racial segregation and the exclusion of women from ministry. But, of course, such "modern" bigotry was nothing new.

19. "Cognitivism" is a slippery term; I use it here as shorthand for a picture of knowledge that reduces knowledge to the propositional. In this respect, I was encouraged to see Robert C. Roberts recognize a similar difficulty with the term "cognition." In a footnote to his discussion of the emotions as "construals," he notes that "cognition" is a word that "does not have well agreed-upon boundaries, but it is perhaps usual that a mental event is a cognition only if it has one or more of the following characteristics: a) it is truth-asserting, b) it is inferred from some other datum" (in Roberts, "What an Emotion Is: A Sketch," *Philosophical Review* 97, no. 2 [April 1988]: 188 n. 12). This is in the ballpark of how I'm using the term when I criticize "cognitiv*ism*." Another near synonym might be what Charles Taylor describes as "intellectualism" — a working picture that sees "the human agent as primarily a subject of representations." This subject, he comments, "is a monological one. She or he is in contact with an 'outside' world, including other agents, the objects she or he and they may deal with, her or his own and others' bodies, but this contact is through the representations she or he has 'within.'" As a result, "what 'I' am, as a being capable of having such representations, the inner space itself, is definable independently of body or other." See Taylor, "To Follow a Rule . . . ," p. 49.

First, postmodernism[20] calls into question the supposed neutrality and universality of reason as proclaimed by the moderns. At the risk of falling into cliché, the postmodern critique of modernity found that what was often touted as "rational" turned out to be what white European males thought would be a good idea.[21] In other words, the lineaments and conclusions of universal reason are, at the end of the day, only one particular perspective writ large as if it were not a perspective but "just the way things really are." So what claimed to be a universal, neutral, God's-eye-view of the world turns out to be only the elevation and deification of one particular perspective pretending and parading as if it were not a "perspective" at all. And what is hailed as "knowledge" and "rationality" is one particular mode or register of calculation and perception — one particular way of "processing" the world according to the rubric of a particular logic.[22]

Second, beyond merely pointing out the reductionist nature of Enlightenment "rationality" and the veiled particularity of modernity's feigned universal reason, postmodernism actually *re*values embodiment and particularity. In other words, postmodernism offers a fundamentally different philosophical anthropology or understanding of human nature that does not reduce human identity to thinking or a disembodied mind. To the contrary, postmodernism takes seriously the particularities of race, gender, class, and geography precisely because it takes seriously the fact that we are embodied creatures who inhabit a world of space and time — and we inhabit this world in particular ways, in particular places, at particular times.[23] This

20. For merely heuristic purposes, I'm going to use the term in a monolithic way. Of course, none of it is as simple and clean as I'm portraying it here. However, the postmodern sensibility I'm describing would be shared by a host of twentieth-century thinkers such as Heidegger, Gadamer, Foucault, Derrida, Polanyi, Kuhn, and many more.

21. Here is another point at which I think the philosophical intuitions implicit in pentecostal spirituality resonate with feminist philosophy. For a representative feminist critique of reductionistic models of rationality (particularly Kant's transcendental logical ego) articulated in relation to the Christian philosophical tradition, see Janet Catherina Wesselius, "Points of Convergence between Dooyeweerdian and Feminist Views of the Philosophic Self," in *Knowing* Other-*wise: Philosophy at the Threshold of Spirituality,* ed. James H. Olthuis (Bronx, NY: Fordham University Press, 1997), pp. 55-68. See also Andrea Nye, *Feminist Theory and the Philosophies of Man* (New York: Routledge, 1988).

22. Cp. Michel Foucault, *The Archaeology of Knowledge,* trans. A. M. Sheridan Smith (New York: Pantheon Books, 1972), pp. 100-101.

23. See, for instance, Linda McDowell's critique of "thinking-thing"-ism in her *Gender, Identity, and Place: Understanding Feminist Geographies* (Minneapolis: University of Minnesota Press, 1999).

is not a regrettable state of affairs to be lamented, but rather an essential aspect of being human that is to be affirmed. And because postmodernism rejects the reductionistic picture of human beings as merely thinking things, it also calls into question the privileging of reason or intellect as queen of the faculties. Instead, postmodernism argues that our orientation to the world is not primarily mediated by intellectual perception, but rather by a more fundamental "passional orientation" — an affective comportment to the world that "construes" the world of experience on the basis of an "understanding" that is precognitive.[24]

So rather than reducing the human person to a disembodied thinking mind, postmodernism revalues embodiment, and in so doing it offers an account of knowing that revalues what, in the philosophical tradition, has often been referred to as the "heart." Thus it is no coincidence that one of the most formative influences on Martin Heidegger's account of "affective" understanding was the work of Blaise Pascal, who was himself retrieving a vision of knowing first articulated by Saint Augustine.[25] As Pascal famously put it, "the heart has reasons of which Reason knows nothing." This is a way of "knowing" the world that cannot be reduced to cognition or intellectual perception — and certainly not to "data" or facts. Thus postmodernism lowers the core of human identity, as it were, from the head to the heart. This, of course, is not some advanced theoretical excuse for kissing our brains good-bye, nor is it philosophical license to endorse some kind of anti-intellectual emotionalism. What we're calling the "heart" or the "affections" does not simply reduce to the emotions, so we're *not* setting up some kind of dichotomous opposition between head and heart, between love and knowledge, between affection and cognition, between thinking and passion. I don't mean to suggest that postmodernism baptizes modes of spirituality that simply retreat into emotional ecstasy, abandoning engagement with the world in order to retreat into a quasi-mystical desire, to be immersed in the private world of a

---

24. See Smith, *Desiring the Kingdom,* chapter 2, where I develop this more explicitly from Heidegger's account of *Verstehen.*

25. See James R. Peters, *The Logic of the Heart: Augustine, Pascal, and the Rationality of Faith* (Grand Rapids: Baker Academic, 2009). As Steven Land has shown, this same Augustinian emphasis was later articulated by Jonathan Edwards in terms of "the affections" (Land, *Pentecostal Spirituality,* pp. 122-36). See also Evan B. Howard, *Affirming the Touch of God: A Psychological and Philosophical Exploration of Christian Discernment* (Lanham, MD: University Press of America, 2000), where he describes discernment as an "affectively-rich act of knowing."

worship "experience" with Jesus. Rather, the point is to affirm the *primacy* of the heart and affections as the *basis* for a rational, intellectual engagement with and interpretation of the world. And precisely because our passional orientation to the world is reflective of the particularities of our embodiment (our geographical location, gender, religious confession, etc.), postmodernism takes seriously the "perspectivalism" that is an essential feature of being embodied, finite creatures. Indeed, we can summarize the differences between modernism and postmodernism by the stark difference between the modern ideal of dispassionate, disinterested objectivism and the postmodern affirmation of a passional, even confessional perspectivalism.

Now, to get back to the task at hand, what does this have to do with pentecostalism? I hope my brief account of the postmodern critique of modern rationalism has already hinted at a fundamental affinity between the postmodern critique of modernity and key aspects of pentecostal spirituality. Indeed, my core claim is that pentecostal worship constitutes a kind of performative postmodernism, an enacted refusal of rationalism. Implicit in the practices of pentecostalism are both a philosophical anthropology and an epistemology that resist the slimmed-down reductionism of modern cognitivism. These practices sustain a "form of life" (in Wittgensteinian terms) that nourishes what Peter Berger would call "a cognitive minority" — a people whose plausibility structures have not succumbed to the de facto naturalism of market-driven, technological construals of the world.[26] Rather, pentecostal spirituality fosters a more expansive, affective understanding of what counts as knowledge and a richer understanding of how we know. "I know that I know that I know" is an almost-nonsensical, quasi-glossolalic mantra that is struggling to articulate what might be inarticulable — a sense that there are ways of knowing that cannot be translated into propositions or syllogisms. Thus I'm suggesting that we "read" the practices of pentecostal spirituality as expressing a tacit, even unwitting, critique of modern rationalism, and carrying an implicit, constructive epistemological vision. In particular, I would highlight two features.

First, the postmodern critique of Enlightenment dualism echoes what

---

26. On the notion of a "cognitive minority," see Peter Berger, *A Rumour of Angels: Modern Society and the Rediscovery of the Supernatural* (Harmondsworth: Penguin, 1969), pp. 18, 31; on "plausibility structures," see Peter L. Berger and Thomas Luckmann, *The Social Construction of Reality: A Treatise in the Sociology of Knowledge* (New York: Anchor/Doubleday, 1967), pp. 154-56.

we might describe as a creational or incarnational affirmation of embodiment and materiality that characterizes pentecostal worship. Rather than the thin, reductionistic picture of the human person bequeathed to us by modernity, postmodernity appreciates the "thickness" of being human — that essential to being-human is being-in-the-world, inhabiting a material environment *as* a body (not just *in* a body). I *am* my body (even if I am also more than my body), and as such my body is an essential aspect of my identity. And as a result, all the things that attend embodiment are not merely accidental "properties," but rather essential features that make up who I am. To be embodied means that I reside in a time and a place — that I am a person with a geography and a history that constitute who I am. It means that my identity is linked with my gender, my race and ethnicity, my desires and passions, my physical gifts and even my incapabilities. Postmodernism takes race, class, and gender seriously precisely because it takes embodiment seriously — unlike the disembodied dualism of modern rationalism.

Such an affirmation of embodiment is essential to the incarnational principle at the heart of Christian confession. The story that God tells us about who we are begins with God's making us flesh, quickening the flesh of Adam *as* a material, embodied creature — and *then* saying it was "very good." This affirmation of the goodness of embodiment finds a reaffirmation in the incarnation of God in Christ, the Word become *flesh*. And it finds its ultimate reaffirmation in the hope of the resurrection. Ours is not a dream of a Platonic eternity, detached from the prison house of the body and liberated to be a disembodied soul. Our hope is not for redemption *from* bodies, but the redemption *of* our bodies — undoing their brokenness in order to be restored to their goodness. Because the goodness of embodiment is consistently affirmed and reaffirmed in the narrative arc of Scripture, we ought to also take seriously the features of being embodied (race, gender, sexuality, geography, history), as well as those ways of being-in-the-world that are unique to embodied creatures: the world of the arts, for instance, which requires ears to hear, eyes to see, hands to touch, bodies to dance.

In this respect pentecostalism is a distinctly embodied practice of Christianity — which is precisely why I think an integral pentecostalism resonates with postmodernism whereas certain strains of (cessationist) evangelicalism, which have significantly absorbed the assumptions of modernity, have been allergic to the postmodern critique of modern rationalism. But pentecostalism is its own critique of rationalism and dualism. Its critique of dualism is implicitly embedded, for instance, in the pentecostal affirmation of bodily healing. To say that God cares enough about bodies to heal them is to recapture the creational affirmation of the goodness of embodiment against the neo-Gnosticism of modernity. In other words, if we really teased out the implications of our central affirmation regarding bodily healing, we ought to reject the dualism that denigrates the body as the source of all evil — a dualism that pentecostals have too often absorbed, and absorbed precisely from the widespread dualism that characterizes generic evangelicalism that reduces faith to a kind of "talking head" Christianity that mirrors the rationalistic dualism of modernity.

In fact, we might say that pentecostalism is a quintessentially incarnational faith and practice — a very embodied way of being-before-God, and being in relation to God. As we've noted, pentecostal spirituality sees the body as essential to worship.[27] Indeed, I still remember making my way to Pentecost from a rabidly fundamentalist and cessationist tradition. I remember how *physically* difficult it was to get my body to participate in worship. I remember the utter awkwardness of raising a hand in praise, almost as if it were cemented to my side. But then I also remember the remarkable sense of release — the almost sacramental dispensation of grace and liberation and renewal that seemed to flow down through upstretched arms, as if the very positioning of my body opened channels for grace to flow where it couldn't otherwise. I remember the remarkable charge of grace that would come with a hand laid on my shoulder in prayer — the very embodied, material connection that was solidified by touch. "Thinking things" can't raise their hands in praise, or fall prostrate in worship; disembodied minds can't lay hands on a brother or sister in prayer; brains-in-a-vat can't dance before the Lord and make their way to the altar. So what have we to do with the stunted dualistic anthropology of modernity?

This affirmation of embodiment and eschewing of dualism have epistemological implications. Early Pentecostals in particular were more attentive to the antithesis between the dreams of modernity and their Spirit-filled visions of the coming kingdom. In fact, we might suggest that the community of faith gathered at Azusa Street had a firsthand acquain-

27. I think the same is true of sacramental, liturgical traditions in which the very material elements of bodily posture, taste, touch, even smell are central to worship formation. This is why I think worship in the kingdom is a catholic charismatic community. In this respect, pentecostalism is a catalyst for recovering ancient Christian emphases — an occasion for creatively recollecting the Christian tradition.

tance with the underside of modernity's myths of reason (recall that one of its most important preachers was a son of former slaves). And their *experience* of meeting God in embodied worship led them to resist and reject the rationalism of modernity, in favor of an understanding that gave primacy to the affections, to the "heart." In other words, the philosophical anthropology embedded in pentecostal faith and practice does not yield merely a "thinking thing," but rather an embodied heart that "understands" the world in ways that are irreducible to the categories and propositions of cognitive "reason." In testimony, when the pentecostal believer claims that "I know that I know that I know," she is trying to express that *how* she knows and what *counts* as knowledge cannot be formulated simply as "I know X" or "I have a justified true belief about Y." She will not reduce the criteria for knowledge to those accepted by the cognitive majority. In pentecostal experience there are construals of the world and an understanding of God that are irreducible to the tidy categories of cognition. That does not constitute a rejection of cognition or propositional truth; but it does situate and relativize that particular mode of knowing. In the next section I will consider how the central pentecostal category of "story" yields an epistemology that situates the narrow mode of knowing associated with cognition within a wider, richer account of embodied knowing.

I Love to Tell the Story: A Narrative Pentecostal Epistemology

In Denise's testimony above, we can note several things of epistemological import: First, she recounts what she knows — what she "knows that she knows that she knows" — in a narrative form. Why doesn't she come up and simply announce that she's pregnant? Why not just provide the requisite information, "just the facts," as it were? But she doesn't merely provide information, articulate propositions, or make factual claims. She recounts a story — a sequence of events with a narrative arc, with a crisis and complications, even with elements of suspense building to a climax.[28] While she begins by telling us she's never done this before, Denise seems to emerge on the scene as an accomplished storyteller. This is because she has been inhaling stories as the oxygen of pentecostal worship. Second, Denise

28. Paul Ricoeur would say that Denise's narrative indicates a process of "emplotment." See Paul Ricoeur, *Time and Narrative*, vol. 1, trans. Kathleen McLaughlin and David Pellauer (Chicago: University of Chicago Press, 1984).

locates her story within another story: her micronarrative from the past several weeks is allusively situated within the macronarrative of Scripture. Her barrenness is situated and signified against the backdrop of barren "exemplars," as it were. This wider story both gives her own story a narrative arc and provides a context for the meaning of her own story. Third, God is a character in Denise's story; the Spirit is an agent, a player, in this narrative. Indeed, one might say that the Spirit is the protagonist of the story even though he's never named.[29] Denise's testimony, then, is a charged practice loaded with core aspects of pentecostal spirituality.[30]

Telling stories is what comes "naturally"[31] to pentecostals. And I am certainly not the first to highlight this. Kenneth Archer in particular has articulated the importance of pentecostalism's narrativity, describing "the Pentecostal story" as the "hermeneutical filter" by which pentecostals make sense of their world and their experience.[32] The world of experience is layered by stories: the believer's experience is situated vis-à-vis the story of the "Last Days" outpouring at Azusa Street, which is read in light of the outpouring at Pentecost (Acts 2), whose significance, in turn, is understood against the prophetic heritage of Israel (Joel 2).[33] Furthermore, Archer has explained how and why such narrativity is constitutive of pente-

---

29. Granted, this is also the point of temptation for pentecostal testimony — to make the story *about me*. Thus "testimony nights" can sometimes seem to turn into spiritual duels of one-upmanship. So I would want to distinguish something like "authentic" pentecostal testimony (in which it is God who is the protagonist) from inauthentic, egocentric, self-centered stories that seek pity or grandstand one's own spirituality. In this respect, I like Christine Overall's notion in her discussion of feminist autobiographical philosophy: "I have only a bit part in my own autobiography" (Overall, "Writing What Comes Naturally?" *Hypatia* 23 [2008]: 229). In pentecostal testimony, while my life might be the stage, it is the Spirit who is the lead actor. (One can see similar contrasts in autobiography and memoir: contrast the egocentric centrality of the author in Barbara Brown Taylor's *Leaving Church* with the persistent deflection to others in Joan Didion's *Year of Magical Thinking*.)

30. Testimony and narrativity would be, I think, an example of why this "pentecostal" spirituality is shared across theological and denominational traditions since such storytelling would be common not only to classical Pentecostal meetings, but also to charismatic and third-wave worship.

31. "Naturally" in the sense of a "second nature," an acquired habit, a disposition. In this respect, the role of testimony in pentecostalism is akin to the lives of the saints in Catholic devotion.

32. Kenneth J. Archer, *A Pentecostal Hermeneutic for the Twenty-first Century: Spirit, Scripture, Community* (London: Continuum, 2004), pp. 94-126.

33. Archer explicates this "Pentecostal story" in particular in *A Pentecostal Hermeneutic*, pp. 100-114.

costal identity. There's no need for me to repeat his important work here. Instead, I want to build on this analysis in order to suggest ways in which the role of story[34] in pentecostal spirituality points up the limits of regnant epistemological paradigms, particularly within Christian (and perhaps especially evangelical) philosophical circles. As will become a pattern in the remaining chapters, I'm seeking here to provide a phenomenology of an aspect of pentecostal spirituality precisely in order for it to function as a liminal case study, pushing back on existing paradigms and thus becoming a productive catalyst for theoretical revision, drawing on a kind of inchoate "genius" embedded in pentecostal experience.

In particular, I want to suggest that pentecostal testimony points to the irreducibility (and perhaps primacy) of "narrative knowledge."[35] I use this term to denote a certain *kind* of knowledge, distinct from run-of-the-mill knowledge, which is usually understood (philosophically) as "justified true belief," where "belief" is understood as assent to propositions, or at least characterized by a propositional attitude. "Narrative knowledge," then, would be a different kind of knowing, knowledge of a different order, on a different register — knowing by other means. There is, on this account, a "distinct understanding that narratives supply" that is "inseparable from its form."[36] And it is just this sort of epistemic intuition that is implicit in pentecostal spirituality. For the pentecostal practice of testimony, narrative is not just a decorative form, a creative medium, a jazzier vehicle for truths that can be distilled and known otherwise. The truth *is* the story; the narrative *is* the knowledge. If the testimony is translated into "mere" facts, codified into propositions, distilled into ideas, then we are dealing with a different animal: I would both "know" something different and "know" it differently.[37]

---

34. For the purposes of my argument, I will treat "story" and "narrative" as synonyms. Other analyses, asking a different set of questions, will want to distinguish stories from narratives (where narratives, for example, will be understood as a particular kind of story with a resolution or conclusion). For discussion of these matters, see Ismay Barwell, "Understanding Narratives and Narrative Understanding," *Journal of Aesthetics and Art Criticism* 67 (2009): 49-59, at p. 49.

35. Normally I would want to make a (Heideggerian) distinction between "understanding" *(Verstehen)* and "knowledge" *(Wissen)*. In the ensuing discussion, I will speak of "narrative knowledge" as distinguished from something like "propositional knowledge." If we were to map this onto the Heideggerian distinction, "*narrative* knowledge" would be that sort of "knowledge" characteristic of "understanding."

36. Barwell, "Understanding Narratives," p. 49.

37. Narrative knowledge is not *opposed to* propositional or quantifiable or "codeable" knowledge, but it does relativize and situate such knowledge. However, the difference between

So, what characterizes "narrative knowledge"? What is irreducible about narrative knowledge? In a way that particularly resonates with pentecostal experience, David Vellman has suggested that what is distinctive about narrative knowledge is found in the connection between narratives and emotions. Narratives articulate a kind of "emotional understanding"; a narrative "means something to an audience in emotional terms."[38] But what does that mean? What's the connection between narrative and emotion? Vellman and others suggest it is twofold: First, the claim indicates that the way narratives work is affective. A narrative makes sense of a life, a series of events, or an experience by a "logic" that is not deductive but affective. The linkage and production of meaning are not the result of a cognitive inference but rather of an affective construal. A story is "a particular way of organizing events into an intelligible whole,"[39] but the mode of this organization "is at bottom an affective one. The essential narrative connection is neither causal nor temporal; instead it is emotive."[40] One is almost tempted to fall back on the old language of "faculties" to try to describe this. With such a lexicon, we could say that narrative is a way of understanding the world that draws upon an affective or emotive faculty (rather than a judgment about the world effected by the intellect). But, second, narrative works on this affective register precisely because the emotions are themselves already "construals" of the world.[41] The emotions

---

the two does present a challenge for pentecostal methodology in theology and philosophy (recall Archer, "A Pentecostal Way of Doing Theology: Method and Manner," *International Journal of Systematic Theology* [2007]: 6, cited above, p. xxiii n. 32). "Pentecostal knowledge," we might say, is narrative knowledge, but the genres of philosophical analysis and theological articulation are decidedly nonnarratival (even "narrative theology" is a genre of propositional and theoretical analysis that makes the case for the importance of narrative in a nonnarratival mode). We will address this methodological challenge in more detail in chapter 5. But in this context I am reminded of Christine Overall's account of "autobiographical philosophy" as a mode of resistance to regnant methodological paradigms in philosophy: "feminists have to continue to resist cultural messages that say women's lives are not important, our experiences have no significance, and our feelings are excessive or uncontrolled and therefore irrational [a pretty common description of pentecostals!]. Autobiographical philosophy is a way of 'talking back' to those messages" (Overall, "Writing What Comes Naturally?" p. 233).

38. David Velleman, "Narrative Explanation," *Philosophical Review* 112 (2003): 1-25, at p. 6.

39. Velleman, "Narrative Explanation," p. 1.

40. Paisley Livingston, "Narrativity and Knowledge," *Journal of Aesthetics and Art Criticism* 67 (2009): 25-36, at p. 31.

41. See Robert C. Roberts, "What an Emotion Is," pp. 183-209, and Roberts, *Emotions: An Essay in Aid of Moral Psychology* (Cambridge: Cambridge University Press, 2003).

themselves are already hermeneutic filters, "noncognitive affective appraisals"[42] doing the work of interpreting our world. Narrative is a mode of explication and articulation that feeds off (and fuels) the sort of affective, imaginative construal of the world that already characterizes the emotions. In other words, there is a kind of "fit" or proportionality between narrative and our affective register; and in concord, both work to "make sense" of our world and our experience in a way that is irreducible.

If there is an irreducibility of narrative knowledge, there may also be a *primacy* of narrative understanding that bubbles up from our embodiment as an adaptive strategy of our evolutionary development. Anthony Damasio, Daniel Dennett, and others have emphasized the ways in which the construction of an "I" — an identity — is bound up with being able to tell a story about oneself.[43] As Oliver Sacks once put it, "each of us constructs and lives a 'narrative,' and . . . this narrative *is* us, our identities."[44] And there might be a sense in which we are "wired" to be storytellers, that storytelling comes "naturally" in a "first nature" sense as well. Damasio argues that "the self" is the narratival product of the neurological structure of the brain that yields what he describes as a "feeling of knowing."[45] The storiedness of our identity, on this account, emerges not just as a cultural construct but from our bodies. As Paul John Eakin summarizes, "narrative is biological before it is linguistic and literary."[46] So if, as he concludes, "the

---

42. Jenefer Robinson, *Deeper Than Reason: Emotion and Its Role in Literature, Music, and Art* (Oxford: Oxford University Press, 1997). Robinson also ties affective appraisal to the physiology of embodiment — a further resonance with pentecostal experience.

43. Perhaps the strongest and most comprehensive version of this claim is Alasdair MacIntyre, *After Virtue*, 2nd ed. (Notre Dame, IN: University of Notre Dame Press, 1984), p. 216: "man is in his actions and practice, as well as in his fictions, essentially a story-telling animal." But MacIntyre does not tend to root this in claims about biology or evolutionary psychology as Damasio and Dennett do (though, in *Dependent, Rational Animals*, MacIntyre clearly honors our "animal nature"). For a critical discussion of these claims, see Peter Goldie, "Narrative Thinking, Emotion, and Planning," *Journal of Aesthetics and Art Criticism* 67 (2009): 97-106, and Bernard Williams, "Life as Narrative," *European Journal of Philosophy* 17 (2007): 305-14.

44. Oliver Sacks, *The Man Who Mistook His Wife for a Hat and Other Clinical Tales* (New York: Harper and Row, 1987), p. 110. The context is a discussion of Mr. Thompson, who, because of a brain impairment, cannot retain memories — and thus at stake is his very identity since a narrative, a biography, requires memory (and anticipation).

45. Anthony Damasio, *The Feeling of What Happens: Body and Emotion in the Making of Consciousness* (New York: Avon, 1995), pp. 6-7.

46. Paul John Eakin, "What Are We Reading When We Read Autobiography?" *Narrative* 12 (2004): 121-32, at p. 128.

identity narrative impulse that autobiographies express is the same that we respond to everyday in talking about ourselves," and if "both may be grounded in the neurobiological rhythms of consciousness," then we might conclude that the pentecostal impetus to narrative and testimony gives expression to this fundamental, bodily impulse.[47]

Story, then, is not just an optional "package" for propositions and facts; nor is narrative just a remedial or elementary form of knowledge that is overcome or outgrown by intellectual maturity. (Even "we moderns," Christian Smith emphasizes, "not only continue to be animals who make stories but also animals who are *made by* our stories.")[48] Rather, narrative is a fundamental and irreducible mode of understanding — and "pentecostal knowledge" attested in testimony bears witness not only to the Spirit's work but also to this epistemic reality. But our existing epistemological paradigms and categories are not well calibrated to deal with "narrative knowledge." Our epistemic tools, as it were, are better suited to discrete "beliefs" and facts, "items" of knowledge that can be articulated in propositions, plugged into syllogisms, and "defended" by apologetic strategies. And while we might even have epistemologies that make room for the Holy Spirit,[49] we don't have an array of epistemological theories or tools that honor and make sense of the *kind* of knowledge that characterizes "narrative knowledge." In short, pentecostal experience and testimony may require us to stretch our epistemologies to account for such knowledge. In this respect, I expect that a pentecostal epistemology will find resonance with a long history of pragmatism, a philosophical tradition that has long contested reductionism in philosophy. Wittgenstein's account of an irreducible "know-how," Peirce's "ab-

---

47. I think there is a further sense in which pentecostal testimony "gives voice" to narrative identity — by providing an occasion and opportunity for the poor to find a story and articulate their own story. In our culture of the twentysomething memoir, we should recognize that the bourgeoisie have no shortage of opportunities to "find their voice" and "tell their story." Indeed, the privilege of a liberal arts education institutionalizes such. But the implicit democracy of pentecostal worship means that *everyone's* story is significant. Pentecostal worship *evokes* a story and gives *all* people an occasion and space to narrate their identity.

48. Christian Smith, *Moral, Believing Animals* (New York: Oxford University Press, 2003), p. 64.

49. Cp. Alvin Plantinga, *Warranted Christian Belief* (New York: Oxford University Press, 2000), pp. 290ff. While I appreciate Plantinga's recognition of an epistemic role for the Holy Spirit, my concern is that the Spirit functions largely as the guarantor of assent to propositions ("teachings" of faith).

duction,"[50] and Brandom's emphasis on practice as the fount for "articulating reasons" are all trying to get at something that is implicit in pentecostal experience: that there is a means of "knowing" before and beyond propositions.

This epistemological push from pentecostal experience might actually press philosophers to also develop epistemological models that honor something more like a "biblical" understanding of knowledge. Indeed, I am struck by the resonance between what I've been describing as pentecostalism's "narrative knowledge" and recent accounts of Paul's epistemology. Consider, for instance, Ian Scott's analysis of "Paul's *way* of knowing" in which we look to Paul as a contemporary resource for thinking about knowledge precisely because "[i]n Paul we have the opportunity to see how someone approached religious knowledge who was at one and the same time foundational in the development of Western culture and yet relatively untouched by epistemological currents which so many now suspect are bankrupt."[51] Scott unearths a "narrative structure to the Apostle's knowledge," a distinct narratival "logic" that is operative beneath his speech (pp. 5-6, 10). In doing so, Scott brings "to the surface [Paul's] tacit assumptions about how people in general can come to knowledge," discerning "assumptions which the Apostle himself may never have brought to full consciousness" (p. 11).

The focus here is less *what* is known and more a matter of *how* we know. So, for example, in Paul's "critique of pure reason," as it were (or perhaps better, echoing Dooyeweerd rather than Kant, Paul's critique of the pretended autonomy of theoretical thought), in Romans 1:21-31 and 1 Corinthians 1:18–2:16, Paul's target of critique is "not reason in and of itself, but reason which has been hijacked by human vices" (p. 44). The root problem is an "unwillingness to accept the limits of human autonomy" (p. 28). So the work of the Spirit is not the provision of new *content,* but instead the gracious granting of "access": "The Spirit appears in these verses [1 Cor. 2:6-16] not as one who uncovers hidden content, but as one who al-

50. For further discussion, see Amos Yong, "The Demise of Foundationalism and the Retention of Truth: What Evangelicals Can Learn from C. S. Peirce," *Christian Scholar's Review* 29 (2000): 563-88.

51. Ian W. Scott, *Paul's Way of Knowing: Story, Experience, and the Spirit* (Grand Rapids: Baker Academic, 2009), p. 4. (In relation to my project of attempting to make explicit the epistemological intuitions that are implicit in pentecostal practice, it's interesting to note that an earlier version of Scott's book, published in Germany, was entitled *Implicit Epistemology in the Letters of Paul.*) Page numbers placed in the text refer to Scott.

lows believers to recognize the (openly presented) message as true" (pp. 46-47). But the Spirit's epistemological operation in this regard is not magical or Gnostic. Rather, the Spirit's gracious epistemic operation is a combination of moral regeneration — "healing the believers' moral constitution" (p. 47)[52] — and narratival location — situating the believing community within a story that provides a new context for understanding their experience. This is a kind of Spirit-induced paradigm shift. In a way that significantly echoes (or rather, anticipates) Archer's account of the role of narrative in pentecostal understanding, Scott notes that "the moment of revelation for Paul comes not in the pre-reflective experience but in the *interpretation* of that experience, when the meaning of the experience is hermeneutically grasped and appropriated" (pp. 75-76). The hermeneutical frame is provided by a story that functions as the "narrative substructure" of Paul's knowledge (pp. 95-96). "When Paul thought about theological matters," Scott summarizes, "his thoughts in fact had a narrative structure. He thought of actions and events which were both causally and temporally related, and which were all governed by the overarching plot of God's rescue of his creation" (p. 118).[53] Thus what Paul preached, and what Paul was calling both Jews and Gentiles to embrace, was not just a constellation of ideas, a set of beliefs, or a collection of doctrines; rather, their salvation depended on affectively and imaginatively absorbing a story — and seeing themselves in that story. Thus for Paul, "ethical knowledge" is not just a cognitive grasp of laws or duties, or knowledge of a set of

---

52. Or as Scott later puts it, "The Spirit would thus be responsible for faith in the sense that he restores the human moral constitution, making it possible for human beings to follow the [narrative] logic which leads to the Gospel" (p. 65). Thus, as Scott notes but does not develop, knowledge becomes a matter of *virtue*. For further discussion of links between virtue and epistemology, see Linda Zagzebski, *Virtues of the Mind* (Cambridge: Cambridge University Press, 1996); Robert C. Roberts, *Intellectual Virtues: An Essay in Regulative Epistemology* (New York: Oxford University Press, 2007); and Daniel J. Treier, *Virtue and the Voice of God* (Grand Rapids: Eerdmans, 2006).

53. Scott raises an important and obvious question: If Paul's thinking and knowledge are so fundamentally shaped by this narrative, "then why do we not find him simply telling the story" (pp. 108-9)? Why are the epistles so didactic, so *un*like the Gospels? Scott suggests that Paul's own letters are a kind of "criticism"; that is, they are written to help us understand and appreciate the story in the same way that, say, the criticism of Edmund Wilson opens up and deepens our appreciation for Nabokov's fiction even though Wilson's criticism is decidedly didactic. The didactic or "reflective" form of the Pauline epistles, however, still grows "organically out of the process of narration." In this way, "the narrative itself would seem to be primary" even if Paul never simply recounts the story in narrative form.

moral principles; ethical knowledge is "the emplotment of one's life in the theological narrative" (p. 10).[54]

Understanding events — which is central to Paul's gospel — is not a matter of logical deduction but rather a kind of narratival reasoning. For example, Paul's understanding of causality is not a linear, efficient causality: "We are rarely presented with cases of a sufficient cause and its inevitable effect. Rather we find the more ambiguous causality which is more common in narrative, in which one event serves as *part of* the reason for another" (p. 104). To understand this distinction between efficient causality and narrative causality, consider our discomfort with some developments in a film. Let's say a film has been following the story of two estranged brothers who have been separated for years. In a climactic scene near the end of the film, the younger brother, distraught and depressed, is on the top of a Brooklyn apartment building, perched there with suicidal intent. In fact, as the camera pans in closely upon his back, he leans forward to take the plunge. In a shot, a hand reaches to grasp him and restrain him from self-destruction. As the younger brother, now on his back, looks up, squinting into the sunshine, he finds himself in the shadow of, you guessed it, his older brother. Now, a filmmaker can deal with the issues of *efficient* causality. They can now sit on the roof of the building, have a beer, with the younger brother asking: "How'd you get here?" The older brother can recount the machinations of how he arrived. But what that won't answer is our *narrative* sense that this "cause" doesn't make any sense. His arrival is a *deus ex machina* — a shorthand term to describe an event or move within a story that violates not efficient causality but narrative causality. If we can recognize the sort of "gut" reaction we have at such moments — a "sense" that something's not right — then we have some intuitive grasp of what I (along with Scott) am calling "narrative knowledge" and "narrative causality." Story makes sense of our world, our experience, and events on a register different from the deductive logic of efficient causality. In short, what Paul "knows" is *more than* just what he "thinks" and

54. Cp. pp. 122-23 where Scott shows this is true of Paul himself: "the 'little story' of Paul's life finds meaning by being related to the 'big story' of which the organizing center is Christ." This then raises interesting questions about Paul's own claims to "knowledge." For example, when Paul says he "knows" *(oida)* that his coming to Rome will be "in the fullness of the blessing of Christ" (Rom. 15:29), what is the ground for that knowledge? What sort of knowledge-claim is this? Is this supported by propositions in Scripture? Propositions from some secret revelation? Or is Paul engaging in his own narrative deduction? Is this more like Paul saying "I know that I know that I know"?

"believes" (p. 156). It is this kind of knowledge — this sort of "know-how" — that is implicit in pentecostal spirituality, particularly the practice of testimony and the centrality of story in pentecostal preaching. Making room for this sort of knowledge would be one of the effects of a distinctly pentecostal philosophy.

Moved by the Spirit: Affective Knowledge

If Denise's knowledge of the Spirit's activity is constituted by narrative — that is, if she "knows that she knows that she knows" *because* she understands the story (or rather, a plurality of stories) — there is also a significant sense in which she "knows" the truth *from experience.*[55] Indeed, what could be more pentecostal than experience? Denise's testimony is embedded within a rich environment of tactile, embodied experience: she has just participated in a service that will have been deeply affective in music and word; she has engaged in a ritual of "coming forward," moving her body through a motion that carries its own significance; she is recounting her testimony while her husband and the pastor are laying hands on her shoulders; she is recounting an earlier embodied experience of communal prayer; her emotions are welling up and expressing themselves in and through her body — even while her own story is affecting others, moving them in a host of different ways. All of this and more constitute the "experience" of pentecostal worship and spirituality.

But what are we naming when we talk about experience? And what does it mean to claim that one knows "on the basis of" experience? The folk discourse of pentecostal spirituality will often speak of being "moved by the Spirit," and without question, charismatic spirituality is moving and emotive (for which it is often denigrated). But is there something "philosophically interesting" going on in this milieu? Might closer phenomenological attention to this scene and this experience also press and stretch our philosophical categories? How might we philosophically make sense of pentecostal experience? And might pentecostal experience carry within it an implicit "sense" that would add to our philosophical repertoire? In this section I will tackle these themes analogically, drawing on Carl Plantinga's

---

55. Scott also discusses a related kind of knowledge in Paul — "noncognitive" modes of knowledge rooted in "experience" (*Paul's Way of Knowing*, pp. 143-55) — which also resonates with pentecostal spirituality.

account of "affect" in film to illuminate the "affect" of pentecostal experience. Pentecostal spirituality is, in a sense, looking for words — for categories and frameworks to articulate its implicit "genius," the intuitions embedded in practice. My engagement with Plantinga's account of film and emotion is meant as an analogical dialogue that will provide a conceptual framework to unpack what's going on in pentecostal experience. In the next section, I'll build on this engagement with film to discuss some wider aesthetic implications of this account, sketching elements of a pentecostal aesthetic.

First, we need to appreciate that there is an incipient philosophical anthropology at work in pentecostal worship — a tacit, assumed model of human persons. The reason why pentecostal worship is so affective, tactile, and emotive is because pentecostal spirituality rejects "cognitivist" pictures of the human person that would construe us as fundamentally "thinking things." Pentecostal worship is "experiential" because it assumes a holistic understanding of personhood and agency — that the essence of the human animal cannot be reduced to reason or the intellect. Or, to put it otherwise, rather than seeing human action and behavior as entirely driven by conscious, cognitive, deliberative processes, pentecostal worship implicitly appreciates that our being-in-the-world is significantly shaped and primed by all sorts of precognitive, nondeliberative "modular" operations. In short, we *feel* our way around the world more than we *think* about it, *before* we think about it. Consider, for instance, a scenario one could glimpse in pentecostal worship: at the conclusion of a service, in response to a "word of knowledge," a pastor issues an altar call to husbands and fathers who have been neglecting their responsibilities, failing to love their wives as Christ loved the church — and perhaps engaged in all sorts of behaviors that are corroding families. When, in response, a man comes forward for an altar call, the embodied acts of coming forward, kneeling at the altar, and even the emotional "work"[56] in tears are not merely emotional adornment, as if some kind of baroque superfluity. The *work* of conviction and transformation is not just an intellectual matter; rather, repentance has to seat itself in the core of the person. In order for this to really effect transformation, what's needed is not just a change of mind but a change of heart, a reorientation of one's comportment to the world, to others, to oneself. And if our most basic comportment to the world is pre-

56. Cp. Jacques Derrida, *The Work of Mourning,* trans. Pascale-Anne Brault and Michael Naas (Chicago: University of Chicago Press, 2003).

cognitive and affective, then such transformation has to be channeled through affective, embodied means. This husband has perhaps been "convinced" for weeks that he needs to make a change; that is, he has "known" (cognitively, intellectually) for a long time that his behavior is inconsistent with his confession. But mere intellectual conviction has not effected change because the "driver" of our behavior is not just (or even for the most part) intellectual. This is why the "experience" — which taps the embodied, affective, and emotional aspects of the person — is not just a superfluous addition, an emotivist add-on. Rather, the experience and its activation of emotion is precisely what reaches the core of the human person as an affective animal.

Carl Plantinga's account of affectivity and emotion in film is out to make a similar claim. Thus we find him contesting reductionistic paradigms of film theory that want to reduce a film to its "message," as when film critics and scholars talk of "reading" a film, implying that "film viewing is a cool, intellectual experience."[57] Thus the critic decodes the film by boiling it down to the hidden meanings that can then be distilled in propositional form. Such a paradigm of criticism assumes that films are basically just elaborate vehicles for information that is ultimately propositional and intellectual. Thus "this way of thinking about film diminishes the art form by reducing it to a bare bones propositional message." And as a result, all that is "moving" about movies is relegated to the nonessential and superfluous. But as Plantinga rightly asks, "Are all of these affective elements of film spectatorship mere epiphenomena, the throwaway detritus of what is worthwhile about the film viewing experience?"[58] The burden of his book is to suggest otherwise: that the affective, emotional aspects of film — precisely those aspects of movies that *move* us — are essential and irreducible. As he comments, "Any abstract meaning that a film might have is ancillary to the *experience* in which that meaning is embodied."[59] What a film *means* cannot be reduced to the propositional "message" that might be gleaned from it. This is because "[e]xperience creates its own meaning, and in some cases the meaning to be taken from the experience of the film may contradict the abstract meaning an interpreter might glean from film dialogue, for ex-

57. Carl Plantinga, *Moving Viewers: American Film and the Spectator's Experience* (Berkeley: University of California Press, 2009), p. 2.
58. Carl Plantinga, *Moving Viewers*, p. 3.
59. Carl Plantinga, *Moving Viewers*, p. 3, italics added.

ample. Affective experience and meaning are neither parallel nor separable, but firmly intertwined."[60]

The cognitivist theory — which would reduce film-viewing to proposition-receiving — assumes a tacit picture of movie *viewers*. In other words, it is not just a theory about films but about spectators. And it assumes that spectators are fundamentally rational, cognitive processors of information who, when watching a film, are coolly engaged in a deliberative process of interpretation, "reading" a film.[61] Plantinga is out to contest a cognitivist[62] theory of film precisely because he thinks it assumes such a reductionistic picture of spectators. Indeed, it is characterized by what he calls a "cognitive fundamentalism" that overemphasizes the role of consciousness and rational deliberation. The cognitivist accounts for emotion by tracing it to prior beliefs; so, for instance, "the experience of fear requires that the fearing subject consciously subsume the feared object under the category 'seriously threatening' or 'dangerous' . . . and that such conscious deliberation must *precede* having the emotion of fear." But we are not fundamentally or even for the most part "cognitive" animals; "[o]n the contrary," he continues, "much of what leads a person to have an emo-

60. Carl Plantinga, *Moving Viewers*, p. 3.

61. As Carl Plantinga later summarizes, "The phrase 'reading a film' mischaracterizes the viewing process as literary, with the effect of distracting us from the medium's sometimes disavowed quality, namely, that film is a powerful sensual medium. . . . When critics talk about reading a film, they infuse film viewing with the patina of intellectual distance and implicitly ally film viewing with the ostensibly more active and legitimate activity of reading. By using the language of reading, however, such critics also downplay the prerational elements of spectatorship" (*Moving Viewers*, p. 112). I think Plantinga's use of the term "literary" in this context might be a bit too broad, since "literary" texts (novels, poetry) move us in ways that are quite similar to films. Perhaps Plantinga could say that he's critical of those critics who reduce films to "texts." I might add that such critics mistakenly fail to appreciate the extent to which reading practices are *also* prerational and automatic. The act of reading calls on a wide panoply of nonconscious processes that are affected by the materiality of the page, print, etc. (This is one aspect that Derrida's "deconstruction" tried to highlight about "texts.")

62. As we've already noted, "cognitivist" is a slippery term. In this context, I would suggest that "cognitivism" refers to a picture of the human person that assumes that human agency and action — our comportment to the world, our being-in-the-world — are directed by conscious, deliberative processing of "beliefs." So, for instance, a "cognitivist" account of emotion would say that beliefs precede emotions. In contrast, Carl Plantinga remarks, "Our affective life, I would argue, is certainly influenced by our beliefs, but it is not wholly determined by them. In many cases, our modular minds generate responses that are in part independent of belief" (*Moving Viewers*, p. 65).

tion must occur at the level of what I call . . . the 'cognitive unconscious.'"[63] Thus our experience of a film — and our experience of the world — is constituted and construed by processes that are "automated" and "automatic."[64] Indeed, film is the supermedium it is precisely because it affects us on so many levels and in so many ways — drawing on visual spectacle, narrative power, musical affect, temporal energy, and more. Viewing a film is a holistic experience that would be reduced and ruined were we to deliberately sit in the theater "reading" for the "message." We would be short-circuiting the affective and emotional experience that the film was meant to engender. Because we are the sorts of animals who are directed not only by cognition but also by affect and emotion, we are able to "understand" a movie by quasi faculties that are operative well beyond the ken of our cognitive deliberation. A film "works on us" because it taps into these automated layers of our being — those affective aspects of the self that elude conscious articulation. So in contrast to cognitivist paradigms (and their attendant assumptions about spectators), Plantinga articulates a "cognitive-perceptual theory" that "preserves room for unconscious and non-conscious spectator responses and for responses that, while not necessarily illogical or irrational, bypass the conscious inference-making that is mistakenly thought to underlie all cognitive film theory."[65]

I want to suggest that something similar is at stake in pentecostal spirituality (on my interpretation) that also contests the "cognitive fundamentalism" that seems to characterize philosophical understandings of Christian faith, construing Christianity as primarily a "message," a constellation of beliefs and propositions to which believers give assent.[66] And just as cognitivist film theory assumes that human persons are, fundamentally and for the most part, conscious deliberators who traffic in propositions

---

63. Carl Plantinga, *Moving Viewers*, p. 49. In *Desiring the Kingdom* (pp. 55-62) I discuss the "adaptive unconscious." Plantinga and I differ slightly insofar as he wants to preserve a cognitive moment to this unconscious; so it seems that his "cognitive unconscious" is unconscious because it is *not* deliberative, and *not* because it is not cognitive. In contrast, I emphasize that the adaptive unconscious harbors a kind of noncognitive understanding. Plantinga may think I tend toward what he calls "conscious inessentialism"— "the view that consciousness matters little in our moment-to-moment response and judgments" (*Moving Viewers*, p. 52). I do think that current research in cognitive science suggests something very close to this. It's the *"little"* that we'd be quibbling over.

64. Carl Plantinga, *Moving Viewers*, pp. 51-52. I discuss automaticity in *Desiring the Kingdom*, pp. 55-62.

65. Carl Plantinga, *Moving Viewers*, p. 8.

66. I'll return to this problem in chapter 5 below.

and beliefs, so cognitivist accounts of faith assume that believers are prop-
osition processors who make their way in the world by conscious deliberation. But what if we are, fundamentally and for the most part, oriented by
the adaptive unconscious? What if we make our way in the world by
construals that are pre- and noncognitive? What if our action and behavior are driven not primarily by conscious deliberation but instead by a
kind of nonconscious "feel" for the world? This would be quite a different
philosophical anthropology, and it is just such an affective, holistic anthropology that is implicit in pentecostal practice. If we are oriented by a kind
of affective "engine," then the Spirit's transformation must tap our emotional core. And if our emotional and affective life is tethered to our embodiment, then the Spirit, in incarnational logic, must reach us through
our bodies.[67] So when the husband makes his way to the altar and kneels in
penitence; and when the ambient music of worship and the chorus of
prayer in tongues elicit his sorrow (and joy); and when brothers and sisters
lay their hands upon his shoulders in prayer; these affective elements are
not just "epiphenomena, the throwaway detritus"[68] of an experiential husk
that can be discarded once we discern the kernel of propositional truth.
Rather, these affective elements are essential and irreducible; they are constitutive of the "truth" of the experience and attest to the fact that we
"know that we know that we know" on levels that elude propositional articulation. Pentecostal worship implicitly understands this.

I would even grant that there is something *like* a psychoanalytic moment to pentecostal worship. I suggest this cautiously since many critics
and skeptics would like to reduce pentecostal experience to psychosis, or at
least to some kind of mass therapeutic paradigm explainable in naturalistic terms. However, I don't mean to suggest that; rather, it seems to me that
affectivity and emotion are central to pentecostal spirituality because they
implicitly recognize that our being-in-the-world is primarily and for the
most part "driven" at an unconscious, affective, predeliberative level. Thus

---

67. I would grant that this implicit intuition is not *only* true of pentecostal worship. I
think the same principle holds for Catholic sacramental traditions. Or, conversely, we might
say that the pentecostal tradition is a kind of sacramental tradition in this respect and thus
shares much in common with the Catholic tradition. For arguments that pentecostal spirituality is sacramental, in a sense, see Frank Macchia, "Tongues as a Sign: Towards a Sacramental Understanding of Pentecostal Experience," *Pneuma: Journal of the Society for Pentecostal Studies* 15 (1993): 61-67, and Simon Chan, *Pentecostal Theology and the Christian
Spiritual Tradition* (Sheffield: Sheffield Academic Press, 2000).

68. Carl Plantinga, *Moving Viewers*, p. 3.

pentecostal worship digs down past and through the cognitive, conscious, and deliberative register to the affective and emotional core of our identity — a noncognitive core that directs much more of our action and behavior than we'd like to admit.[69] A *life* of discipleship — a life of obedience and joy, a life of repentance and transformation — is not the fruit of merely intellectual assent or conviction. Indeed, the spiritual giants throughout the ages (think of book 8 of Augustine's *Confessions*) regularly attest that the challenge of discipleship is not solely one of *knowledge,* but more a matter of *will* and *desire.* The husband can *know* he's not supposed to be doing X and Y but still finds himself almost helpless to stop. Why is that? Augustine would say that this is because his *love* remains disordered; pentecostal spirituality implicitly says that the affective and emotional core of his identity needs to be reformed and redirected. Changes in a *way of life* will not take place until that affective core is reached.[70] And that is exactly what the tactile, visceral, and emotional nature of pentecostal worship aims to effect.[71]

My point is that pentecostal worship is primed to reach us on a different register.[72] This is not properly "psychoanalytic" since it does not re-

---

69. For a non-Freudian way of articulating this, see Timothy Wilson, *Strangers to Ourselves: Discovering the Adaptive Unconscious* (Cambridge, MA: Harvard University Press, 2004).

70. It is this, I think, that makes pentecostalism a "mystical" tradition as expressed, say, in the disciplines of Saint John of the Cross, *Dark Night of the Soul.*

71. I can attest to this from experience: As a young family in grad school, we had never developed very good habits of tithing and giving; in short, we hadn't really made economic discipleship a way of life. And even though, over several months, we became (intellectually) convinced that we *ought* to, and even that it would be *good* to do so, this didn't touch our ingrained habits. But then one night during a prayer service in Lansdale, Pennsylvania (not our "home" church), an altar call specifically invited families who were struggling financially to find God's provision in a commitment to principled giving. And the pastor did the strangest thing — though just the sort of thing that caricatures of Pentecostal televangelists would lead us to expect: he asked us to come to the altar with our wallets! Not in order to give money (they didn't ask for a dime), but in order for the prayer team to pray over us with our pocketbooks in hand. This was an absolute turning point in our economic well-being. At the same time, we began to adopt practices concerned with economic justice. I "know that I know that I know" that this visceral experience, charged by the presence of the Spirit, made a difference for our *practices.*

72. I think this is precisely the way to understand the centrality of music in pentecostal worship. Rather than being seen as an instrument for fostering emotional frenzy (to which, I admit, it is easily prone and often used), I would suggest that music in pentecostal worship effects a certain effacement of the cognitive, a displacement of the "executive" function of deliberation, *opening* the person to operations of the Spirit on the affective register (which

quire assuming a Freudian or Lacanian theory about the unconscious.[73] But it does recognize that our being-in-the-world is governed by habituations that are sedimented in our unconscious, and that these unconscious habitualities orient and guide our actions and behavior. If this preconscious or unconscious aspect of the self is identified with affect or emotion, then we could say that we *feel* our way around the world more than we *think* our way through it. Here, too, Plantinga's account of film and emotion provides a helpful analogue. Plantinga also draws on Roberts's account of emotions as "concern-based construals," which we've noted above. As we emphasized, this means that emotions are not just reflexive responses or the "irrational" detritus of experience.[74] Emotions are themselves "takes" on the world — irreducible, precognitive construals and interpretations that constitute the world for us in particular ways even *before* we "think" about it or "perceive" it. In phenomenological terms, we'd say that emotions *mean* — they intend the world, constitute phenomena, giving "sense" to the world even if on a register that is not intellectual or cognitive. As a concern-based construal, an emotion "is like a perception in the extended sense of the word."[75] And if our emotions construe the world

---

can also include a process of unearthing repressed desires and sins, but also opening up the core of our affections to redirection and renewal). In this sense, music in pentecostal worship has a kind of *mystical* function. This reading of pentecostal music does not preclude also seeing it as a unique means of expression with its own irreducible "sense." Thus David Daniels, in his "acoustemology" of pentecostalism, rightly describes the unique mode of sound "as a way of knowing," a hermeneutic, a "sonic way of knowing." See David D. Daniels, "'Gotta Moan Sometime': A Sonic Exploration of Earwitnesses to Early Pentecostal Sound in North America," *Pneuma: Journal of the Society for Pentecostal Studies* 30 (2008): 5-32, especially pp. 26-29. Cp. Jeannette Bicknell, *Why Music Moves Us* (New York: Palgrave Macmillan, 2009).

73. It's interesting that Plantinga, since he's also trying to make room for the non- and unconscious in film viewing, also has to ward off the specter of psychoanalysis by distinguishing his understanding of the unconscious (drawing on recent cognitive psychology) and a Freudian understanding of the unconscious (see Carl Plantinga, *Moving Viewers*, pp. 18-19).

74. Carl Plantinga distinguishes between "affect" more broadly and "emotions" in particular. Affects are more reflexive responses, "felt bodily states" (*Moving Viewers*, p. 57), whereas emotions "have a stronger cognitive component" — that is, they are *about* something (p. 29). Affects are more visceral and "cognitively impenetrable" whereas emotions, as construals, can be "understood" in a sense. Or one could simply say that emotions are "intentional": "not in the sense of being deliberative and considered but in their 'aboutness'" (p. 55). However, Plantinga cautions that "[t]his distinction between affect and emotion is not meant to carry any heavy theoretical weight" (p. 57).

75. Carl Plantinga, *Moving Viewers*, p. 56.

before and *more often* than our intellectual, cognitive perceptions, then the shape of our emotions *makes* our world most of the time — in which case, discipleship would be more a matter of training our emotions than of changing our minds. It is this intuition that I think is inchoately central in pentecostal worship and spirituality.

So how might the role of emotion in film be an illuminating analogue? Two features are suggestive. First, Plantinga emphasizes that the affective experiences generated by movies "may burn themselves into the memories of audiences and may become templates for thinking and behavior."[76] The cinematic experience becomes an emotional template, embedding certain emotional habits that then become templates for later, extracinematic, thinking and behavior. Because in movies emotions are embedded in narratives,[77] the power of movies in this respect is amplified, to the extent that Plantinga claims "[m]ovies are influential enough that they have the potential to attach emotions and affects to kinds of stories, thus regulating emotional experience."[78] This "regulative" role of paradigmatic experiences engendered by movie watching is further specified in terms of "priming" and "disposition." Movie effects and strategies can prime us to experience certain emotions in certain situations, and can even embed in us a long-term disposition or "propensity to experience certain emotions in relation to situations and construals."[79] In sum, we might simply say that the affective experiences staged by movies *train* us emotionally, thereby priming and disposing us to affectively construe the world in particular ways.

Second, while the film provides an affective experience that can become a template for emotional habits, the film itself always already embodies a certain emotional "take" — it is itself an embodiment of a certain construal of the world (even if the film cannot be reduced to auteur

76. Carl Plantinga, *Moving Viewers*, p. 6. Later he briefly emphasizes that the "memory" here is *bodily* (pp. 119, 129), more like "muscle memory" than conscious recall. For further discussion of such bodily memory, operative outside the mechanisms of conscious recall, see Edward S. Casey, "Habitual Body and Memory in Merleau-Ponty," *Man and World* 17 (1984): 279-97, and Casey, *Remembering: A Phenomenological Case Study*, 2nd ed. (Bloomington: Indiana University Press, 2000), chapter 8 ("Body Memory").

77. "As concern-based construals," Plantinga remarks, "emotions can be communicated as stories — stories we tell ourselves about our experiences" (*Moving Viewers*, p. 80). This resonates with our exploration of narratival knowledge in the preceding section and confirms the implicit wisdom of the pentecostal conjunction of narrativity and affectivity.

78. Carl Plantinga, *Moving Viewers*, p. 60.

79. Carl Plantinga, *Moving Viewers*, p. 61.

expressivism). Plantinga refers to this as "affective prefocusing" and claims that "all films are affectively prefocused to some extent." Just as "emotions direct us to salient elements of our environment, bringing relevant percep- tual phenomena to our attention,"[80] so do films "direct" our emotional at- tention and focus our affective engagement. The prefocused narratives of movies are already "ways of interpreting the world."[81] So if movies "train" our emotions, and thus shape our affective construal of the world, this "education" of emotion is not neutral or generic. It is always already an in- culcation into a particular focus and interpretation.

It seems to me that this provides a way of understanding what hap- pens in pentecostal worship. The tangible, visceral, emotional nature of pentecostal spirituality works as a pedagogy of the affects, an education of the emotions, priming disciples to precognitively construe the world of their experience in a certain way *outside* of worship. In other words, in its best moments, the emotional fervor of pentecostal worship is not an escape from the "realities" of a cruel world, nor is it merely a quasi- narcissistic immersion in an emotional "high." Rather, what's going on in the affectivity of pentecostal worship is emotion training that amounts to construal training — it is the inculcation of a preconscious herme- neutic, shaping and forming our "concern-based construals." Pentecostal worship is affectively prefocused, patterned to highlight certain aspects of experience as salient; it is also regulative or exemplary, seeking to in- culcate certain emotional habits that, when inscribed and sedimented in the believer, become part of her emotional repertoire beyond gathered worship, thus priming and disposing her to construe the world of her ex- perience in certain ways. In this way we might see pentecostal experience as epistemic and hermeneutic training.

Imagining the World Otherwise: A Pentecostal Aesthetic

Pentecostal worship operates on the tacit assumption that we are moved by stories. As we've already seen, film operates on the same assumption — as does literature. One could see, then, how the affectivity of pentecostal spirituality resonates with the imaginative arts. Indeed, I would suggest that a pentecostal epistemology is always already a kind of *aesthetic,* an

---

80. Carl Plantinga, *Moving Viewers,* p. 79.
81. Carl Plantinga, *Moving Viewers,* p. 80.

epistemic grammar that privileges *aisthesis* (experience) before *noesis* (intellection).[82] Thus our schematic reflections on the outline of a pentecostal epistemology invite reflection on the shape of a pentecostal aesthetic. Are there inchoate intuitions in pentecostal spirituality that suggest the shape of a pentecostal cinema? Are there aspects of the pentecostal social imaginary that invite the articulation of a pentecostal literature?[83] Might there be ways that the art of filmmaking resonates with core assumptions of pentecostal spirituality and practice?

Pentecostalism is marked, even defined, by an openness to "signs and wonders"; as such, it is a spirituality of signs, of the visible and the invisible — it is a religion of manifesting, displaying, and showing.[84] Pentecostal spirituality and worship are very much a visual economy, a spectacular, visible, fantastic world of the sort created by the fantastic world of film. Like the visual world of film, pentecostal worship is semiotic; but also like film, it is *more* than visual, affecting other senses and affecting us via narrative, etc. So I will argue that given certain distinctive features of a pentecostal worldview, pentecostals should be creatively engaged in the production of visual culture.

In the discussion of the pentecostal social imaginary in chapter 2, I emphasized that implicit in pentecostal spirituality is a holistic affirmation of embodiment — that there is a kind of sacramentality of pentecos-

---

82. I suggested something similar in James K. A. Smith, "Staging the Incarnation: Revisioning Augustine's Critique of Theatre," *Literature and Theology* 15 (2001): 129-30.

83. Here we would first have to distinguish between a descriptive and a constructive pursuit of these questions. Of course, on the one hand, one could find artifacts of pentecostal film (the classic *The Cross and the Switchblade* immediately comes to mind). My project, however, is more concerned with a constructive analysis: What would be some of the elements that would shape an integral pentecostal aesthetic? (There is also another line of exploration I can't explore, namely, the perceived tensions between pentecostal "supernaturalism" and the worldwide pentecostal embrace of media technologies, including film. However, my concern here is the aesthetic rather than the technical side. For a discussion of the tensions in pentecostal appropriation of technology, see Birgit Meyer, "Religious Revelation, Secrecy, and the Limits of Visual Representation," *Anthropological Theory* 6 [2006]: 431-53.)

84. As such, I think pentecostal spirituality and practice — marked by a central role for the spectacular and visual — contest traditional "Protestant" privileging of hearing and voice (cf. Stephen Webb, *The Divine Voice: Christian Proclamation and the Theology of Sound* [Grand Rapids: Brazos, 2004]), and the correlate Protestant critique of *theologia gloria* and economies of visibility. In sum, the pentecostal economy of signs and wonders is further evidence of its Catholicity and sacramentality. So this renewal framework maps better onto Orthodoxy and Catholic paradigms than Protestant ones (cp. Amos Yong, *Spirit-Word-Community: Theological Hermeneutics in Trinitarian Perspective* [Aldershot: Ashgate, 2002]).

tal worship that sees the material as a good and necessary mediator of the Spirit's work and presence. There could be no pentecostal spirituality without the matter of bodies; in other words, for pentecostalism, *bodies matter.*[85] Furthermore, in this chapter we have seen that same affirmation of embodiment expressed in the pentecostal emphasis on narrative, affectivity, and emotion, yielding an epistemology that prioritizes "narrative knowledge." This is a kind of intuitive, even "emotional" knowing ("I know that I know that I know") that is the basis for "intellectual" knowledge, but is irreducible to such knowledge. Our most primary and fundamental mode of "understanding" is more literary than logical; we are the kind of creatures who make our way in the world more by metaphor than mathematics. The way we "know" is more like a dance than deduction. Both of these elements of a pentecostal worldview are fertile soil for articulating a pentecostal aesthetic. In short, pentecostal worship tacitly appreciates that we are *aesthetic* creatures: we are shaped, moved, and influenced by the fictive-like movements of stories more than we are by the enumeration of propositions. The way story (even fiction) communicates truth affects us more deeply than the presentation of "facts." The film *Schindler's List* affects us more deeply and significantly than a textbook presentation of facts about the Holocaust. Why is that? Because we are aesthetic animals; stories are the air we breathe. In addition to these, I would also highlight a third element of a pentecostal worldview as relevant: the eschatological orientation of pentecostalism that prioritizes *hope.* As I'll suggest below, this futural orientation — with its implicitly political envisioning of the coming kingdom — would also shape a pentecostal aesthetic sensibility.

How might these elements of a pentecostal worldview inform a pentecostal aesthetic, or at least a certain aesthetic sensibility? Let me just briefly imagine the shape of a pentecostal aesthetic by imagining a particular genre — the possibility of a pentecostal cinema.[86] Documentary filmmaker Francisco Newman — who speaks a lot about the influence of his upbringing in a storefront Pentecostal church, often participating in dramas

85. Here is yet another point of contact for further dialogue between feminism and a pentecostal philosophy. Springboards for such a conversation should include Elizabeth Grosz, *Volatile Bodies: Toward a Corporeal Feminism* (Bloomington: Indiana University Press, 1994), and Judith Butler, *Bodies That Matter* (New York: Routledge, 1993).

86. There is, I grant, a certain irony (or opportunity) here: many pentecostal churches occupy former cinemas. In a way, I'm suggesting that there could be good reason for pentecostals to recover these spaces *as* cinemas as well.

staged by the church[87] — once said in an interview (speaking about an article on Jean-Luc Godard): "Before that, I'd never thought about being a filmmaker, but that article got me interested in making films because, growing up as a Pentecostal, we were taught that movies were of the devil. It wasn't until I grew up that I found out they were right! Well, they just assumed that all movies were from the devil because of what we see coming out of Hollywood. So they just didn't watch any kind of movies. It never occurred to them that it's possible to make a film that isn't demonic."[88] I would suggest that given what pentecostals implicitly affirm about human nature — that we are embodied, imaginative, affective, narrative animals — pentecostals should see film and movies as an almost uniquely pentecostal aesthetic medium! Pentecostals and charismatic Christians should see filmmaking as a cultural expression uniquely fitted to their sensibilities. Indeed, film is a unique medium — what someone has called a "supermedium" — that is aesthetically powerful precisely because it reaches multiple aspects of our affective nature. Images coupled with the music of a score reach right into the heart region of our affective imaginations and get hold of our attention and desires.[89] And the ability of film to *narrate*, to tell us a story that invites us to relate to characters over time, draws us into an experience of a world that can be transformative. As a medium uniquely equipped to be imaginative, affective, and narrative, film presents a powerful opportunity to pentecostals to tell stories about the world that offer renarrations and counternarrations to competing stories being offered. (However, I should note that I don't mean that pentecostals should just start making movies about the Holy Spirit or Jesus or even explicitly "religious" films.[90] Rather, a "pentecostal" film would tell the truth, but tell it slant.)

87. Francisco Newman, "Cinema of the Oppressed," *Callaloo* 27 (2004): 715-33. Newman emphasizes the "theatricality" of pentecostal worship (pp. 717-19).

88. Newman, "Cinema of the Oppressed," p. 722.

89. For a few discussions related to this, see three essays in Richard Allen and Murray Smith, eds., *Film Theory and Philosophy* (Oxford: Oxford University Press, 1997): Edward Branigan, "Sound, Epistemology, Film" (pp. 95-125), George Wilson, "On Film Narrative and Narrative Meaning" (pp. 221-38), and Carl Plantinga, "Notes on Spectator Emotion and Ideological Film Criticism" (pp. 372-93).

90. "Religious" films almost always reduce to propaganda; that is, they let the "facts" of a "message" or doctrine trump the imaginative, aesthetic aspect of the art. For a discussion of the tendency of "Christian" art to devolve to propaganda (shutting down "allusivity"), see Calvin Seerveld, *Bearing Fresh Olive Leaves: Alternative Steps in Understanding Art* (Carlisle, U.K.: Piquant, 2000), pp. 117-57. I have not addressed an important theme given the Holiness

If film presents an opportunity to renarrate the world, it also provides a unique medium to *imagine the world otherwise* — and I think that is at the heart of the pentecostal experience, and pentecostal eschatology in particular. Pentecostal spirituality is enlivened by a vision of a coming kingdom that imagines the world otherwise — a world no longer plagued by racism or disease or poverty — the world as envisioned at the end of the book of Revelation. However, to be able to *imagine* that, our imaginations need to be converted, freed from the logics of power, scarcity, and consumption that constitute "rationality" in our world. In short, there is a significant way in which we need to contest what counts as "rational," and that is at the heart of the pentecostal social imaginary. As Margaret Poloma has noted, "When most reflective of its distinct identity, Pentecostal/charismatic ritual reflects a worldview that in many ways is at odds with the metanarrative of materialism, scientism and instrumental rationality that characterizes Western culture."[91] In many ways the broader culture lacks the imagination to imagine the world otherwise, and it is the pentecostal vision of a coming kingdom that can both contest and loosen up the petrified imagination of a world culture bent on consumption, violence, and the pursuit of power and exploitation.

Filmmaking would be most pentecostal when it offered a renarration of the world that breaks the stranglehold of modern instrumental rationality and frees the imagination to imagine the world otherwise. In terms suggested by Herbert Marcuse, "phantasy" or imagination is a mode of intending the world that retains a high degree of freedom vis-à-vis the "reality principle" of modernist instrumental rationality.[92] In fact, it is phantasy or imagination that subverts the regnant paradigms of "rationality" (what Marcuse, following Freud, would call "the reality principle") that would consign our hoped-for world to the impossible realm of "uto-

---

impetus of pentecostal spirituality, namely, the importance of not just producing "sanitized" or "safe" films, but the necessity for *true* films to grapple with the *brokenness* of the world. For a discussion, see James K. A. Smith, "Faith in the Flesh in *American Beauty:* Christian Reflections on Film," in *Imagination and Interpretation: Christian Perspectives,* ed. Hans Boersma (Vancouver: Regent College Publishing, 2005), pp. 179-89.

91. Margaret Poloma, "Glossolalia, Liminality, and Empowered Kingdom Building: A Sociological Perspective," in *Speaking in Tongues: Multi-Disciplinary Perspectives,* ed. Mark Cartledge (Milton Keynes, U.K.: Paternoster, 2006), p. 156. I would only emphasize that the "ritual" (i.e., the practices) *precedes* "the worldview"; that is, rather than ritual "reflecting" a worldview, I would say that a worldview is an articulation of an "understanding" that is embedded in practice (Taylor).

92. Marcuse, *Eros and Civilization* (Boston: Beacon Press, 1966), p. 140.

pia."[93] "While this harmony has been removed into utopia by the established reality principle, phantasy insists that it must and can become real, that behind the illusion lies *knowledge*. The truths of imagination are first realized when phantasy itself takes form, in which it creates a universe of perception and comprehension."[94] And this, Marcuse rightly emphasizes, happens in *art* that instantiates "the truth value of the imagination."[95] In this way art plays a critical, we might say "prophetic," function: it refuses to accept the limitations of "rationality" dictated by a stunted "reality principle." It is in art that the dream of a coming kingdom is made real in the here and now, as a foretaste of what is to come. But since our imaginations are so restricted by the dictates of the logic of an instrumental rationality, art must free up the imagination, break its bonds and loosen its shackles. Thus Marcuse points to the crazy, fantastic, magical world of surrealist art as a medium in which the imagination is set free to imagine the world otherwise.[96] Surrealism breaks the rules; it stops us short because its images and movements defy the conventions of rationality, even the conventions of sensory perceptions. Its graphic images and visual contortions make the world strange even for our affective habits, thereby inviting us to acquire new habits of vision and imagination.

In this way, I think pentecostal filmmaking — and a pentecostal aesthetic more generally — would be a kind of surrealism, constantly pushing back against what "they" say is possible. Film presents a unique medium to embody the *fantastic,* but to do so, it will have to traffic in tropes and visions that seem surreal to our contemporary rationality. As such, I think that pentecostal filmmaking will be more like the fantastic, magical surrealism of *Pan's Labyrinth* than the so-called realism of *The Passion of the Christ*. In this way, pentecostal filmmaking might be an analogue of pentecostal worship: a space in which God's Spirit breaks in to fantastically give a foretaste of the coming kingdom.

93. "The relegation of real possibilities to the no-man's land of utopia is itself an essential element of the ideology of the performance principle" (Marcuse, *Eros and Civilization,* p. 150).

94. Marcuse, *Eros and Civilization,* p. 143.

95. Marcuse, *Eros and Civilization,* p. 148. Marcuse goes on to claim, alluding to André Breton: "That the propositions of artistic imagination are untrue in terms of the actual organization of the facts belongs to the essence of their truth" (p. 149).

96. It is perhaps also of interest to pentecostals that Breton, in his first Surrealist Manifesto (1924), was concerned to redeem "dreams," as it were, from their Freudian denigration. For surrealism, dreams — rather than being merely portals into pathology — were a means of envisioning what *could* be real.

4 Shattering Paradigms, Opening the World

Science, Spirit, and a Pentecostal Ontology

Pentecostalism, Modernity, and the Disenchantment of the World

Pentecostal and charismatic Christianity is nothing if not fantastic. Particularly in its global expressions, pentecostalism inhabits a world that is very much "enchanted." The world of pentecostal worship and spirituality replays what Bultmann dismissed as the "mythical" world of the New Testament: a world of "signs and wonders," a space where the community *expects* the unexpected and testifies to events of miraculous healing, divine revelation in tongues-speech, divine illumination, prophecy, and other "supernatural" phenomena. One of the central features of pentecostal spirituality is the unique combination of a gritty, material, physical mode of worship that is radically open to transcendence. Thus above I have argued that one of the core components of a pentecostal worldview is a sense of radical openness to God, with a distinct emphasis on the continued operation of the Holy Spirit in the world and the church.

However, this clearly has ontological implications that need to be worked out, as well as implications for pentecostal participation in (and appropriation of) regnant paradigms in the natural and social sciences — as well as paradigms that govern the science/theology dialogue. If it is an essential feature of pentecostal belief and practice to be open to God's surprises, this presupposes a sense that the universe and natural world must also remain *open systems*. But this ontological claim would seem to stand in opposition to two key affirmations of contemporary science: (1) what we could call "metaphysical naturalism," which affirms (beyond strictly "scientific" evidence) that the universe *is* a determined, closed, immanent system of natural processes; and (2) "methodological naturalism," which, while it may remain agnostic with respect to metaphysical naturalism, nevertheless claims that science qua science must operate *as if* the universe were a closed system.

Given the enchanted worldview of pentecostalism, is there any room for a pentecostal contribution to metaphysics? And given the naturalist vogue in contemporary metaphysics, what possibility is there for a uniquely pentecostal intervention in the science/theology dialogue? By asserting the centrality of the "miraculous" and the fantastic, and being fundamentally committed to a universe open to surprise, doesn't pentecostalism thereby forfeit admission to the conversation? A pentecostal contribution to the science/theology dialogue would be inevitably gauche precisely because it would transgress an unspoken taboo in the parlor of the science/theology conversation, namely, that one not question the "science" side of the conversation, and in particular, one not ruin the party by calling into question the governing naturalistic assumptions of science. In such an environment with a settled genteel etiquette dominated by deference to "what science says," pentecostals would spill into the parlor as a rather raucous bunch, refusing to defer to the implied rules of such parlor games. As such, response to pentecostals in the parlor of the science/theology dialogue will not be unlike the response to the revival at Azusa Street, which was also dismissed by the gentry.

With the hopes of avoiding such an awkward scene, in this chapter I would like to work out some of the ontological implications of a pentecostal worldview in order to make a preliminary contribution to the science/theology dialogue *as* a pentecostal scholar working unapologetically from a pentecostal worldview. My project is a bit of a two-edged sword: on the one hand, I want to suggest that a pentecostal worldview need not (and *should* not) entail a "naive" supernaturalism — even that the language of *super*naturalism is a kind of Deistic hangover that is problematic. There will be an element of internal critique here, suggesting that pentecostals have too often and too easily adopted a simplistic or hyper-"supernaturalism." On the other hand, pentecostal spirituality is defined by the miraculous, by ontological surprises that naturalism wants to deny (or rather, refuses to recognize). Thus I will suggest that pentecostals should push back against the regnant assumptions regarding naturalism that govern not only scientific practice, but also the parameters of the science/theology dialogue in particular. If we run with the parlor metaphor above, one might say that my goal is to dust off pentecostalism and show that it's not quite as boorish and naive as those in the parlor might suspect. However, I will also suggest that an integral pentecostal engagement with science will not be simply a deferential guest. While we're not out to ruin the party, we are going to be interested in loosening things up a bit — which might involve what could be a rather rude questioning of the host.

My central thesis is this: Embedded in pentecostal practice is a worldview — or better, social imaginary — whose ontology is one of radical openness and thus resistant to closed, immanentist systems of the sort that emerge from reductionistic metaphysical naturalism. I believe that a pentecostal contribution to metaphysics — and to the related science/theology dialogue — should begin from and draw on this experience of the elasticity of "nature" as always already inhabited by the Spirit.[1] Such an approach is its own kind of empiricism that seeks to honor and take seriously the observation and experience of the miraculous (rather than, ironically, the sort of aprioristic naturalism that, in the name of scientific observation, rules such experiences out of court de jure). So any pentecostal engagement with the sciences must begin from an experience of the Spirit's transcendence and surprise that is central to the fantastic nature of pentecostal worship and spirituality. However, pentecostal practice also attests to a strong sense of the *immanence* of the Spirit's presence and activity.[2] As such, a pentecostal ontology would resist both dualistic and Deistic supernaturalisms and naturalisms of various stripes, both reductionist and nonreductionist. This is why I will suggest that the "understanding" of nature that is implicit in pentecostal practice can find resources for articulation in the "participatory ontology" articulated by "Radical Orthodoxy."

To undertake this project I will first provide a map of "naturalisms"

---

1. This methodology for a distinctly pentecostal engagement is analogous to Alexei Nesteruk's model of engaging science from the distinctive "experience" of Eastern Christianity (Nesteruk, *Light from the East: Theology, Science, and the Eastern Orthodox Tradition* [Minneapolis: Fortress, 2003], p. 4). Nesteruk emphasizes the "specialness" of Orthodox relationship to science as being rooted in the essential (and distinct) "theological underpinnings" regarding the nature of the human person, etc., as understood in the Orthodox "experience." So, too, should pentecostal engagements in the science/religion dialogue begin from the distinctives of pentecostal "experience" and the distinct elements of the pentecostal social imaginary.

2. Amos Yong, "*Ruach,* the Primordial Waters, and the Breath of Life: Emergence Theory and the Creation Narratives in Pneumatological Perspective," in *The Work of the Spirit: Pneumatology and Pentecostalism,* ed. Michael Welker (Grand Rapids: Eerdmans, 2006), pp. 183-204.

and the correlate "supernaturalisms" that they take themselves to be rejecting. I will then sketch how a pentecostal ontology (implicit in pentecostal
practice) refuses the distinctions behind both these naturalisms and rejected supernaturalisms. Instead, a pentecostal ontology — akin to Radical
Orthodoxy's participatory ontology — is characterized as an "enchanted
naturalism" that differs from reductionistic naturalism, as well as naive supernaturalism. I will also be concerned to show how this pentecostal ontology of "enchanted naturalism" (a noninterventionist en-spirited naturalism) differs from a close cousin: Clayton and Griffin's nonreductive
naturalism (or monism). It will be important to note the differences between these, precisely because they share so many concerns in common.
Finally, I will indicate the opportunities and challenges that this ontology
brings to the science/theology conversation.

Whose Naturalism? Which Supernaturalism?
Topography and Taxonomy

A pentecostal engagement with science will quickly run up against the issue of "naturalism." Such a "super"-natural religion would seem to be at
direct odds with the naturalistic orthodoxy of contemporary scientific
practice, as well as the widespread commitment to the incontestability of
naturalism in the theology/science dialogue. The price of admission to the
dialogue would seem to be giving up extravagant claims to supernatural
phenomena of just the sort that are central to pentecostal spirituality and
practice. Of course, there is a sense in which this is true for any Christian
tradition that would affirm, for example, the physical, bodily resurrection
of Christ. However, I am suggesting that the issue is intensified and also
more "mundane" for pentecostalism precisely because the miraculous and
"supernatural" are not only attributed to past events but are also expected
(and witnessed) in contemporary worship and experience. This would
seem to bring us to an impasse: either pentecostals give up their claims to
miraculous phenomena or they remain outside science and the science/
theology conversation.

However, upon closer inspection things are more complicated. This is
because "naturalism" is a more contested concept than one might expect.
Indeed, rather than speaking of "naturalism," we would do better to speak
of "naturalisms." This has a correlate implication: what such naturalisms
reject under the banner of "supernaturalism" is also rather slippery. As

such, one might legitimately ask whether the supernaturalism rejected by, say, Dennett is actually a description of the "supernaturalism" embedded in the pentecostal social imaginary. For instance, if "supernaturalism" for Dennett refers to an interventionist framework (a picture where a transcendent God intervenes and interrupts the "laws" of nature), and if (as I hope to show) pentecostal spirituality implicitly rejects such an interventionist framework, then Dennett's rejection of interventionist supernaturalism would not constitute a rejection of pentecostal supernaturalism. To sort out the complexities of this terrain, we need to ask (in the spirit of MacIntyre): Whose naturalism? Which supernaturalism?

I think we can identify at least two naturalisms. The *reductionistic*[3] naturalism of folks like Dennett, Dawkins, Jaegwon Kim, and others is a "nothing buttery" naturalism: there is "nothing but" the material or physical, and thus all phenomena can be explained by reference to physical laws and processes. There is no nonphysical something-other in the universe. This naturalism is a *physicalism:* all entities are physical entities. This is sometimes described as "metaphysical" (as opposed to "methodological") naturalism insofar as it makes ontological claims about the sorts of things that constitute the furniture of the universe. Alvin Plantinga (along with others) refers to it as "philosophical naturalism," which he describes as "the belief that there aren't any supernatural beings."[4] In any case, such reductionistic naturalisms are understood to be disenchantments par excellence, evacuating the world of any spirits or magic or mystery — any stuff that is not material and subject to the laws of matter.

The second set of naturalisms we might call *nonreductionistic* naturalisms (Griffin, Clayton, Peacocke). Such nonreductionistic naturalisms are fighting on two fronts: on the one hand, they reject the reductive physicalism of the usual naturalisms. On the other hand, nonreductionistic naturalism

3. For an account that happily owns up to the reductionism of this form of naturalism, see Michael Devitt, "Naturalism and the A Priori," *Philosophical Studies* 92 (1998): 45-65.

4. Alvin Plantinga, "The Evolutionary Argument against Naturalism: An Initial Statement of the Argument," in *Naturalism Defeated? Essays on Plantinga's Evolutionary Argument against Naturalism,* ed. James Beilby (Ithaca, NY: Cornell University Press, 2002), pp. 1-14, at p. 1. It should be noted that the heart of Plantinga's argument against naturalism actually stems from his epistemological project, which he describes as a "radical naturalism." Thus he seeks to demonstrate that "naturalism in epistemology flourishes best in the context of a theistic view of human beings: naturalism in epistemology requires supernaturalism in anthropology" (Plantinga, *Warrant and Proper Function* [Oxford: Oxford University Press, 1993], p. 46; the argument is fully developed on pp. 194-237).

remains very critical of supernaturalism. David Ray Griffin, for instance, criticizes the reigning form of naturalism — what I've called reductionistic naturalism — as an overreaching form of naturalism. Thus he distinguishes this reductionistic naturalism, which he calls naturalism$_{sam}$ ("sam" symbolizing "sensationist-atheistic-materialistic") from a more minimalist naturalism, called naturalism$_{ns}$ (where "ns" is simply "nonsupernaturalist").[5] In a similar way, Philip Clayton articulates an "emergent" monism that simply "presumes" naturalism because "if we do not make [this presumption], science as we know it would be impossible."[6] However, his emphasis on the emergence of complexities that then function as top-down causalities yields a naturalism that does not assume that all phenomena can be explained by or reduced to physical laws. What makes Griffin's and Clayton's ontology "naturalisms" is the fact that they are still *monisms*, allergic to any "dualism" that would posit some ontological "stuff" that is not physical. There is nothing "super"-natural, nothing beyond "nature." Thus Clayton: "[O]ne must acknowledge an initial presumption in favour of metaphysical naturalism — though here the presumption is once again weaker than before. By metaphysical naturalism I mean the view that there are no things, qualities, or causes other than those that might be qualities of the natural world itself or agents within it."[7] It takes only a little philosophical suspicion, it seems to me, to ask just what "natural" means in this claim.

However, what's interesting is that both of these naturalisms (reductionistic and nonreductionistic) seem to be rejecting the *same* "supernaturalism," what we'll call an "interventionist" supernaturalism. (My enemy's enemy is my friend!) In fact, one might suggest that what defines both of these sorts of naturalisms is *only* their rejection of any supernaturalism. In that case, "naturalism" seems to be defined as "antisupernaturalism."[8] Thus Dennett, in defining religion as a "natural" phenomenon, says the claim amounts to saying that "religion is natural as opposed to *supernatu-*

---

5. David Ray Griffin, *Reenchantment without Supernaturalism: A Process Philosophy of Religion* (Ithaca, NY: Cornell University Press, 2001), p. 22.

6. Philip Clayton, *Mind and Emergence: From Quantum to Consciousness* (Oxford: Oxford University Press, 2004), p. 163. Technically, and empirically, it seems to me that this claim is invalid. Both historically and in the present there are scientists who do experimental work who do not presume naturalism. Clayton concedes that "here the arguments are not decisive" (p. 165).

7. Clayton, *Mind and Emergence*, p. 164.

8. Michael Bergmann, "Commonsense Naturalism," in *Naturalism Defeated?* p. 83 n. 40.

ral, that it is a human phenomenon composed of events, organisms, objects, structures, patterns, and the like that all obey the laws of physics or biology, and hence do not involve miracles."[9] In a similar way, when David Ray Griffin describes Whitehead's process philosophy as a form of naturalism, he emphasizes, "To say that it is a new form of *naturalism* is to say, and *only* to say, that it *rejects supernaturalism,* meaning the idea of *a divine being who could (and perhaps does) occasionally interrupt the world's most fundamental causal processes.*"[10] While nonreductionistic naturalists like Griffin and Peacocke seem to have room for a greater diversity of metaphysical furniture in the universe (stuff such as emergent minds and spirits), they share with reductionistic naturalism a conviction regarding the ironclad nature of natural "laws."

Indeed, the essence of naturalism is often less defined by an articulated conception of "nature" and more often by an opposition to supernaturalism. Naturalism isn't quite sure what it is, but it is absolutely certain what it is *not.* This is confirmed by Owen Flanagan's topography of naturalism. Following Barry Stroud, Flanagan concludes that "anti-supernaturalism is pretty much the only determinate, contentful meaning of the term 'naturalism.'" So while it's clear what naturalism is against, what it means positively is not spelled out. Instead, it remains "a very general thesis; neither what is 'natural', 'a natural law', or 'a natural force', nor what is 'non-natural', 'supernatural', or 'spiritual' are remotely specified. All the important details are left out or need to be spelled out."[11] In short, naturalists are not very forthcoming about just what they mean by "nature."

---

9. Daniel Dennett, *Breaking the Spell: Religion as a Natural Phenomenon* (New York: Viking, 2006), p. 25. Dennett also defines "religion" as "belief in a supernatural agent" and then stipulates that part of the defining creed of "brights" (Dennett's term for the "church" of enlightened antisupernaturalists) is that they do not believe in the supernatural (p. 21). Dennett has a remarkably confident grasp of what constitutes "nature." Or rather, one should say that, remarkably, Dennett — like most naturalists — spends little time interrogating the concept of "nature." I would say the same tends to be true of discussions of "nature" in the science/theology conversation.

10. Griffin, *Reenchantment without Supernaturalism,* p. 21, italics in original.

11. Owen Flanagan, "Varieties of Naturalism," in *The Oxford Handbook of Religion and Science,* ed. Philip Clayton (Oxford: Oxford University Press, 2006), p. 433. Flanagan goes on to concede a distinction that Griffin and others do not, viz., a distinction between "ontological" and "methological" naturalism, or what Flanagan calls "strong" versus "weak" naturalism. "Weak" naturalism simply emphasizes that "one should dispense with the supernatural in *explaining* things" (p. 434). He concedes that one could be, say, a weak naturalist about economics, but nonetheless be an ontological nonnaturalist (pp. 434-35).

So all varieties of naturalism are marked by this trenchant rejection of the supernatural. As Flanagan summarizes, across the varieties of naturalisms, "some kind of exclusion of the supernatural, of the spiritual, is *required*."[12] These naturalisms across the spectrum are defined by a rejection of ontological dualism (no "stuff" other than "natural" stuff) and a rejection of the miraculous as violations of the "laws" of nature. This common rejection of "supernaturalism" raises at least two questions:

1. Just *what* is being rejected in this rejection of supernaturalism? If, as we've seen, there are a variety of naturalisms, then avoiding caricature requires us to admit that there might be a variety of "super"-naturalisms. If that's the case, then we would need to determine just *which* supernaturalism is being rejected by naturalism. Could there be other models?
2. *Why* the rejection of supernaturalism? What is it that motivates the rejection of the supernatural, and often so vehemently?

On the first point, it seems clear that the supernaturalism being rejected is what we might call an *interventionist* supernaturalism. This assumes an ontology whereby a basically autonomous world operates for the most part according to a "normal" causal order — but this order is not *closed*, and therefore the system is open to *interruptions* or *interventions* from outside the system by a transcendent God.[13] Such "interventions" are taken to suspend the "normal" causal order and therefore cannot be explained and cannot be anticipated. Thus Griffin summarizes his "ontological naturalism" as stipulating "that there are never any divine interruptions of the world's *normal* causal relations," and as "the doctrine that there can be no supernatural interruptions of the world's *normal* cause-effect relations."[14]

This then explains why naturalists are so keen to reject supernaturalism.

---

12. Flanagan, "Varieties of Naturalism," p. 433. It should be noted that rejection of the supernatural is "required" *in order to be a naturalist*. Flanagan does not articulate just *why* one should be required to be a naturalist.

13. This is also the "supernaturalism" (or model of "miracle") rejected by Hume, *Enquiries concerning Human Understanding and the Principles of Morals*, ed. P. Nidditch (Oxford: Oxford University Press, 1975 [1777]), section X, where he considers "prophecy" as an instance of the miraculous. This should remind us that "supernatural" and "miraculous" seem to be almost synonymous here — which is why pentecostalism has such a vested interest in these issues.

14. Griffin, *Reenchantment without Supernaturalism*, p. 182, italics added.

Because "science" is governed by commitment to the regularities of cause-and-effect (and the successes of science have been the fruit of the predictive power of just such a "normal" causal structure), any theology that would remain viable must concede naturalism. Or, to put it conversely, to cling to supernaturalism is to forfeit the ontology that underwrites the overwhelming success of "science."[15] It is this primary concern of acceding to the naturalism of science that motivates the growing commitment to naturalism by theologians engaged in the theology/science dialogue.[16] I would describe this as a "correlationist" project: a theological project that cedes the "truth" of a particular sphere to a "secular" and supposedly neutral, rational science and then seeks to "correlate" theological claims to conform to the standards established by the secular (Bultmann remains a classic case).[17] In this particular case, "science" is the primary authority and is the first to stipulate what could be theoretically acceptable. Theology then looks for places that remain "open" to theological intervention. After science has made first and preeminent claim to the territory, theology can then look for remaining corners of the realm where it can set up shop. The natural sciences, then, are taken to be "objective" arbiters of "the way things *really* are," and theology (and religious communities) is expected to modify and conform ("correlate") its beliefs and practices to the dispensations of the scientific magisterium. Failure to accede to these conditions of engagement entails refusal of admission to the "parlor," and being written off as a "fundamentalist."

This correlationism is starkly exhibited in the project of Arthur Peacocke, but also that of John Polkinghorne — and, in a way particularly relevant here, in Polkinghorne's account of the "Spirit" in the cosmos.[18] As he says, he is out to "find room" for theology in contemporary cosmology and ontology.[19] Quantum cosmology — "that science puts forward" —

15. Griffin is particularly critical of halfway attempts that opt for a "methodological" naturalism but cling to an ontological supernaturalism (Griffin, *Reenchantment without Supernaturalism*, pp. 25-26).

16. For some critical discussion of this tendency, see Alvin Plantinga, "What Is 'Intervention'?" *Theology and Science* 6 (2008): 369-401, especially pp. 371-73.

17. I have discussed correlationist methodology in more detail in Smith, *Introducing Radical Orthodoxy: Mapping a Post-secular Theology* (Grand Rapids: Baker Academic, 2004), pp. 35-37. I hint specifically about an application of this to the science/theology dialogue on p. 148 n. 19.

18. Peacocke, *All That Is: A Naturalistic Faith for the Twenty-first Century*, ed. Philip Clayton (Minneapolis: Fortress, 2007); John Polkinghorne, "The Hidden Spirit and the Cosmos," in *The Work of the Spirit*, pp. 169-82.

19. Polkinghorne, "The Hidden Spirit," p. 169.

discloses an "intrinsic cloudiness" and unpredictability that leave room for a hidden Spirit to be at work. Thus he concludes that "the scientific picture" is "open to" the possibility of the Spirit's presence in the world.[20] But on this picture, it is "science" that is the gatekeeper and bouncer. The gatekeeper will not tolerate unanticipated interventions, but is perhaps open to leaving room for "cloudiness" as a space for theological claims ("fogginess" might be more apt!). In short, theologians are motivated to accede to naturalism because that is the price of admission for scientific respectability. This is repeatedly exemplified by Griffin and Peacocke.

We can see the same methodological push in Clayton's rich articulation of an emergent monism. For instance, consider just one example of a common trope in Clayton's work: "I have assumed, on the one hand, that if a given account of mental influence is incompatible with natural science, that would be a telling argument against it."[21] Thus the general stance is one of deference since, for example, "our knowledge of physics represents the most rigorous, most lawlike knowledge humans have of the world."[22] Thus theological claims must wilt before "scientific" knowledge. Otherwise one would "obviate" scientific study.[23] J. Wentzel van Huyssteen rightly criticizes Clayton's strategy (and *mutatis mutandis,* that of Griffin and Peacocke). As he summarizes, Clayton's project is focused on what sorts of "altered notions of divine creation and providence would be required for any theology that would seek to be consistent with the natural sciences." But in doing so, "Clayton still seems to yield to an allegedly superior scientific rationality. . . . This move, taken to the extreme, could be fatal for theology, because it reveals a total commitment to the epistemic priority of science — and at the expense of theological boundaries."[24] He goes on to note a tension: "These arguments of Clayton suggest a proper epistemic respect for the natural limitations of scientific knowledge and scientific explanations but remain strangely in tension with his earlier argument for divine action at a personal level. . . . As became clear earlier, on this view God's action (and our theological understanding of it) clearly seemed to be limited by a 'superior' scientific explanation."[25]

20. Polkinghorne, "The Hidden Spirit," p. 177.
21. Clayton, *Mind and Emergence*, p. 139.
22. Clayton, *Mind and Emergence*, p. 188.
23. Clayton, *Mind and Emergence*, p. 187.
24. J. Wentzel van Huyssteen, "Emergence and Human Uniqueness: Limiting or Delimiting Evolutionary Explanation," *Zygon* 41 (2006): 649-64, at pp. 657-58.
25. Van Huyssteen, "Emergence and Human Uniqueness," p. 659.

So all varieties of naturalism reject supernaturalism; more specifically, they reject an *interventionist* supernaturalism, and they reject this precisely because such interventionism is not scientifically admissible. However, from a pentecostal perspective, this raises several questions: Could we imagine another option or ontological model? I would suggest that the supernaturalism rejected by these naturalisms is not the ontology that is implicit in pentecostal spirituality and practice. So, if there can be a variety of naturalisms, could we — on the other end of the continuum — recognize some nuance and differences between what might traffic under the banner of supernaturalism? Could we perhaps imagine something like a *non*interventionist "supernaturalism"? Flanagan seems to leave the door open to this possibility. As he stipulates, naturalism requires the rejection of "the *objectionable form of* supernaturalism."[26] The qualifier is significant for my project. He goes on to suggest that the requirements of naturalism do not preclude affirming "spirituality or religion." They only require rejecting versions of such that espouse "the objectionable form of 'supernaturalism'" or "supernaturalism in the objectionable sense."[27] While Flanagan wants to leave his door open for naturalistic spiritualities, and while I suspect he would still find pentecostal claims to the miraculous highly "objectionable," he does at least make room for some nuance and complexity on the "supernaturalist" end of the spectrum. Does he not also leave the door open to the possibility of not only nonobjectionable spiritualities, but also perhaps a nonobjectionable supernaturalism? If we make room for a variety of supernaturalisms, could we imagine a model of "supernaturalism" (I have reservations with the word) that might not fall prey to aspects of the naturalist rejection (the ontological concern about interventions and interruptions) — but nonetheless retains features that even the nonreductionist naturalist paradigm will not admit (e.g., miracles)?

Already the "super" prefix might be a misnomer. An alternative model — which I will suggest is implicit in pentecostal spirituality — will both stretch and question the "super" here. Indeed, I have concerns that "super"-language almost inevitably communicates an interventionist dualism. But I have equal concern that *losing* the "super" means a collapse of transcendence, shutting down surprise, and de jure ruling pentecostal experience of the miraculous an impossibility. (We might say this is a Chalcedonian challenge, seeking to retain immanence without reduction,

---

26. Flanagan, "Varieties of Naturalism," p. 433, italics added.
27. Flanagan, "Varieties of Naturalism," p. 436.

and transcendence without dualism.) Thus in what follows I will suggest that this "third way," rather than being described as a noninterventionist *super*naturalism, might be better described as an "enchanted naturalism" or an "en-Spirited naturalism."

We might summarize or map the terrain of our discussion so far by noting at least these ontological options, plotted along something of a continuum:

(1) reductionistic naturalism (Dennett, Kim)	(2) nonreductionistic naturalism (Clayton, Peacocke, Griffin)	(3) enchanted naturalism or noninterventionist supernaturalism (implicit in pentecostal spirituality)	(4) interventionist supernaturalism (often expressed in pentecostal language)

It is the middle of the continuum that is most interesting and most complex, since both (2) and (3) are fighting on two different fronts. These options are "close" to one another in some respects but different in others. In particular, I propose that (3) — which I'm suggesting is the ontology implicit in pentecostal spirituality — is unique with respect to all the others precisely because it rejects the notion of an *autonomous,* self-sufficient "world" that runs on its own steam, as it were. In other words, I actually think that (1), (2), and (4) ironically share a very similar conception of "the world" as an independent (basically) closed system to which God is "Other." But again, I grant that (2) is unique in this regard insofar as the panentheism that usually attends this position emphasizes the *immanence* of God to the world as the world's dynamic principle. This differs from the pentecostal ontology (3) insofar as the "God" internal to the world, as it were, does not, would not, and cannot act outside of the "laws" of nature. In short, the key difference between (2) and (3) is the question of miracles. And I don't believe that nonreductionistic naturalism has shown sufficient reason to reject miracles apart from the desire to concede to "what science says." Or, in terms I'll use below, I don't think reductionistic naturalism has ever questioned whether the price of admission to modern, scientific "respectability" has perhaps been a bit inflated.

Granted, for (4), God can intervene and interrupt this order. But one could suggest that the "world" of (1) and (2) is just the sort of world that would be left after the extrinsic God of (4) is eliminated.[28] Even nonreductionistic naturalism still accedes to the false dichotomy of Dennett's reductionistic naturalism — "natural *as opposed to* supernatural"; this is because both work with a static ontology of an *autonomous* universe and an account of *causality* that refuses surprise. But this is also true of (4): even interventionist supernaturalism still works with a notion of an *autonomous* "nature." In contrast, the ontology of (3) would refuse such compartmentalizations and false dichotomies; it would refuse to see the natural as "opposed to" the supernatural (and vice versa). In fact, it would argue that one can only have a robust "nature" insofar as it is charged by grace. This is just to say that model (3) works with a very different ontological picture of "nature."

In the next section I want to argue that embedded in pentecostal practice and the pentecostal social imaginary are the resources for articulating a unique, noninterventionist supernaturalism. I should note here (and will explain further below) that I don't mean to suggest that pentecostals "in the pew" (or rolling on the floor, perhaps!) would articulate it in this way. That is, I concede that pentecostals, when pressed, would speak in terms of interventionist supernaturalism — and I have, to this point, tried to concede to that practice. However, I want to suggest that they should stop talking that way *because of their own pentecostal commitments:* the ontological framework that is assumed by interventionist supernaturalism mitigates against the pentecostal experience of the Spirit *as natural.* Part of the genius and uniqueness of pentecostal experience is precisely that one does not see the Spirit's care and activity as exceptions or interruptions of the "normal" ordering of the universe. A feature of the strange and fantastic world of pentecostal spirituality is a sense that the miraculous is normal, that the surprises of the Spirit are normal, whereas interventionist language still presumes the steady, static ontology of "nature" that informs both naturalism and Deism. So when pentecostals adopt interventionist-speak, I believe they are picking up a foreign tongue that is inadequate to articulate their own experience and the theological intuitions implicit in their spirituality. In other words, I think implicit in pentecostal spirituality are the resources for a unique ontology. And because this ontology is walking a tightrope between naturalism and supernaturalism, I suggest that the

---

28. In short, it would be just the kind of world that emerged after Scotus's bifurcation of an "autonomous" world, culminating in Kant. For discussion, see Smith, *Introducing Radical Orthodoxy,* pp. 95-103.

elucidation and articulation of this implicit ontological aspect of the pentecostal social imaginary will find assistance in the "participatory" ontology associated with the *nouvelle théologie* and its contemporary rendition in "Radical Orthodoxy."

A Pentecostal Ontological Intervention in the Science/Theology Dialogue

I have been emphasizing that embedded in pentecostal practice is an "understanding" of the world that eschews the dualistic opposition[29] of the "natural" and the "supernatural." Pentecostal spirituality is not escapist, disembodied mysticism, nor is it merely pragmatic materialism. Instead, pentecostal worship and practice are characterized by a kind of gritty materiality as space for work of the Spirit. Thus some pentecostal theologians have described pentecostal spirituality as *sacramental* in character.[30] We might say that the ontology embedded in pentecostal practice is a material supernaturalism or a supernatural materialism. Again, our lexicon is limited as the very prefix "super" has us falling back into old paradigms. Perhaps we need to adopt a strategy of the young Derrida who recognized such inadequacies of language and suggested that we write *sous rature*, under erasure. In that sense, one might say I'm articulating a ~~super~~natural materialism. As such, it contests the natural/supernatural distinction[31] — which is why I've argued that we need to revisit the identification of pentecostalism as a "supernaturalism."

In this respect, the ontology implicit in pentecostal practice is very much akin to the vision articulated by those theologians associated with *nouvelle théologie*, particularly Henri de Lubac. As such, I am suggesting that their earlier articulation of such a nondualistic supernaturalism can provide resources and conceptual tools for pentecostals to articulate the on-

29. As noted earlier, I'm using the term "dualistic" in a strong sense as including not just the *distinction* between the natural and supernatural (or material and spiritual) but also the *opposition* between the two and the denigration of materiality. Thus by dualism in this context I mean a kind of Gnosticism — one not entirely foreign to some strains of evangelical piety.

30. Frank Macchia, "Tongues as a Sign: Towards a Sacramental Understanding of Pentecostal Experience," *Pneuma: Journal of the Society for Pentecostal Studies* 15 (1993): 61-76.

31. Amos Yong, *The Spirit Poured Out on All Flesh: Pentecostalism and the Possibility of Global Theology* (Grand Rapids: Baker Academic, 2005), pp. 292-301.

tological "understanding" embedded in the pentecostal social imaginary. By eschewing the simple distinction between discrete realms of "nature" and "super-nature," de Lubac struggled to articulate a paradoxical phenomenon, namely, that nature is oriented to the supernatural and that this orientation to the supernatural is "natural" (i.e., constitutive of creaturehood). John Milbank notes the tightrope de Lubac was walking: "this insistence could appear to the ecclesiastical authorities at once 'radically' to threaten the gratuity of the supernatural and the revealed order, and 'conservatively' to threaten the autonomy of the natural domain of reason."[32] Creation *is* (and "nature" *is*) insofar as it participates in and is indwelled by God, in whom we live and move and have our being. Thus the shape of de Lubac's "blurring" of the natural/supernatural distinction[33] finds a more detailed ontological articulation in Radical Orthodoxy's "participatory" ontology, which provides a dynamic sense of the God/world relation that would eschew both naturalism and supernaturalism.

The shape of this theological or participatory ontology is *non*reductive and incarnational: on the one hand, it affirms that matter *as created* exceeds itself and *is* only insofar as it participates in or is suspended from the transcendent Creator; on the other hand, it affirms that there is a significant sense in which the transcendent inheres in immanence. "Things," then — and the created order in general — do not have any kind of "sheer" or "autonomous" existence, as if possessing some kind of inalienable right to be. Rather, being is a *gift* from the transcendent Creator such that things exist only insofar as they participate in the being of the Creator — whose Being is Goodness. Thus Graham Ward suggests that the very words of institution in the Eucharist ("This is my body") already require a more dynamic ontology.[34] If one begins with a radical sense of creation's dependence or gift-character, then the autonomous stasis of materiality must be

32. John Milbank, *The Suspended Middle: Henri de Lubac and the Debate concerning the Supernatural* (Grand Rapids: Eerdmans, 2005), p. 10.

33. Indeed, doesn't the very notion of *creation* blur this distinction? See Yong, "*Ruach*, the Primordial Waters, and the Breath of Life."

34. Graham Ward, *Cities of God* (London: Routledge, 2001), pp. 90-91. It would be interesting to compare and contrast how Ward and Peacocke approach the Eucharist. For Ward, the eucharistic pronouncement is an occasion for theology to "push back" on philosophy and science, and in particular the ontologies bequeathed to us by modernity. In Peacocke, by contrast (see *All That Is,* chapter 8), eucharistic theology needs to submit to revision on the basis of "what science tells us." Thus Ward and Peacocke represent two paths for pentecostals considering the theology/science dialogue. I would suggest that walking down the path with Arthur Peacocke would entail the evisceration of pentecostal spirituality.

revised in such a way that this ontological scandal of the eucharistic pronouncement can be absorbed — just as the doctrines of Christ's bodily
resurrection and ascension must entail a distinctly Christian ontology of
materiality. Hence "[t]here is only one radical critique of modernity — the
critique that denies the existence of the secular as self-subsisting, that immanent self-ordering of the world which ultimately had no need for
God. . . . The Christian doctrines of incarnation and creation stand opposed to closed, immanentalist systems."[35] Thus, to counter the politics
and epistemology of secular modernity, it is necessary to subject its *ontology* to critique (and unveil its status as a *mythos*), then articulate the only
counterontology that is able to do justice to materiality and embodiment
as such. Such a participatory ontology provides a groundwork for rethinking the God/world relation, and so reconsidering several key themes in sci-
ence/theology dialogue, including questions about divine action in the
world, the nature of scientific "laws," a nonreductive materialist account of
the human person, and perhaps even a "naturalized" account of the sacra-
ments. In sum, Radical Orthodoxy's participatory ontology provides the
groundwork for thinking about the reenchantment of the world in dialogue with science.

The key here is that this dynamic, participatory ontology refuses the
static ontologies that presume the autonomy of nature. While I would pre-
fer to drop "nature" from our lexicon, working with it we might say that
nature is always already suspended in and inhabited by the Spirit such that
it is always already *primed* for the Spirit's manifestations. Pentecostal spirituality and practice don't merely expect that God could "interrupt" the so-
called "order" of nature; rather, they assume that the Spirit is always already at work in creation, animating (and reanimating) bodies, grabbing
hold of vocal cords, taking up aspects of creation to manifest the glory of
God. Thus Amos Yong has recently offered a "pneumatological assist" to
this participatory ontology, which I received with thanks.[36] Specifically,
Yong points to the Spirit as the agent of "suspension," the triune person *in*
whom the material world is suspended. This only further invites us to see
Radical Orthodoxy as a resource, ally, or partner in the explication of dis-

35. Ward, *Cities of God*, p. 94.
36. Amos Yong, "Radically Orthodox, Reformed, and Pentecostal: Rethinking the Intersection of Post/modernity and the Religions in Conversation with James K. A. Smith,"
Journal of Pentecostal Theology 15 (2007): 233-50; James K. A. Smith, "The Spirit, Religions,
and the World as Sacrament: A Response to Amos Yong's Pneumatological Assist," *Journal of
Pentecostal Theology* 15 (2007): 251-61.

tinctly pentecostal ontology. In response to Yong's pneumatological assist I have articulated an account of the God/world relation in the Spirit in terms of *intensities* of participation. While all that is participates in God through the Spirit, there are sites and events that exhibit a more *intense* participation. Thus phenomena that might be described as "miraculous" are not instances of God "breaking into" the world, as if God were outside it prior to such events; rather, they are instances of a unique and special mode of participation that always already characterizes creation.

Thus the participatory pneumatological ontology I'm suggesting is *not* an "interventionist" model; in short, it is not really a "super"-naturalism. Hence I'm even somewhat cautious about adopting the language of an "open" creation since this still seems to presume a picture of "nature" as basically autonomous but open to intervention by God from the outside. But such language of "intervention" has at least two problems:[37]

1. A scientific problem: it fails to honor the overwhelming success of science predicated on the predictability of nature's lawlike regularity (it also tends to punt on questions about the *mechanics* of intervention).
2. A theological problem: it assumes a picture of the world, and of the God/world relation, that actually cedes an *autonomy* to the natural order akin to Deism. I would call this the "discretion" model because it carves out "the world" as a discrete, autonomous realm that God then has to "enter," a closed system that God comes to "interrupt" or in which God "intervenes." This "discretion" model — the sense that God and the world are "discrete" — is shared by both the naturalists who reject such interventions and the supernaturalists who claim such interventions. Both basically see "nature" as an autonomous system; what they *dis*agree about is whether or not God can/does intervene into this discrete, closed system.

But should we think of the cosmos ("nature") as a discrete, closed, autonomous system, as both naturalists and supernaturalists assume? I think such an assumption rests on a problematic theology of creation. In particular, I think it rests on a theology of creation that is devoid of any sense of the essential, constitutive, dynamic presence of God the Spirit *in* creation.[38] I

37. I don't think the problems I enumerate here are the same ones addressed in Plantinga, "What Is 'Intervention'?" pp. 383-88.

38. As I've suggested, a close cousin of this position (an enchanted naturalism or non-

suggest that embedded in a pentecostal social imaginary is an "understanding" of the God/world relation that eschews the "discretion" model and refuses to grant "nature" the autonomy of a closed system. Rather, the Spirit is always already present at and in creation. The Spirit's presence is not a postlapsarian or soteriological "visiting" of a creation that is otherwise without God; rather, the Spirit is always already dynamically active in the cosmos/world/nature. God doesn't have to "enter" nature as a visitor and alien; God is always already present in the world. Thus creation is *primed* for the Spirit's action.

Nature as En-Spirited

According to this pentecostal ontology, nature is always already en-Spirited. Thus it begins from a picture of creation that emphasizes the Spirit's essential and dynamic presence in nature. This nuanced, dynamic ontological picture makes it possible to account for both the *regularity* of natural processes and the *special* action of the miraculous (in contrast to even the nonreductionistic naturalism of Griffin and Clayton).

1. *Regularity.* Science's successes and insights are predicated on the regularity and (relative) constancy of natural processes. Naturalism claims that this must entail an understanding of nature as a closed system of "laws," but this is not a properly scientific (empirical) claim. The affirmation of the Spirit's dynamic presence in creation is not opposed to recognizing that, for the most part, this presence is manifested by God's steady, sustaining care of the universe along the lines of what seem like "laws." For pentecostals, it would be spurning God's faithful, steady presence to not recognize this. So I think it is important to note that a pentecostal worldview does not require rejecting a sense of a

---

interventionist ~~super~~naturalism) is something like Clayton's panentheism. I am in some ways sympathetic to such panentheism (and would follow Jonathan Edwards on this score) *except* to the extent that it assumes an ontological rigidity to "natural law." That is, I think Clayton's panentheism does not start from a sufficiently dynamic sense of the *contingency* of the "laws" of nature. This will require an account of the *regularity* of "natural" processes without attributing to them a reified lawlike character. In general, I find that process theologians such as Griffin and Clayton tend to ignore questions about science as a contingent, cultural institution, and are somewhat naive about scientific *practice*, including the contingent role of metaphor (such as "law") in describing the world.

steady, faithful presence of the Spirit in creation — even if it does remain open to the ways in which God might surprise us (ontological surprises!). This is particularly important given that some pentecostal and charismatic traditions have been given to a kind of *hyper-supernaturalism* that refuses medical (scientific) treatment of illness and disease. I'm suggesting that this is not only bad science, it is also bad pentecostal theology, working from a caricatured pneumatology that sets the Spirit in opposition to the creation that the same Spirit sustains. Therefore there is nothing inconsistent about working from a pentecostal worldview and affirming a minimal disenchantment or methodological naturalism. I think this is important to emphasize precisely because some Pentecostals have thought that the confession of God's dynamic work in creation required ignoring this steady, lawlike manifestation of the Spirit's presence in the world. While a pentecostal worldview affirms both the dynamic presence of the Spirit in creation and a nondualistic emphasis on bodily healing, I think some Pentecostal traditions try to be more spiritual than the Spirit by rejecting the Spirit's more mundane operations that are discerned by medical science. It is precisely this hyper-supernaturalism that makes me think that a healthy dose of minimal disenchantment and methodological naturalism might actually be a *better* way to recognize *all* the ways that the Spirit is dynamically present in creation.[39]

2. *Special Action.* Because nature is always already inhabited by the Spirit, it is also primed for (not merely "open to") special or unique singularities; these will not be "antinature," because nature is not a discrete, autonomous entity. Rather, we can think of these "special" miraculous manifestations of the Spirit's presence in creation as more *intense* instances of the Spirit in creation — or as "sped-up" modes of the Spirit's more "regular" presences.[40] Augustine describes them as "extraordinary" actions that are meant to refocus our semiotic attention on the "miraculous" nature of the ordinary. A "miracle" is not an

---

39. It should be noted, however, that this is an alternative description of what passes under the banner of "methodological naturalism." I am not suggesting that pentecostals accede to methodological naturalism to secure intellectual respectability or to bow to "what science says." Rather, I'm suggesting that the kind of attentive observation of nature that constitutes science yields fruit by recognizing regularity — without thereby ramping such regularity up into the de jure, ironclad status of a "law" of nature. In this respect, I actually think I agree with David Hume.

40. Cp. C. S. Lewis, *Miracles* (New York: Macmillan, 1947), pp. 132-42.

event that "breaks" any "laws" of nature, since nature does not have such a reified character; rather, a miracle is a manifestation of the Spirit's presence that is "out of the ordinary"; but even the ordinary is a manifestation of the Spirit's presence. Augustine enjoins us to see nature *as* miracle.[41]

We are told by naturalists (both reductionist and nonreductionist) that the price of admission to the theology/science dialogue (yea, to science and the proverbial "modern world") is naturalism. Thus the theology/science dialogue is a kind of Rawlsian original position that requires believers to strip down at the entry, leaving them with only what all "rational" people hold in common. But paying that price of admission requires pentecostals to pawn what is essential to pentecostal spirituality: the Spirit's miraculous surprises. What I have tried to argue is that the so-called price of admission has been illegitimately inflated — that certain gatekeepers of science (and of the science/theology dialogue) have suggested that the price of admission to science (and "scientific respectability") was metaphysical naturalism, or at least ontological monism, coupled with rigid conceptions of the "laws" of nature. I have tried to offer an alternative description of nature that, negatively, points out the illegitimate inflation stemming from a *con*flation of science with naturalism, and positively, provides a rationale for careful empirical observation and prediction without a priori ruling out the miraculous. Such, I hope, begins to make room for pentecostals in the science/theology dialogue, and encourages pentecostals to engage the sciences.[42]

41. For a discussion of Augustine on this point, see Chris Gousmett, "Creation Order and Miracle according to Augustine," *Evangelical Quarterly* 60 (1988): 217-40.

42. For further development of these themes, see James K. A. Smith and Amos Yong, eds., *Science and the Spirit: A Pentecostal Engagement with the Sciences* (Bloomington: Indiana University Press, 2010).

5 From Beliefs to Altar Calls

A Pentecostal Critique of Philosophy of Religion

I would like to invite you to a tiny little mission church in north Philadelphia. It is the site of one of my most treasured memories of ministry, but also an event that constantly challenges my inherited paradigms in philosophy of religion.

It is an early winter evening, so darkness presses against the windows of the rented sanctuary as a small group of believers are gathering; light and song push back against that darkness and ooze out of the cracks of the aging, tiny structure. We have gathered for an evening service of celebration as several members of a neighborhood family, new to the church, have presented themselves for baptism. Over the past several months we have witnessed a transformation in the mother and some of her children, and tonight they make public profession of their newfound faith by dying and rising in the waters of baptism. The father and some uncles have come for the service to honor those being baptized, but as with previous visits to Sunday worship, they remain aloof, distant, and unengaged. But tonight that will change. Baptism in a Pentecostal church brings together the charismatic and the sacramental: their baptism is situated in a narrative enacted through song and sermon, echoed in the story of their testimonies as they present themselves for baptism. And as they are baptized, the pastor draws upon the materiality and physicality of the sacrament as a picture of the gospel itself. Tonight it's not just a matter of *telling*, but a matter of *showing*. As the mother emerges from the water it feels as if we are witnessing the resurrection itself. Pastor and parishioner embrace in tears as the congregation can no longer contain its "Hallelujah's" and shouts of praise;

their songs and prayers become the sound track of resurrection. He is risen! *She* is risen! As the teenagers are baptized, they each renounce the Evil One and pledge allegiance to the coming King. They have a new story, a new love, a new desire.

And then we notice that slowly the father has made his way to the front of the sanctuary. He has been gripped by something in what he has witnessed. As others notice, a hush comes over the congregation. His brothers with him, the father quietly but urgently speaks with the pastor, and then a laugh of surprise and joy breaks across the pastor's face as he embraces the father and assures him, "Of course!" The men have come asking: "Can we be baptized, too? Can we become Christians?" The waters of baptism stir once again and the sound track of resurrection becomes even louder as an entire family is enfolded into the family of God.

Just what happened there? More to the point, to what extent can the regnant paradigms in philosophy of religion understand or explain a scene like this one? This father's desire to embrace the Christian story — and be embraced by Christ — was not an instance of intellectual resolution. Christ was not the "answer" to a "question." Jorge was not drawn to "theism," and when he, too, emerged from the waters of baptism he did not rise with a new "perspective" or "worldview." He didn't die to skepticism and rise to "knowledge" (cf. Rom. 6:1-14). Something other, something different, something both ordinary and extraordinary was witnessed there. Are the dominant frameworks in philosophy of religion able to do justice to what happened there in that tiny sanctuary on a winter night? Or are they plagued by a kind of reductionism and rationalism that is poorly calibrated to understand a scenario like this one? What picture of the "believer" is assumed in our philosophies of religion? In this chapter I want to consider how pentecostal spirituality functions as a liminal case that stretches the conceptual assumptions operative in contemporary philosophy of religion.

Limits of the "Renaissance" in Philosophy of Religion

There has been much discussion of the "renaissance" in the philosophy of religion in the last several decades of the twentieth century. After the last gasp of positivism and the final attempt to police philosophical discourse through ordinary language philosophy, there emerged the space for a renewed consideration of religion within the halls of philosophy in two

senses: on the one hand, religious themes and questions once again became legitimate topics for philosophical reflection; on the other hand, and
perhaps more radically, a critique of the supposed neutrality and objectivity of philosophical reason opened the space for *religious* philosophy —
that is, philosophical reflection undertaken from a perspective and orientation that were unapologetically religious and confessional. The "of" in
this renewal in philosophy *of* religion was both an objective and subjective
genitive: religion was reintroduced as a legitimate mainstream topic of
consideration (objective genitive), and religion was admitted as a legitimate orienting perspective for philosophical research and reflection (subjective genitive).

Work along the former lines included renewed interest in religious
phenomena such as miracles, the perennial problem of evil, as well as the
conditions of possibility of religious language or "God-talk."[1] This developed into a more robust renewal of "philosophical theology" now exemplified in the work of Eleonore Stump, Marilyn Adams, Stephen Davis,
Brian Hebblethwaite, Brian Leftow, and many others.[2]

Developments along the latter lines of a *religious* philosophy were
closely connected with the development of "Reformed epistemology" as
articulated by Nicholas Wolterstorff and Alvin Plantinga — a distinctly
nonfoundationalist epistemological project that sought to contest the
criteria of "rationality" that had been marshaled to exclude religious belief from both the halls of philosophy and the sphere of public discourse.[3] Articulating a critique of the supposed neutrality and autonomy

---

1. As an example of this development, consider, for instance, the work of Antony Flew: *Hume's Philosophy of Belief* (London: Routledge, 1961); *God and Philosophy* (New York: Dell, 1966); and Antony Flew and Alasdair MacIntyre, eds., *New Essays in Philosophical Theology* (London: SCM, 1955).

2. For just a sample of representative work in this vein, see Kelly James Clark, ed., *Our Knowledge of God: Essays on Natural and Philosophical Theology* (The Hague: Kluwer, 1992); Eleonore Stump, ed., *Reasoned Faith: Essays in Philosophical Theology in Honor of Norman Kretzmann* (Ithaca, NY: Cornell University Press, 1993); Marilyn McCord Adams, *Horrendous Evils and the Goodness of God* (Ithaca, NY: Cornell University Press, 2000); Brian Hebblethwaite, *Philosophical Theology and Christian Doctrine* (Oxford: Blackwell, 2005); and Stephen T. Davis, *Christian Philosophical Theology* (Oxford: Oxford University Press, 2006).

3. There is also a European and Catholic story to be told here associated with Blondel and, later, Gilson's claims regarding a "Christian philosophy." As usual, at stake here is how we receive the legacy of Thomas Aquinas — a debate that has come to the fore again with contemporary retrievals of *nouvelle théologie*. However, I cannot do justice to these issues

of reason, Wolterstorff and Plantinga argued that religious belief was *just as* "warranted" as other presuppositions in philosophy that, in fact, shared the same epistemic status.[4] Thus Reformed epistemology undercut the foundationalist rationalism of philosophy and thereby opened a path of legitimacy for philosophical reflection oriented and informed by religious presuppositions. This critique of foundationalism and neutrality resonated with other developments in philosophy, including Alasdair MacIntyre's account of the "traditioned" nature of rationality,[5] as well as the tradition of "hermeneutic" philosophy associated with Heidegger and Gadamer which emphasized the constitutive role of presuppositions in shaping rationality — anticipating the shape of a "postmodern" critique of foundationalist reason.[6] While these different schools of thought are not often associated (indeed, Reformed epistemology remains virulently allergic to "postmodernism"), I would suggest that, in fact, these tensions represent a kind of sibling rivalry.[7] Their work, as I've already noted, made room for the very idea of a "Christian philosophy," which in turn made it possible to imagine something like a "pentecostal philosophy."

In this chapter I want to offer an appreciative critique of these devel-

---

here. For relevant discussion see Francesca Aran Murphy, "Gilson and Chenu: The Structure of the *Summa* and the Shape of Dominican Life," *New Blackfriars* 85 (2004): 290-303; D. Stephen Long, "The Way of Aquinas: Its Importance for Moral Theology," *Studies in Christian Ethics* 19 (2006): 339-56; and Adam C. English, *The Possibility of Christian Philosophy: Maurice Blondel at the Intersection of Theology and Philosophy,* Radical Orthodoxy Series (London: Routledge, 2006).

4. Most famously, Plantinga pointed out the analogy between the epistemic status of belief in "other minds" and belief in God. See Alvin Plantinga, *God and Other Minds: A Study of Rational Justification of Belief in God* (Ithaca, NY: Cornell University Press, 1967).

5. MacIntyre, *Whose Justice? Which Rationality?* (South Bend, IN: University of Notre Dame Press, 1989).

6. For a summary of this related to philosophy of religion, see James K. A. Smith, *The Fall of Interpretation: Philosophical Foundations for a Creational Hermeneutic* (Downers Grove, IL: InterVarsity, 2000), and Smith, "The Art of Christian Atheism: Faith and Philosophy in Early Heidegger," *Faith and Philosophy* 14 (1997): 71-81.

7. Much work remains to be done on this score, and I can't pursue it further here. Suffice it to say that Plantinga's critique of "postmodernism" (*Warranted Christian Belief* [New York: Oxford University Press, 2000], part III) is a rejection of a straw man, and that, in fact, his nonfoundationalist account of warranted belief has much in common with Heidegger, Rorty, and perhaps even Derrida. For some recent hints along this line, see the discussion of Plantinga and Rorty in G. Elijah Dann, *After Rorty: The Possibilities for Ethics and Religious Belief* (London: Continuum, 2006).

opments in philosophy of religion. Recognizing my own indebtedness to this earlier work, I nonetheless want to suggest a significant lacuna, or blind spot, namely, the absence of any rigorous attention to worship, liturgy, or the *practices* of religious communities. In sum, one could argue that philosophy of religion has been attentive to *beliefs* but not *believers*. It has been characterized by a kind of epistemological fixation that myopically focuses on either the epistemic status of religious belief or an explication of the propositional content of specific beliefs (e.g., the goodness of God, God's eternity, or resurrection). But philosophy of religion has spent very little time being attentive to how embodied, flesh-and-blood believers experience religion primarily as a form of life. A formative and usually central aspect of that form of life — across religious traditions — is participation in corporate worship, liturgical practices, and other forms of shared spiritual disciplines. In other words, believers tend to focus on faith as a way of life ("what we *do*") whereas contemporary philosophy of religion tends to treat faith as a way of thinking ("what we *believe*"). In this respect, I think pentecostal experience can function as a case study that will press a way forward for a philosophy of religion that seeks to overcome this blind spot and direct the attention of philosophy of religion to *practice*.

Cartesian Ghosts: A Lingering Rationalism in Philosophy of Religion

Levinas famously remarked that Dasein is never hungry.[8] And yet, does Dasein ever eat? In the same vein we might ask: Does Dasein ever worship? Or more pointedly, do the believers countenanced in contemporary philosophy of religion ever kneel or sing?[9] Do they ever respond to an altar call, weeping on their knees? In fact, do *believers* ever really make an appearance in philosophy of religion? Is it not most often taken up instead

---

8. Emmanuel Levinas, *Totality and Infinity,* trans. Alphonso Lingis (Pittsburgh: Duquesne University Press, 1969), p. 134.

9. To his credit, it should be noted that in the later Heidegger, believers dance and pray. See Martin Heidegger, "The Onto-Theo-logical Constitution of Metaphysics," in *Identity and Difference,* trans. Joan Stambaugh (San Francisco: Harper and Row, 1969), p. 72. For further discussion, see Merold Westphal, "Overcoming Onto-Theology," in *God, the Gift, and Postmodernism,* ed. John D. Caputo and Michael Scanlon (Bloomington: Indiana University Press, 1999), pp. 146-63.

with *beliefs?* Judging from the shape of the conversation in contemporary philosophy of religion, one would guess that "religion" is a feature of brains-in-a-vat, lingering in a particularly spiritual ether but never really bumping into the grittiness of practices and community. Indeed, one wonders whether such "believers" really even need to go through the hassle of getting up on Sunday morning. Once the beliefs are "deposited," it's hard to see what more is needed to be faithful.

The renaissance in philosophy of religion in the past thirty years has been beholden, I would contend, to a lingering rationalism that remains at least haunted (if not perhaps *governed*) by a sort of Cartesian anthropology that tends to construe the human person as, in essence, a "thinking thing." Because it assumes a philosophical anthropology that privileges the cognitive and rational (an anthropology criticized in chapter 3 above), philosophy of religion thus construes religion as a primarily epistemological phenomenon. As a result, the "religion" in philosophy *of religion* is a very cognitive, "heady" phenomenon — reduced to beliefs, propositions, and cognitive content, which are the only phenomena that can make it through the narrow theoretical gate that attends such rationalism. Believers, insofar as they appear, seem to be little more than talking heads. The result is a reductionism: religion, which is primarily a "form of life" and lived experience, is slimmed down to the more abstract phenomena of beliefs and doctrines. The rich, dynamic, lived experience of worshiping communities is reduced to propositions that can be culled from artifacts produced by these communities (e.g., documents, creeds, scriptures). If philosophy of religion pays any attention to liturgy or other religious practices, it is usually only in order to mine the artifacts of liturgy for new ideas and propositions.

Thus philosophy of religion as currently practiced tends to reflect a working (or at least functional) assumption that doctrine is prior to worship and thus ideas and propositions trump practices. Practiced in this rationalist mode, philosophy of religion finds a ready-made proportionality to theological doctrines, ideas, and propositions. Hence what has flourished in philosophy of religion has been philosophical theology of a particular sort.[10] At

10. For instance, when philosophers of religion consider prayer, they focus primarily on the epistemological challenges, or how prayer can be reconciled with the doctrines of God's omniscience and omnipotence. See, for example, Eleonore Stump, "Petitionary Prayer," *American Philosophical Quarterly* 16 (1979): 81-91, and Lawrence Masek, "Petitionary Prayer to an Omnipotent and Omnibenevolent God," in *Philosophical Theology: Reason and Theological Doctrine,* Proceedings of the American Catholic Philosophical Association 74

best, this amounts to a reduction of "religion" to propositional thinking, a narrowing of the richness of religious lived experience. At worst, the result is not just a "thinning" of religion, but a falsification of it, insofar as religion construed as primarily a cognitive or propositional or epistemological phenomenon fails to discern the heart of religion as practice. What one works on is often a reflection of one's tools. If all I have is a hammer and nails, I'm not equipped to work on an electric circuit. In that vein, contemporary philosophy of religion is equipped with a tool belt made for thinking about thinking — analyzing concepts of a certain sort. As a result, the philosopher of religion is equipped only to "work on" religion insofar as it can be made (and thus cut down) to the measure of conceptual, cognitive thinking.[11] Attention to aspects of religion as a form of life and set of practices would require a different, or at least expanded, tool belt.[12]

A new renaissance in philosophy of religion could be sparked by reversing this assumption and taking seriously the priority of religious practices to doctrinal formulations. I have been describing pentecostalism as a "spirituality" (rather than a system of doctrines) in order to appreciate that pentecostalism is what Wittgenstein would describe as a "form of life" — a constellation of practices, rituals, and embodied habits that "carry" a story and an understanding. A philosophy of religion that would do justice to pentecostal experience will have to recover a sense of religion as a form of life and embodied experience — and that will require challenging the rationalist philosophical anthropology that underlies contemporary philosophy of religion. In a way, pentecostal spirituality already does this: pentecostal experience — and the ways of life associated with pentecostal communities — resists rationalist reduction and exhibits a way of being-in-the-world that manifests the fundamentally affective nature of the hu-

---

(2000): 273-83. For a contrasting philosophical engagement with prayer, see Peter Ochs, "Morning Prayer as Redemptive Thinking," in *Liturgy, Time, and the Politics of Redemption*, ed. C. C. Pecknold and Randi Rashkover (Grand Rapids: Eerdmans, 2006), pp. 50-90. For further discussion of Ochs's work in this regard, see James K. A. Smith, "How Religious Practices Matter: Peter Ochs' 'Alternative Nurturance' of Philosophy of Religion," *Modern Theology* 24 (2008): 469-78.

11. I don't think this is a phenomenon unique to "analytic" or Anglo-American philosophy. Much "continental" philosophy of religion also exhibits an epistemological fixation.

12. In *Speech and Theology: Language and the Logic of Incarnation* (London: Routledge, 2002), I argue that this was precisely the project of the young Heidegger: to come up with a new "concept" that could do justice to the richness of lived experience, and *religious* lived experience in particular (see pp. 67-113).

man person.[13] In sum, it is precisely the phenomenon of religious life that points up the paucity and thinness of the Cartesian "thinking thing" as a very *un*natural beast. It's not that a cognitivist philosophical anthropology is just too narrow or selective, but that it actually falsifies the engaged, embodied character of our being-in-the-world. So attention to religion *as* a form of life and nexus of liturgical practices brings us up against a phenomenon that challenges and deconstructs the lingering rationalist anthropologies that continue to shape method in philosophy of religion. There is, one could say, a very different, nonrationalist philosophical anthropology implicit in pentecostal spirituality such that worship becomes a catalyst, even a "revelation," that unsettles overly-cognitivist pictures of the human person. In sum, it is the very phenomenon of religion as liturgical practice that functions as a "shot in the arm" to philosophy of religion by calling for a philosophical anthropology that honors our primarily affective, precognitive, communal, and "practiced" mode of being-in-the-world. Thus there is a dialectical relationship envisioned between philosophy and liturgy: on the one hand, the lived religious experience embodied in liturgical practice points to the necessity of an affective (nonrationalist) philosophical anthropology; on the other hand, the development and assumption of an affective philosophical anthropology enable philosophy of religion to be primed for dealing better with the more fundamental phenomena associated with religion, namely, practices rather than doctrines.

In fact, it was just this impetus — this interjection of embodied, lived religious experience as a "shock" to regnant philosophical method — that was the prompt for the young Heidegger's critique of the lingering Cartesian rationalism that characterized Husserl's early phenomenology.[14] Thus we can find the resources for this retooling philosophy of religion by considering an analogous critique in the rudimentary elements of Heidegger's critique of Descartes and Husserl. A central aspect of Heidegger's project in *Being and Time* was to call into question the rationalist anthropology

13. Social scientific accounts of pentecostal spirituality must grapple with a similar challenge. For a relevant discussion in this regard, see the nuanced methodological appendix in Ralph W. Hood, Jr., and W. Paul Williamson, *Them That Believe: The Power and Meaning of the Christian Serpent-Handling Tradition* (Berkeley: University of California Press, 2008), pp. 247-56.

14. Another impetus was the messiness of lived ethical experience as analyzed by Aristotle. For a discussion of Aristotle in these terms, see Martin Heidegger, "Phenomenological Interpretations with Respect to Aristotle: Indications of the Hermeneutic Situation [1922]," trans. Michael Baur, *Man and World* 25 (1992): 355-93.

assumed by Husserl, who still tended to construe human beings as primarily perceiving things — as if we inhabited the world as observers and spectators who spend time *thinking* about the world. In contrast, Heidegger argued that primarily and for the most part, we don't *think* about a world of objects; rather, we are *involved* with the world as traditioned actors. The world is the environment in which we swim, not a picture that we look at as distanced observers.[15]

Careful phenomenological attention to the dynamics of religious life — that is, religion as a way of life (Hadot) or form of life (Wittgenstein) — manifests something about the nature of human being-in-the-world that is missed by the overly-cognitivist paradigms that currently govern philosophy of religion. In particular, the communal practices that shape religion show us that human being-in-the-world is oriented more fundamentally by desire than thinking, and manifests itself more in what we do than in what we think.[16] As such, it is precisely the visceral, embodied nature of religious life[17] that calls for a revision of the *philosophy* at work in "philosophy of religion."

Against Minimalist Theism: Pentecostal Philosophy and Canonical Theism in Dialogue

I want to close by suggesting that a pentecostal philosophy of religion will find an ally in the work of William Abraham, *Crossing the Threshold of Di-*

15. I have unpacked this in more detail in *Speech and Theology*, pp. 67-82.

16. Religion as a form of life ("what we *do*") also confirms important developments in philosophy of mind, cognitive science, and neuroplasticity, which emphasize the ways and extent to which our comportment to the world happens at the level of the bodily, tactile, and preconscious. Philosophy of religion has yet to engage these conversations, but a turn to liturgy provides the catalyst for such explorations. For relevant discussions, see Timothy D. Wilson, *Strangers to Ourselves: Discovering the Adaptive Unconscious* (Cambridge, MA: Harvard University Press, 2002), and Shaun Gallagher, *How the Body Shapes the Mind* (Oxford: Clarendon, 2005). This just comes down to requiring that philosophy of religion take embodiment seriously. For an important beginning, see Sarah Coakley, ed., *Religion and the Body* (Cambridge: Cambridge University Press, 2003).

17. I should clarify that I think *all* modes of religious life are embodied — whether pentecostal, Catholic, Muslim, or Buddhist. I mean to suggest only that this aspect of religious practice is particularly amplified (and affirmed) in pentecostal spirituality, making pentecostalism a fruitful catalyst for pressing this methodological paradigm shift in philosophy of religion.

vine Revelation, in particular because I believe he provides hints of a paradigm shift that can do justice to the religious experience of "ordinary believers."[18] In a spirit of charitable critique, humble boldness, and no-holds-barred irenics, he manages to call out almost every existing school in contemporary philosophy of religion for uncritically buying into various versions of the "standard strategy" that obfuscates the nature of faith precisely by canonizing some epistemological theory. Granted, Abraham's charm might fool us into missing the fact that he's calling us to the mat for pawning the family jewels to the highest epistemological bidder.[19] The "standard strategy," as Abraham describes it, is a widespread project that seeks to "secure the rationality of theism" by first articulating a "general" epistemology that then provides a foothold for demonstrating the rationality of theistic belief. The general epistemology provides "a foothold outside of theology" that functions as an anchor to which theistic belief can be tethered (p. 6).[20] This standard strategy is characteristic of a wide range of particular epistemological theories; it is a big tent under which one will find an eclectic collection, from classic natural theologians and "Wittgensteinian fideists" to Schubert Ogden and Reformed epistemologists (a lot of folks who would be surprised to find themselves on the same team, as it were).

I can't here adjudicate Abraham's claims regarding who is and is not a practitioner of the standard strategy. I am more interested in his insightful critique of two significant problems that are often outcomes of this strategy. The first he describes as "methodism" (surely a playful suggestion to make from the halls of SMU). The standard strategy opts for a kind of one-size-fits-all epistemology that establishes general criteria for knowledge — and often the bar is set very (perhaps even impossibly) high.[21] As a result,

18. William J. Abraham, *Crossing the Threshold of Divine Revelation* (Grand Rapids: Eerdmans, 2006). Subsequent parenthetical references in the text refer to this book.

19. I'm reminded of Kierkegaard's quip about theology selling itself to philosophy: "Theology sits all rouged and powdered in the window and courts its favor, offers its charms to philosophy." Kierkegaard, *Fear and Trembling/Repetition,* ed. and trans. Howard V. Hong and Edna H. Hong (Princeton, NJ: Princeton University Press, 1983), p. 32. Abraham's critique suggests that "Christian philosophy" might actually be playing the pimpish mediator in this process.

20. One might wonder whether there is a certain return of a standard strategy in Abraham's account of divine revelation, which begins by first placing it in "the conceptual field of revelation" per se (p. 60) or from what we know about "personal human agents that we know" (p. 65). However, I won't pursue this here.

21. This is why methodism breeds skepticism (p. 33). I think Abraham's critique of

all sorts of beliefs that don't meet these criteria or can't make it over the bar are denigrated as mere opinion, "faith," and thus subject to doubt. What's going on here is a sort of vanilla-izing of epistemology: the map of knowledge is flat and monolithic. It shows no signs of attention to texture, depth, or gradations in the epistemic terrain. In contrast to the methodist, the "particularist" comes to questions of knowledge with a more fine-grained map of the epistemic landscape. She rejects the monolithic (and hegemonic) assumptions of the methodist's one-size-fits-all epistemology and instead embraces an Aristotelian (p. 29 n. 10) principle of "appropriate epistemic fit," which means that she is primed to "look for relevant differences in the way we adjudicate different kinds of claims" (p. 45).[22] The particularist is an epistemic pluralist and expects to find different habits of belief and justification when we are dealing with different subject matter and objects of belief. Whereas the methodist is an "epistemic miser" (p. 34) who countenances only a small range of legitimate modes of belief, the particularist is epistemically generous and is not surprised by different epistemological habits when it comes to different subjects of knowledge.

Because philosophy of religion is dominated by methodists (the preponderance of Reformed epistemologists notwithstanding!), contemporary paradigms in philosophy of religion are prone to impose on religious belief epistemic criteria that are inappropriate to the subject at hand. Animated by the standard strategy, methodists in philosophy of religion adopt a generic epistemology and then require "believers" to exhibit those modes of believing and knowing. And it is just this generic methodism that leads philosophers of religion to ignore or even rule out of court *particular* Christian claims to knowledge such as "revelation." Thus Abraham's bold project of making the particularity and specificity of divine revelation central to Christian epistemology is an outcome of his desire to abide by the particularist principle of appropriate epistemic fit — a principle spurned by methodists.

---

skepticism applies well to certain schools in "postmodern" philosophy of religion (p. 39 n. 24), though I think he misunderstands Radical Orthodoxy on this point.

22. As a way of bridging the analytic/continental divide in philosophy of religion, it might be interesting to note that the young Heidegger, whose theoretical breakthroughs were very much motivated by a desire to do justice to the realities of lived religious experience, was directly influenced by this same Aristotelian principle of finding concepts "appropriate" to the subject matter *(Sache)* under consideration (Aristotle, *Nichomachean Ethics* 1094.24-25). See Heidegger, "Phenomenological Interpretations with Respect to Aristotle." For relevant discussion, see Smith, *Speech and Theology,* pp. 75-79.

There is a second important outcome of the standard strategy in philosophy of religion: what emerges on the other side of the project is a very "thin" version of religious belief, a "minimalist version of theism" (p. 10) in which "crucial theological claims are systematically ignored or set aside because they would not fit the schema in hand" (p. 9). Abraham aptly describes this as "the mere theism that normally detains the philosopher of religion" (p. 95): "rarely, if at all, do these proposals secure the deep content of Christian belief" (p. 9). Furthermore, the "mere theism" of contemporary philosophy of religion, while failing to do justice to the "thickness" and particularity of Christian belief, also fails to do justice to "the *way* in which a host of Christian believers actually believe" (p. 10, italics added). Here Abraham names a problem that motivates this chapter: Just what sort of animal is pictured when contemporary philosophy of religion talks about "believers"? And I think the most promising and radical aspect of Abraham's project is his clarion call for philosophy of religion to develop "an account that will begin to do justice both to the faith of the ordinary believer and to the faith of the saints and martyrs" (p. 10). This will require retooling the conceptual framework in philosophy of religion to do justice to the thickness and particularity of Christian faith, which Abraham describes as "canonical theism,"[23] in contrast to the thinned-out, "mere" theism that is usually the currency of philosophers of religion. Canonical theism is

> that rich vision of God, creation, and redemption developed over time in the scriptures, articulated in the Nicene Creed, celebrated in the liturgy of the church, enacted in the lives of the saints, handed over and received in the sacraments, depicted in iconography, articulated by canonical teachers, mulled over in the Fathers, and treasured, preserved, and guarded by the episcopate. (p. 43)[24]

The Christian does not just believe in God as *causa sui* or a fine-tuner of the universe; she believes in the God of Abraham, Isaac, and Jesus Christ.

---

23. I cannot do justice to his earlier articulations of this notion. In *Crossing the Threshold* Abraham helpfully points to relevant earlier accounts of canonical theism in Abraham, *The Logic of Evangelism* (Grand Rapids: Eerdmans, 1988) and *Canon and Criterion in Christian Theology* (Oxford: Clarendon, 1998). For further explication see William J. Abraham, Jason E. Vickers, and Natalie B. Van Kirk, eds., *Canonical Theism: A Proposal for Theology and the Church* (Grand Rapids: Eerdmans, 2008).

24. We might note that mere theism has no bishops.

Abraham's articulation of a specifically *canonical* theism might be seen as a kind of Pascalian project.

In addition to the thickness and specificity of the *content* of canonical theism, Abraham is also attentive to *how* Christians come to believe. One does not come to canonical faith magically or by a merely interior operation of the Holy Spirit (*pace* Plantinga?). Abraham's proposal stems directly from his work on the history of evangelism and conversion, particularly the role of catechesis and material practices of formation (p. 51).[25] On the basis of this he "became convinced that becoming a Christian — or better, Christian initiation — was not first and foremost gaining a theory of knowledge but was coming to love the God identified in the rich canonical heritage of the church. In bringing people to faith the church articulated a very particular vision of God, creation, and redemption that had to be seen as a whole and received as a whole" (p. xiii). Because of its rationalism or intellectualism, philosophy of religion has been inattentive to the material practices that nurture and give rise to the thick particularity of Christian faith.[26] Thus Abraham rightly and persistently calls for an account of belief and knowledge that can "take seriously the kind of epistemic suggestions advanced by the ordinary believer" (p. 45).[27] And I have tried to provide a brief exposition of the project precisely because I think Abraham's project hints at a paradigm shift in philosophy of religion that can do justice to understanding just what was happening on that winter night of baptismal resurrection — in a way that intellectualist paradigms cannot. Thus I suggest that Abraham begins to articulate an epistemology for the rest of us. In this respect, I'm reminded of the book *How the Other Half Worships*,[28] a photographic essay documenting the varied spaces in which many Christians worship. Outside the few who actually worship in cathedrals and pristine New England oak-lined sanctuaries, the

25. See Abraham, *The Logic of Evangelism.*

26. I think a similar criticism is articulated by Evan Fales's critique of Plantinga in "Proper Basicality," *Philosophy and Phenomenological Research* 68 (2004): 373-83.

27. The interests or concerns of the "ordinary believer" are not those of the tenured academician: "Those who heard the word of God had more on their minds than recording the phenomenological features of their experience" (p. 61). On the flip side, Abraham also rightly reminds the philosophers that the Word did not become flesh in order to generate dissertations in epistemology: "Nor did God send his Son so that we might hold extended seminars on ontology and metaphysics" (p. 63).

28. Camilo Jose Vergara, *How the Other Half Worships* (New Brunswick, NJ: Rutgers University Press, 2005).

majority of Christians worship the risen Lord in storefronts and mud huts, ramshackle lean-tos and dark, dingy basements. Intellectualist philosophy of religion has given us cathedral epistemologies; Abraham's canonical theism points toward a storefront epistemology.

My deep sympathy with this project leads me to one critical question: Are "ordinary believers" really canonical theists? Is another — albeit thick, particular — *theism* really a radical alternative to the "mere" theism that has been the staple of philosophy of religion? Is this perhaps still too intellectualist? Here I mean only to invite Abraham to consider what it might look like to pursue his project even further.[29] While he rightly rejects the cognitivism or intellectualism that reigns in contemporary philosophy of religion, does a concern with canonical *theism* still remain rather distant from the lived religion of "ordinary believers"? While he rightly contests the "primacy of epistemology" (p. 21), do Abraham's "ordinary believers" still seem a bit fixated on the propositional content (p. 43) and doctrinal assertions (p. 41) embedded in canonical theism? Though he is surely right to note that "[i]t is odd to think of Jesus conducting seminars on epistemology for his disciples" (p. 20), might it not also be odd to think that Jorge was drawn to the baptismal tank because he longed to become a "canonical theist"? I suspect, in fact, that Jorge would have a hard time knowing just what a canonical theist is and would be surprised to learn that he is one. I think Jorge would be especially surprised to find out that "canonical theism is first and foremost a rich ontology" (p. 44).

My concern is that Abraham doesn't follow up on his own hints of a paradigm shift. Instead, the account remains fixated on the "intellectual content" of canonical theism (pp. 41, 45) and the "assertions" and "propositions" that constitute it as an "intellectual entity" in a way that would remain foreign, I think, to many "ordinary believers." This is crystallized, for instance, in his nuanced account of the "logic or grammar of revelation" (p. 81). While Abraham criticizes the "explanatory hypothesis" as "too intellectualist and rationalistic" because it construes belief formation as "fundamentally a matter of forming theories and then testing them by data and evidence" (p. 71), I worry that his own phenomenology of divine revelation still construes the confrontation as a primarily *cognitive* or *intellectual* affair.[30] Suggesting that the "core meaning" of revelation is "disclo-

---

29. For a response, see William J. Abraham, "Response to Professors Long, Smith, and Beilby," *Philosophia Christi* 10 (2008): 363-76.

30. Abraham suggests that "a prophet or apostle occupies a radically different intellec-

sure" (p. 84) keeps revelation quite solidly tied to a theoretical or intellectual lexicon, a matter of "seeing" things differently — as if the primary
telos of revelation was to engender "belief." He takes it that "revelation involves the crossing of an *intellectual* threshold" (p. 92, italics added). Or, in
other words, "the acceptance of divine revelation" is "a world-constituting
experience for the believer" (p. 92).

My question is whether the phenomenology of the *confrontation*
(p. 64) that characterizes divine revelation is aptly or adequately characterized in terms of intellectual content. Does the construal of divine revela-
tion/confrontation as an intellectual event indicate a lingering intellectualism that characterizes canonical theism? Is the event of revelation and
divine confrontation primarily an event of illumination and crossing an
"intellectual threshold"? Or should our phenomenology of revelation recognize it as first and foremost a kind of precognitive, affective *seizure* of
our desire — a *capturing* of our imagination on a register that is not
readily commensurate with the intellect? A more persistent rejection of intellectualism and rationalism in philosophy of religion will eschew
intellectualist pictures of the human person and instead emphasize that we
are primarily affective, desiring animals — and that the thickness and particularity of the gospel (which, it seems to me, remains still thicker than
"canonical theism") grip our "hearts" before it ever gets articulated as a
"theism" — even a rich, canonical theism.[31] While the event of revelation/
divine confrontation is "world-constituting," it is important to emphasize
— following Heidegger — that constitution happens at a level that is
precognitive. Before they're ever "intellectual," "ordinary believers" are
gripped by divine revelation in a way that is irreducible to the cognitive.[32]

---

tual space. . . . What sets a prophet apart is epistemology. The critical appeal is to divine encounter and divine speaking" (p. 82). While he means to emphasize that this is a *different* intellectual space or appeal, I'm asking whether we should think about it first and foremost as
an *intellectual* event.

31. I mean to echo Charles Taylor's claim regarding "social imaginaries": "Humans op-
erated with a social imaginary well before they ever got into the business of theorizing about
themselves" (Taylor, *Modern Social Imaginaries* [Durham, NC: Duke University Press, 2004],
p. 26). I can't develop this further here, but pursue this in more detail in Smith, *Desiring the
Kingdom*, pp. 63-71.

32. And I don't mean to suggest that this is just true of "simple" or uneducated believers. I think it remains true of theologians with academic credentials, too — despite all the
stories/theories we might develop otherwise, theories that paint us as primarily cognitive
animals.

Conclusion

William Abraham's project is animated by a desire for philosophy of religion to remember "ordinary believers" and the ways ordinary folks come to faith in Jesus Christ. This is informed by his historical understanding of conversion and catechesis in the early church, but also by a contemporary sensitivity to the dynamics of conversion (chapter 7).[33] Our philosophical accounts of the nature of Christian belief will be fitting and illuminating only to the extent that they can help us to understand how "ordinary" folks believe — that is, folks without Ph.D.s or college degrees, who don't share the philosophers' fixation on epistemology. Too often our *Christian* philosophizing betrays the fact that we tend to paint all believers in our own rationalist image, as if all believers spend their time fretting about coherentist accounts of truth, or are vexed by issues of warrant that plague testimony, or are persistently haunted by the specter of antirealism. We do well to be reminded otherwise — to discipline our theoretical reflection by regularly confronting it with "ordinary" believers with whom we worship each Sunday.[34]

As I think about these matters, I try to regularly ask myself: Is this true of Tom? Tom is my neighbor on the west side of our home. He lives in a house that is home to quite an eclectic crew, and sometimes quite volatile (let's just say the police are familiar with the address). His face is carved with lines that speak of a difficult life shuffling below the shadows of middle-class comfort most of us take for granted. We don't share very much in common, but we can talk for an hour about two things: NASCAR and Jesus. Several years ago Tom underwent a conversion, and since that time he has been our neighborhood's most vocal witness. His catechesis, from what I gather, has been a blend of Alpha courses, a twelve-step program, and Mel Gibson's *The Passion of the Christ*. But he is always eager to come over and share with me stories of "the powerful One"; he is a *believer* in ways that I'll never be. It is clear that the gospel is not, for him, an ontol-

---

33. It seems to me that in the literature of Reformed epistemology, very rarely do we find prototypical "believers" who are *converts;* more often than not, "Jane" and "Jones" just find themselves believing, have never *not* believed. Does this indicate the theological and ecclesiastical experiences that inform our philosophizing?

34. Unfortunately, Sunday worship is not always a corrective in this score given the realities of class division and the common phenomenon of "the university church" — a congregation where, in fact, many *do* exhibit the kinds of "believing" that one finds in the dominant paradigm in philosophy of religion.

ogy or an epistemology — or even an "answer" to his "questions." It is the good news that someone loves him, that the God of heaven would endure death on a cross to embrace him. For Tom, faith is not a matter of knowledge — it's a matter of love. Over my desk I have an image of Jesus that Tom photocopied for me — one of those terribly sappy, sentimental images that looks like it has been photocopied a thousand times. But for Tom it is an icon, the real presence of the God of love. We might say that, metaphorically, William Abraham's project invites us to do the same: to hang a picture of a photocopied Jesus over our desk as a reminder that the church is perhaps more Tom's than ours, and then get to work articulating an epistemology for the rest of us.

6 At the Limits of Speech

A Pentecostal Contribution
to Philosophy of Language

Perhaps nothing is so synonymous with pentecostalism as "speaking in tongues." But in order that pentecostalism not be reduced to this admittedly strange practice, I have saved consideration of glossolalia until this final chapter. And as with our previous "case studies," I want to consider tongues-speech as a liminal case in philosophy of language. Dominated as it has been (at least in Anglo-analytic circles) by a valorization of "ordinary language philosophy," philosophy of language has had little room for considering a strange, quite extraordinary phenomenon such as glossolalia. As a kind of speech or discourse that hovers on the very fringe of language, there is a deep sense in which tongues-speech resists philosophical analysis or conceptual description. However, in this chapter I want to argue that this resistant nature of tongues-speech is what is precisely most philosophically interesting — that it is part of the very nature of tongues-speech to be a discourse of resistance, in a dual sense: on the one hand, it is a kind of speech (or, as we will say below, a speech act) that resists categories currently on hand in philosophy of language; on the other hand, I also want to argue that tongues-speech is a kind of discourse that arises out of resistance to given cultural norms and institutions. In other words, we could say that tongues-speech is the language of communities of resistance who seek to defy the "powers that be." To describe tongues as a discourse of resistance, then, is to indicate both a *conceptual* and an *ethical* aspect. Thus, in this philosophical analysis of tongues, I want to take a wider view of tongues-speech, considering it not only within the purview of philosophy of language, but also briefly with respect to ethics and social philosophy.

I will first offer an account of tongues-speech through the lens of philosophy of language; more specifically, I consider glossolalia in light of
three contemporary modes of philosophical analysis of language: (1) phenomenology, engaging Husserl and Derrida in particular; (2) philosophical hermeneutics, drawing on Heidegger and Gadamer; and (3) speech act
theory in the wake of Austin and Searle. In the final section (the most "experimental" part of the chapter), I turn to the ethical and social implications of tongues-speech viewed through the lens of what we could vari-
ously describe as critical theory, socialism, or "New Left" categories.

Before proceeding, let me make one methodological prefatory note: in
what follows I have, for the most part, bracketed specifically theological
questions about glossolalia. My analysis, for example, takes no stand on
whether tongues is the "initial physical evidence of baptism in the Holy
Spirit" (as classical Pentecostals would assert) or whether it is simply one
of the charismatic gifts that remains available to the *ekklesia*.[1] Nor do I take
a position on whether glossolalia is the utterance of existing languages pre-
viously unknown to the speaker *(xenolalia)* or simply ecstatic speech uttered by the power of the Spirit (though our analysis below will require us
to consider the implications of such accounts).[2] Insofar as I hope my analysis is not simply antiquarian or historical, the one theological assumption
that remains relevant is that tongues-speech remains a viable and authentic mode of discourse for the believing community, which is the Christian
ekklesia.[3] However, someone who does not share this theological assumption but nevertheless believes that tongues-speech *was* a viable mode of
Spirit-led discourse (as a cessationist would, for example), may find at
least historical significance in my analysis. And in either case, I hope
tongues-speech can function as a kind of limit case that will illuminate
questions and issues in philosophy of language — that is, as a case or in-

---

1. This is not to say, however, that I don't take a position on this. As a "charismatic" —
not Pentecostal — Christian, theologically I reject the claim that tongues is the initial and
only physical evidence of baptism in the Holy Spirit (and would also suggest, philosophically, that such language of "evidence" is linked to a problematic, modernist, and foundationalist epistemology — but cannot expand on that here). But for the purposes of this essay, these questions are not relevant.

2. In the analyses below, I tend to focus on tongues as ecstatic speech. This is because instances of tongues as xenolalia could be easily subsumed under existing categories in philosophy of language; I am interested in those cases that resist the categories currently on offer.

3. Though, again, for the most part I will bracket — as far as possible — theological
evaluations of whether what is currently practiced in Pentecostal and charismatic congregations qualifies as authentic tongues-speech.

stance of utterance that challenges the current conceptual categories in philosophy of language and thus might push us to transgress the limits of these categories. So it could even be possible that someone who holds no theological affirmation of tongues-speech might still find the notion a productive thought experiment for philosophy of language.

A final methodological preface: my analysis of tongues-speech will constitute something of a phenomenology of glossolalia. As such, I want to take seriously the normative accounts of practice in the New Testament, but also consider the ways in which tongues-speech is currently practiced in pentecostal communities. At some points the contemporary practice is difficult to map onto the normative account in the New Testament, and the attempts to warrant contemporary practice often rely on a kind of interpretive injustice of these New Testament texts. However, if tongues-speech constitutes an illuminating limit case for philosophy, these instances for illuminating resistance might also be found in contemporary practices.

Resisting (and Producing) Concepts: Tongues and Philosophy of Language

Though I want to argue that tongues-speech resists the categories of analysis currently employed in philosophy of language, I want to suggest that this resistance to given categories is actually philosophically *productive;*[4] in other words, because tongues-speech constitutes a limit case for available modes of philosophical analysis, it provides an opportunity for rethinking, expanding, and revising these philosophical methodologies and lexica of concepts. The fact that glossolalia cannot easily fit existing categories can be an opportunity to revisit these categories and call into question the regnant paradigm (though, admittedly, it can also be an occasion to disregard glossolalia).[5] The resistance of tongues-speech to analysis can be an occasion for illumination.

4. Gilles Deleuze and Felix Guattari suggest that the essence of the philosophical project is the production of concepts. See Deleuze and Guattari, *What Is Philosophy?* trans. Hugh Tomlinson (New York: Columbia University Press, 1996).

5. We might recall here Thomas Kuhn's account of the way in which existing paradigms tend to simply not see what does not fit with the paradigm's expectations (in *The Structure of Scientific Revolutions* [Chicago: University of Chicago Press, 1970]). "Normal science" (what Kuhn describes as the regnant "orthodoxy" within a discipline) in philosophy of lan-

In this section I will consider tongues-speech in light of three promi-
nent modes of analysis in philosophy of language in the order of their historical emergence.[6] Each poses an important question for tongues-speech;
and the phenomenon of tongues-speech poses challenges to the conceptual
categories of these philosophical analyses. Husserl's phenomenological
analysis poses perhaps the most basic question: *What is* tongues-speech?
What does it mean to "speak" in tongues? Hermeneutics raises the question
of interpretation or meaning: How is tongues-speech "understood"? What
"gets said" in tongues? And speech act theory poses a question about *action:*
What "gets done" in tongues-speech? What does glossolalia *effect?*

These three modes of philosophical analysis are complementary, but
also discrete. As such, each section seeks to provide an account of tongues-
speech from a particular "camp" within contemporary philosophy of language. I think it is important to utilize all three approaches because each
approach offers a unique perspective on tongues; but together, they provide a well-rounded philosophical engagement.[7]

"Tongues Are for a Sign": Phenomenology

The longest and richest tradition of philosophical reflection on language is
what we would now loosely describe as "semiotics" — an account of language in terms of *signs (semeia)*. While the notion of semiotics is most often linked to twentieth-century figures such as Ferdinand de Saussure and
C. S. Peirce, this tradition of reflection has a long pedigree reaching back
through Augustine to the Stoics.[8] One of the most powerful and influential

---

guage, coupled with a general bias against distinct (and admittedly strange) religious phenomena such as tongues-speech, would almost guarantee that glossolalia would not be suggested as an arena for research. Hopefully the present essay can go some way to resisting this
tendency.

6. One could also consider tongues-speech along the lines of accounts of orality and
literacy developed by Walter Ong and others. I will not pursue this line of inquiry here, but
have provided a sketch in James K. A. Smith, "The Closing of the Book: Pentecostals, Evangelicals, and the Sacred Writings," *Journal of Pentecostal Theology* 11 (1997): 49-71.

7. This is not to say I am providing an exhaustive account. Further research should consider tongues from the perspectives of C. S. Peirce's pragmatic semiotics and Wittgenstein's
notion of "language games." But space here does not permit such an investigation.

8. For an account of an Augustinian semiotics (and references to the relevant literature), see James K. A. Smith, *Speech and Theology: Language and the Logic of Incarnation,*
Radical Orthodoxy Series (London: Routledge, 2002), chapter 4. For a lucid introduction to

restatements of such an analysis of language was offered by Edmund Husserl, most especially in his earlier work, the *Logical Investigations,* and a later piece, *The Origin of Geometry.*⁹ Because Husserl's phenomenology of language was so foundational for much of the work that would follow in the twentieth century, and because it provided the first impetus for my thinking about tongues and philosophy of language, I want to consider his philosophical framework fairly closely.¹⁰

In the first of the *Logical Investigations* ("Expression and Meaning"), Husserl seeks to map the different modes of expression and speech by asserting a number of distinctions. For Husserl, the overarching category is that of *signs,* so what we get in the First Investigation is not really his account of language, but most specifically (yet more broadly) his theory of signs — of which language is a subset. Within the broad category of "signs" *(Zeigen),* Husserl asserts a first, fundamental distinction between those signs that *express* something — an "expression" *(Ausdruck)* — and those signs that do not express or "mean" something — what he calls "indications" *(Anzeigen).* Expressions are "significant" insofar as they "signify" or "mean" *(Bedeuten)* something, whereas indications are only "indicative" and serve merely as pointers (*LI,* p. 269). However, one should not overstate or misunderstand this distinction between "expression" and "indication." For instance, the two are not mutually exclusive: it is possible, Husserl notes, for a sign to be indicative but also "happen to fulfil a significant" function as well. Moreover, the distinction between expression and

---

semiotic theory in a context related to tongues-speech, see Graham Hughes, *Worship as Meaning: A Liturgical Theology for Late Modernity* (Cambridge: Cambridge University Press, 2003), especially chapter 3.

9. Edmund Husserl, *Logical Investigations,* trans. J. N. Findlay (New York: Humanities Press, 1970 [1900; 2nd. ed., 1913]), vol. 1, henceforth abbreviated in the text as *LI;* Husserl, "The Origin of Geometry," in *The Crisis of the European Sciences and Transcendental Phenomenology,* trans. David Carr (Evanston, IL: Northwestern University Press, 1970). Both of these works captured the attention of the young Jacques Derrida. On the *Logical Investigations,* see Derrida's *Speech and Phenomena,* trans. D. B. Allison (Evanston, IL: Northwestern University Press, 1973). Derrida was the translator of *Origin of Geometry* into French (1962), and his extensive introduction to the translation was Derrida's first major publication (see Derrida, *An Introduction to Husserl's "Origin of Geometry,"* trans. John P. Leavey, Jr. [Lincoln: University of Nebraska Press, 1989]).

10. Others have thought about tongues as "sign," but not explicitly within a semiotic context. See, for example, Frank D. Macchia, "Tongues as a Sign: Towards a Sacramental Understanding of Pentecostal Experience," *Pneuma: Journal of the Society for Pentecostal Studies* 15 (1993): 61-76.

indication should not be understood on the register of genus and species; it is not the case that expression is really a particular kind of indication.[11] Indeed, Husserl's most surprising (and most contested) claim is that there can be modes of expression that do not involve any aspect of indication; in other words, there is a sphere — what Husserl calls "isolated mental life" — in which there is meaning without indication.[12]

Indications are pointers that stand for something else; in this sense, Husserl notes, "a brand is the sign of a slave, a flag the sign of a nation" (p. 270) — the indications aid us in recognizing some thing to which the sign is attached. In some cases this attachment is contingent, even arbitrary (as in the case of a flag or brand); but other attachments of signs to their referents are more "natural"; it is in this sense that we can say, "Martian canals are signs of the existence of intelligent beings on Mars," or, "fossil vertebrae are signs of the existence of prediluvian animals" (p. 270). In short, smoke is a sign of fire in the sense of being an *indication (Anzeige)*. The relation between the indicative sign and its referent is *motivational:* what is *given* (the indicative sign) motivates me to consider what is not given, but only indicated in its absence: the referent. On the podium in Greece, the flag of the United States motivates the consideration of a nation-state on the other side of the globe, etc. Essential to the nature of indication, then, is an *absence* of the referent; indication operates on the basis of a certain lack.[13]

Indicative signs are to be distinguished from *expressions,* which are "*meaningful* signs" (p. 275). Thus Husserl wants to reserve the term "expression" for a specific instance of signification, drastically narrowing what we might describe, in ordinary language, as an indication. For instance, we often speak of "facial expressions," but on Husserl's register these are not properly *Ausdrucken* ("expressions") because, according to him, such bodily signs "involuntarily accompany speech without commu-

---

11. "The two notions of sign do not therefore really stand in the relation of more extensive genus to narrower species" (*LI*, p. 269).

12. It is precisely this central claim that is subjected to relentless critique in Derrida's *Speech and Phenomena.* Indeed, the core thesis of *Speech and Phenomena* is that there is an essential "entanglement" *(Verflechtung)* between expression and indication. I have dealt with Derrida's critique in detail in James K. A. Smith, "A Principle of Incarnation in Derrida's *(Theologische?) Jugendschriften,*" *Modern Theology* 18 (2002): 217-30. For Husserl, meaning is always "bound up" with indication only in the case of *communicative* speech (*LI,* p. 269). As we shall see below, this has implications with respect to tongues-speech.

13. This, of course, is a central theme in Derrida's critique (and gives rise to what he will describe as "the metaphysics of presence").

nicative intent" (p. 275).[14] "In such manifestations," he continues, "one man communicates nothing to another: their utterance involves no intent to put certain 'thoughts' on record expressively, whether for the man himself [i.e., the one making the bodily gesture], in his solitary state, or for others. Such 'expressions,' in short, have properly speaking, *no meaning*" (p. 275, italics in original). In other words, they are not properly "expressions" at all because they are not communicative. The question is, are these bodily gestures still a mode of *language?* Could there be an instance of noncommunicative, nonexpressive *language?* What would that be? We will return to this below.

When Husserl considers expression, his focus is on *speech* because it is in speech that we find *intention:* a speaker, by means of a sign, means to communicate something to a listener. The connection between sign and referent with respect to expression is, we might say, "tighter" than it is with indication; as Husserl puts it, in speech the signs given (the "expressions") are "phenomenally one with the experiences made manifest in them in the consciousness of the man who manifests them" (p. 275). There is almost a sense in which the referent inheres in the expressive sign in a way it does not in the indicative sign. Indeed, he goes on to describe an expression as "a verbal sound *infused* with sense" or meaning (p. 281, italics added). Thus Husserl privileges speech as the site of expression.

However, here we find an interesting twist (which is also the fulcrum of Derrida's critique). Speech is the best exemplar of expression for Husserl, but not all speech is communicative for him. In fact, insofar as speech is *communicative* (that is, involves the intersubjective exchange of expressions), it is necessarily implicated with *indication*. "All expressions in *communicative* speech function as *indications*" (p. 277). This is because there is a kind of essential *absence* in the intersubjective relation between speaker and listener. Expressions in speech "serve the hearer as signs of the 'thoughts' of the speaker . . . as well as of the other inner experiences which are part of his communicative intention" (p. 277). The word-signs that I utter are given to the hearer and thus are *present* to the hearer, but they serve to *indicate* what can never be present to the other person, namely, my inner thoughts and consciousness. Nevertheless, insofar as these utter-

14. It should be noted that Husserl has no sense of an "unconscious" or "subconscious," which we almost assume in a post-Freudian, psychoanalytic climate. For Husserl, the "Freudian slip" and body language are meaningless (whereas for Freud they are oblique access to what one *really* means).

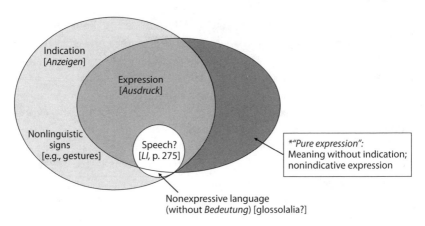

Indication
[*Anzeigen*]

Expression
[*Ausdruck*]

Nonlinguistic
signs
[e.g., gestures]

Speech?
[*LI*, p. 275]

*"Pure expression":
Meaning without indication;
nonindicative expression

Nonexpressive language
(without *Bedeutung*) [glossolalia?]

ances are intentionally given by me to communicate or express meaning, they count as expression. Communicative speech involves the interweaving of both expression and indication.

But what other kind of speech could there be? If intersubjective communication always involves indication, could there be a kind of expression that is not always already "bound up" with indication? Could there be a kind of "pure expression"? For Husserl, yes: and we find this in "solitary mental life," in the inner soliloquy of consciousness (pp. 278-79). Properly speaking, for Husserl (who again, we must recall, does not admit any unconscious), we do not "talk to ourselves" in our interior mental life;[15] we do not need to employ signs (as indications) of our own inner experiences. This is because he sees interior mental life characterized by a kind of immediate self-presence, which does not admit any absence or lack. There are no secret parts of consciousness for Husserl; I am master of my thoughts and intentions. So insofar as indication is a kind of sign *given* to point to what is *absent,* such signs would be superfluous for interior consciousness. The main point is that Husserl sees this interior soliloquy of consciousness as the site of "pure" expression (pp. 279-80).

In the figure at the top of the page I have tried to provide something of a map of Husserl's theory of signs. While for Derrida the most interesting (and problematic) part of Husserl's account is the suggestion regarding "pure expression" (which Derrida contests), for our study of glossolalia I am most interested in an unstable quadrant of this map: Husserl's hints

15. Husserl does grant that one could, very loosely, speak of "talking to oneself," but this would only be metaphorical and by analogy (*LI*, pp. 279-80).

about a kind of nonexpressive speech. On Husserl's account, there are indications that are nonexpressive (e.g., bodily gestures); on the other hand, there are expressions that are nonindicative (e.g., the soliloquy of solitary mental life); there is also a third, intermediate category, which constitutes the bulk of what we consider "communication" or speaking — intersubjective communication — which involves both expression and indication. When we overlay this with a consideration of "speech" in particular, Husserl would contend that speech is essentially communicative, and thus essentially indicative (p. 277); in the soliloquy of solitary mental life, "there is no speech in such cases" (p. 280).

However, Husserl's precise distinctions become unstable at this point, on a couple of levels. First, though "speech" is clearly an important category for his account, it is left quite undefined. As such, he seems to simply link speech to "verbal utterance" — though he clearly wants to specify this as verbal utterance *with meaning* (that is, "infused" with intention). The question is whether Husserl can have what he wants. Must "speech" as vocal utterance always conform to the patterns of a discernible language to count *as* speech? Husserl stipulates that the "articulate sound-complex, the written sign etc., first becomes a spoken *word* or communicative bit of speech, when a speaker produces it with the intention of 'expressing himself about something' through its means" (pp. 276-77, italics added). But what counts as a word? Must the meaning of a vocal utterance be "intentional" — and only intend to communicate a "thought" — to count as a "word"? Could a vocal utterance *mean* without the referent of that meaning being a "thought" in the (intentional) consciousness of the utterer?

Second, Husserl's account relies on a highly questionable rejection of facial expression and bodily gestures as "expressive"; they are, for him, meaning-less because they communicate nothing (p. 275). While one could contest this by calling into question the theory of self-present consciousness behind this,[16] we could also simply cite counterexamples. For instance, in the American presidential debates of 1988, when George H. W. Bush merely glanced at his watch during the broadcast, this clearly "said" something to the American public (the gesture was often cited after Clinton won the election). This gesture, though perhaps not "intentional," was neverthe-

---

16. This is a major aspect of Derrida's critique of Husserl in *Speech and Phenomena*. In addition, one could say that Derrida sets out to show that all "words" function as "gestures," thus erasing the hierarchical distinction made by Husserl. See *Speech and Phenomena*, pp. 37-38.

less expressive. This is not to say that all bodily movements "mean" something; obviously a nervous tick or reaching for a glass of milk does not "mean" in this way. But the question is whether it is legitimate for Husserl to cast *all* bodily gestures into the outer regions of mere indication.

Within this schema, where could we map tongues-speech? Could glossolalia perhaps be a case that would help us in revising Husserl's schema according to the hints above? Is it "speech," properly speaking? Is it a mode of expression bound up with indication (as is everyday speech)? Insofar as it involves vocalization, we can be certain it is not characteristic of the "pure expression" of soliloquy.[17] To go further, we should recall a theological question bracketed earlier: if we think of tongues as *xenolalia* (the utterance of an identifiable language by one without previous knowledge of the language), then tongues-speech would be an instance of communicative speech. This is clearly the case in the instance of the Pentecostal outpouring in Acts 2. In fact, in that case, it is clear that the primary reason for the miracle of glossolalia was to provide a witness to the gospel in terms that could be readily received and understood by the hearers. "How is it that we each hear them in our own language to which we were born?" the listeners asked (Acts 2:8). *Glossolalia* as *xenolalia* is a clear case of communicative speech.

The cases suggested in Paul's letter to the Corinthians are a little more complicated. On the one hand, Paul seems to chastise the Corinthians for tongues-speech that does not properly communicate *meaning*: "There are perhaps a great many kinds of languages in the world," the apostle notes, "and no kind is without meaning. If then I do not know the meaning of the language, I shall be to the one who speaks a barbarian, and the one who speaks will be a barbarian to me" (1 Cor. 14:10-11). This is why Paul requires that tongues-speech be accompanied by interpretation (or translation,

---

17. I will bracket here any consideration of whether one could speak in tongues "to oneself" or "in one's mind." I am not aware of this as a common spiritual practice among charismatic Christians. Of course, there is a practice of praying by oneself in tongues (and some advocate the notion of tongues as a "private prayer language"), but *prayer*, insofar as it is directed to God, is essentially communicative. (Even if one prayed *silently* in tongues, insofar as this is *prayer*, it would be communicative.) On Husserl's register, prayer in tongues is another interesting limit case. On the one hand, according to the theological presuppositions of charismatic prayer, my thoughts are fully present to God (just as Husserl considers my own thoughts to be fully present to myself). In this respect, prayer in tongues-speech could, curiously enough, be an instance of pure expression. But on the other hand, it remains vocalized, in which case it remains "tainted" by indication, on Husserl's terms.

1 Cor. 14:13, 27). So here the goal of tongues-speech is *communicative*, in which case it again can be mapped onto Husserl's schema.

But there are hints in this Corinthian correspondence of a different understanding of tongues-speech, not as primarily communicative but as a testimony, which is not properly "intentional" but nevertheless expressive. First, Paul suggests that "one who speaks in a tongue does not speak to men, but to God; for no one understands, but in his spirit he speaks mysteries. . . . One who speaks in a tongue edifies himself" (1 Cor. 14:2, 4). Here Paul hints at a kind of private use for tongues-speech, which is not necessarily linked to existing natural languages, but is perhaps more akin to ecstatic religious speech.[18] In this case, the point of tongues-speech does not appear to be primarily communicative. Second, later in the chapter Paul notes that "tongues are for a sign" (14:22) in the way that the "signs and wonders" of the apostles were a testimony to the divine authority of their message. In these cases, miraculous phenomena such as tongues are aimed not just (or perhaps even primarily) at the penultimate end of communicating something (or healing a person) but rather at the ultimate end of indicating the Spirit's presence and activity within the believing community. In fact, the category of "signs and wonders" is illuminative for our semiotic discussion: in both the Gospels and Acts, the miraculous works of Jesus and the apostles — usually bodily healing — are persistently described as *signs*.[19] The "signs and wonders" were a mode of attestation that, rather than communicating an "idea" in the consciousness of an "utterer," nevertheless *expressed* something, namely, the power and grace of the God of Jesus Christ attested in the Gospel. Thus these signs functioned as a mode of expression without being linked to a kind of authorial intent.

It seems to me that the case of tongues-speech as a sign operates in the same manner, and destabilizes Husserl's tidy distinctions. In the case of tongues as an ecstatic utterance (perhaps without interpretation), the *fact* of this kind of utterance — though it does not "communicate" because it is not a discernible language — nevertheless "says" something, attests to a divine reality (e.g., the presence of the Spirit in the community). In this re-

18. In charismatic justification of the practice, this is often linked (mistakenly, I think) to Paul's hyperbolic talk of "tongues of angels" earlier in the letter (1 Cor. 13:1).

19. This is a central theme in John's Gospel; see John 2:11; 3:2; 4:54; 6:2-30; 7:31; 9:16; 10:41; 11:47; 12:18; 20:30. In John 9, these signs operate in the *absence* of Jesus, who is absent for most of the narrative, appearing in only the opening and closing "scenes." But he asserts that the miracle that healed the blind man's sight was performed "in order that the works of God might be displayed in him" (v. 3).

spect, we might say that tongues-speech is a kind of speech that functions as a *gesture,* but the kind of gesture that calls into question Husserl's exclusion of gesture from the realm of expression.[20] Glossolalia (understood here as ecstatic religious speech), we might say, is a mode of *speech* that does not employ *words* (in Husserl's sense) but nevertheless is expressive. If the phenomenon of tongues-speech points up the limits of Husserl's phenomenological schema, it may also point us to another mode of linguistic analysis. Below I will suggest that the notion of "speech acts" will give us some conceptual tools to consider the "work" that tongues-speech does in these instances, such that speech act theory might be considered a kind of supplement to Husserl's phenomenological semiotics.

There remains another mode of contemporary pentecostal glossolalic practice that I have not yet considered. In the above, I have largely been concerned with the *public* exercise of tongues-speech within the ecclesial gathering. But in current practice, many pentecostals employ tongues-speech in *private* prayer (as a "prayer language"). Beyond citing 1 Corinthians 14, the practice often draws on a reading of the Spirit's work noted in Romans 8, where Paul asserts that "the Spirit also helps our weakness; for we do not know how to pray as we should, but the Spirit himself intercedes for us with groanings too deep for words" (Rom. 8:26). In this prayer practice, the Christian "prays in tongues" when she lacks the words to properly express her longings or anguish or desires. The practice is deeply cathartic and represents a kind of spiritual discipline. On the Husserlian schema we have unpacked, one might suggest that such a practice is communicative insofar as the prayer is directed to God as "listener." But the vocalization is not necessary for a prayer to be heard. Therefore, I would suggest that such a practice is an instance that may conform to the marginal category engendered by Husserl's distinctions; namely, the practice would be an instance of nonexpressive speech.

---

20. It is interesting to note that some have even attested to a kind of *gestural tongues,* or what is sometimes described as "manual glossolalia," where the "utterer" "speaks" in hand signs. For a discussion, see J. L. Smith, "Glossolalia, Manual," in *The New International Dictionary of Pentecostal and Charismatic Movements,* ed. Stanley M. Burgess and Eduard M. Van der Maas (Grand Rapids: Zondervan, 2002), pp. 677-78.

"Let the One Who Speaks in a Tongue
Pray That He May Interpret": Hermeneutics

What is known as hermeneutics — or more specifically philosophical hermeneutics or hermeneutic phenomenology — emerges from the phenomenological tradition through Husserl's most important student, Martin
Heidegger, and one of Heidegger's students, Hans-Georg Gadamer.[21] This
hermeneutic tradition has been one of the — if not *the* — most significant
developments in philosophy of language over the past century. Its influence is perhaps most powerfully felt in what has come to be known as the
"linguistic turn": the fundamental assertion (now the received position, as
it were) that our being-in-the-world is fundamentally constituted by language, or at least by an interpretive mode.[22] In other words, there is no naive, simple, pure "access" to "the way things are" apart from a way of *construing* the world through a kind of semiotic lens (though the language of
a "lens" still gives a false sense that this is extrinsic to being human).[23] This
was first and most forcefully delineated by Heidegger, who noted that we
inhabit the world as interpreting creatures. We encounter things in the
world not as things "in themselves" but as things that we *use,* as things
"for" something. Because we encounter entities in the world as things "for"
something, we also encounter them always already "as" something. This is
something like the fundamental axiom of hermeneutics: the as-structure
of our being-in-the-world.[24] Our construal of the world *as* something is

21. Paul Ricoeur is another important figure here, but I will not draw on his work in the
present essay. For a helpful introduction to philosophical hermeneutics, see two recent
works: Jean Grondin, *Introduction to Philosophical Hermeneutics,* trans. Joel Weinsheimer
(New Haven, CT: Yale University Press, 1997), and Jens Zimmerman, *Recovering Theological
Hermeneutics: An Incarnational-Trinitarian Theory of Interpretation* (Grand Rapids: Baker
Academic, 2004).

22. See Richard Rorty, ed., *The Linguistic Turn* (Chicago: University of Chicago Press,
1992), and Rorty, *Philosophy and the Mirror of Nature* (Princeton, NJ: Princeton University
Press, 1979).

23. Again, this comes back to Derrida's critique of Husserl in *Speech and Phenomena* in
the *Logical Investigations,* Husserl asserts a realm of pure, unconditioned consciousness; the
point of Derrida's critique is to say that signs go all the way down: consciousness, we might
say, is semiotically conditioned. It is neither a "blank slate" nor a pure conduit.

24. See Martin Heidegger, *Being and Time,* trans. John Macquarrie and Edward Robinson (San Francisco: Harper and Row, 1962), pp. 190-91. I have unpacked Heidegger's hermeneutic theory in more detail in James K. A. Smith, *The Fall of Interpretation: Philosophical
Foundations for a Creational Hermeneutic* (Downers Grove, IL: InterVarsity, 2000), pp. 87-113.

informed *by* the world or environment that we inhabit, insofar as that environment constitutes a horizon within which these construals take place. "Whenever something is interpreted as something," Heidegger notes, "the interpretation will be founded essentially upon fore-having, fore-sight, and fore-concept. An interpretation is never a presuppositionless apprehending of something presented to us."[25] The world I always already inhabit constitutes the horizons of possibility for my understanding and construal of the world and things in the world.

Heidegger, and Gadamer after him, established the hermeneutical character of existence: that we engage the world from a set of presuppositions (or "fore-havings") that orients us *to* the world in a certain way. Both were preeminent philosophers of finitude who recognized the situationality of our knowledge.[26] Another related and central theme of hermeneutics is the role of *tradition* in constituting this world: the environment that provides the conditions of possibility for understanding the world is *handed down* to me by tradition (linguistic, cultural, religious, etc.). So rather than being ahistorical, disembodied egos who encounter the world with a blank slate, I come (in)to the world tradition*ed* — indebted to a tradition (or plurality of traditions) that primes me to engage the world with certain habits of construal.[27] Even those communities who eschew tradition (such as "primitivist" Pentecostal and charismatic communities) have a tradition of rejecting tradition (just as Gadamer points out the Enlightenment prejudice against prejudice).[28]

Finally, in addition to the situationality and traditionality of human being-in-the-world (what Heidegger called the *interpretedness* of Dasein),[29] hermeneutics asserts the *ubiquity* of interpretation. Interpretation is not a specialized activity we engage in when reading texts, discerning legal briefs, or viewing a work of art. Interpretation is synonymous with being-in-the-world. "Experience" is interpretive. As such, it is a fundamental, pretheoretical aspect of being human. "Interpretation is carried out primordially not in a theoretical statement but in an action of circumspective con-

25. Heidegger, *Being and Time*, p. 192.

26. See, for instance, Hans-Georg Gadamer, *Truth and Method,* trans. Joel Weinsheimer and Donald G. Marshal, rev. ed. (New York: Continuum, 1989), pp. 276-307.

27. See Gadamer, *Truth and Method,* pp. 277-85.

28. Gadamer, *Truth and Method,* p. 276.

29. Martin Heidegger, "Phenomenological Interpretations with Respect to Aristotle: Indication of the Hermeneutical Situation," trans. Michael Bauer, *Man and World* 25 (1992): 363.

cern. . . . From the fact that words are absent, it may not be concluded that interpretation is absent."[30] To be human is to interpret; to experience the world is to interpret the world.[31]

Hermeneutics has a complex relationship to the philosophy of language. On the one hand, it clearly draws on notions of language since interpretation has always been linked to lingual phenomena (whether spoken or written). On the other hand, hermeneutics seeks to expand our understanding of interpretation *beyond* merely lingual phenomena (books, utterances, etc.) to the entire panoply of what we encounter in the world. But even with this expansion, the link to language remains insofar as hermeneutics tends to then consider the world a kind of macrotext.[32]

Now, in what ways could hermeneutics provide a framework for thinking about glossolalia? The relationship between interpretation and tongues-speech is intriguing. On the one hand, even within the New Testament witness, glossolalia is bound up with the question of interpretation. Paul's account of this is a rich field for hermeneutical reflection, given the distinct interest of hermeneutics in *understanding*:

> [O]ne who speaks in a tongue does not speak to men, but to God; for no one understands [or hears], but by the Spirit he speaks mysteries. But one who prophesies speaks to men for edification and exhortation and consolation. One who speaks in a tongue edifies himself; but one who prophesies edifies the church. Now I wish that you all spoke in tongues, but even more that you would prophesy; and greater is one who prophesies than one who speaks in tongues, *unless he interprets,* so that the church may receive edification. But now, brothers and sisters, if I come to you speaking in tongues, what shall I profit you, unless I speak to you either by way of revelation or of knowledge or of prophecy or of teaching? Yet even lifeless things, either flute or harp, in producing a sound, if they do not produce a distinction in the tones, how will it be known what is played on the flute or on the harp? . . . So also you, unless you utter by the tongue speech that is clear, how will it be known what is spoken? For you will be speaking into the air. There are, perhaps, a great many kinds of languages in the world, and none is without meaning. If then I do not know the meaning of the language, I shall be to the one

30. Heidegger, *Being and Time,* p. 200.

31. For a fuller thematic consideration of these core themes of hermeneutics, see Smith, *The Fall of Interpretation,* pp. 149-59.

32. This last move is not essential to hermeneutics, but is a commonly related one.

who speaks a barbarian, and the one who speaks will be a barbarian to me. . . . Therefore let one who speaks in a tongue pray that he may interpret. (1 Cor. 14:2-13 NASB, modified)

Tongues, in this excursus, are necessarily linked to interpretation. The primary concern here is for *understanding* — a connection between utterer and listener via the utterance, which requires the interpretation/translation of the utterance into terms that can be received by the listener.[33] So with respect to tongues *as communicative speech* (to recall a Husserlian category), the telos of such speech is understanding, which requires that the utterance be mediated through the structures of interpretation. In this respect, Paul's concern that tongues-speech be aimed at understanding, and his recognition that this required interpretation, makes his account a kind of proto-hermeneutics. His affirmation of the supernatural activity of the Spirit within the ecclesial community did not lead him to posit some kind of magical (or Gnostic) conduit for secret knowledge; rather, his account emphasizes the way in which even the miraculous operates according to the conditions of finitude that characterize the human community — even that distinct community of the Spirit that is the *ekklesia*.[34]

However, on the other hand, in contemporary pentecostal practice and understanding, one often encounters a sense that tongues (and prophecy) are immediate deliveries from the divine, without mediation or translation. In other words, in the popular imagination, glossolalia is often thought to be a quintessentially unmediated, divinely given, ecstatic discourse that bypasses the conditions of interpretation — a kind of pure conduit from God, without the static or supposed distortion of semiotic mediation.[35] An appreciation of the conclusions of hermeneutics must challenge and mitigate such claims: no revelation is ever unmediated. Notions to the contrary would be a kind of neo-Gnosticism of

33. It is not illegitimate to say that all interpretation constitutes a kind of translation whereby an utterance, statement, or text is "translated" into terms that can be "received" by the finite listener or reader, facilitating what Gadamer calls the "miracle of understanding" (*Truth and Method*, p. 292). For a further analysis of the conditions of reception by finite interpreters, see Smith, *Speech and Theology*, pp. 153-76.

34. In *Speech and Theology* I argue that this mode of divine accommodation to finitude is exemplified par excellence in the Incarnation, and that this provides the model for all modes of revelation and communication.

35. Granted, many who think of tongues this way also tend to think of the Bible in the same way, despite its obvious textuality and semiotic character. For a critique of such an "immediacy" model of interpretation, see Smith, *The Fall of Interpretation*, pp. 37-60.

the sort that Paul decidedly rejected in the hermeneutic conditions specified in 1 Corinthians 14.

But I think there is a further line of hermeneutic inquiry relevant to tongues-speech. Central to hermeneutic philosophy is an appreciation of the way our environment and tradition provide the conditions of possibility for how we can interpret our experience — they establish the horizons for our "as" construals. This is not to be understood as a limitation or hindrance, but more positively as the conditions of possibility for *opening up* a world of experience. But as such, the presuppositions or "fore-havings" that we bring to our experience do condition our engagement with the world. It seems to me that a community that is open to the authentic possibility of tongues-speech as both a voice of the Spirit and a sign of God's presence has a distinct set of "fore-havings" that opens up the world of experience in a distinct way. To put it differently, the role of tongues-speech within a community would seem to be necessarily linked to a "worldview" that would eschew reductionistic naturalism and would encounter the world as a kind of "open system" — as a site for the inbreaking of the divine.[36] This would seem to entail that the pentecostal community would/ should inhabit its world differently than others. I hope to explore the nature of this difference in the final part of this chapter.

"Let All Things Be Done for Edification": Speech Act Theory

Perhaps the most fruitful development in philosophy of language for reflection on glossolalia is the speech act theory of language developed by J. L. Austin and John Searle.[37] This work grows out of the groundbreaking theories of the later Wittgenstein (of the *Philosophical Investigations*).[38] Rejecting his own earlier account (in the *Tractatus*) of language as some kind

36. For early suggestions along this line, from within the Pentecostal tradition, see Howard M. Ervin, "Hermeneutics: A Pentecostal Option," *Pneuma: Journal of the Society for Pentecostal Studies* 3, no. 2 (1981): 11-25.

37. See J. L. Austin, *How to Do Things with Words* (Oxford: Oxford University Press, 1962); John R. Searle, *Speech Acts: An Essay in the Philosophy of Language* (Cambridge: Cambridge University Press, 1969); and Searle, *Expression and Meaning: Studies in the Theory of Speech Acts* (Cambridge: Cambridge University Press, 1979).

38. For a helpful and accessible overview of the emergence of speech act theory, see Kevin Vanhoozer, *Is There a Meaning in This Text?* (Grand Rapids: Zondervan, 1998), pp. 207-14.

of representational "picture" of the world, Wittgenstein began to appreciate that language is not always — and perhaps not even primarily — about "reference" or representing a state of affairs. Rather, language is a medium of *action:* words, when used in different ways, *do* different things. A statement or sentence or utterance can "get things done" or "make things happen" — and the same sentence or utterance can get different things done when the context (or "rules of the [language] game") is changed.[39]

It is this linkage of language to *action* that characterizes the speech act theory of Austin and Searle. As Searle puts it, "a theory of language is part of a theory of action, simply because speaking is a rule-governed form of behaviour."[40] A helpful element of speech act theory, then, is its appreciation of language as a *social* phenomenon, governed by rules that are constituted by a community. As such, speech act theory emphasizes the *conventional* nature of language use. It is a social community that constitutes the rules of a "language game."[41]

Austin's unpacking of speech acts emphasizes the *performative* nature of utterances. Utterances are more like dramatic statements on a stage than abstract points in geometry; that is, speakers are *actors,* who speak to get something done. And what they want their speaking to *do* is not always to express a thought (as Husserl seems to think); rather, sometimes we speak to make something happen, or to effect a state of affairs. Most often when I say to my wife, "I love you," my primary motivation for the utterance is not the communication of a piece of knowledge, but a testimony meant to effect comfort or intimacy. When I say "I love you" in such contexts, my utterance is not the expression of an idea; it is meant to *do* something else. In this respect we could suggest that the picture of language we get from Husserl's semiotics tends to be more rationalistic; that is, it tends to be reductionistic, only imaging that speech is a conduit for thoughts. Speech act theory, in contrast, has a richer understanding of language and speech that recognizes that language does *more* than just shuttle ideas from one mind to another. In this respect, and with its appreciation for community,

39. There tends to be an assumption in speech act theory that the *sentence* (rather than the *word*) is the most basic unit of language. (Speech act theorists criticize semiotics for mistaking the *word* as the basic component.) However, in the brief analysis below, I will suggest that the case of tongues-speech should be an occasion to call into question this valorization of the *sentence* as the unit of language that "gets things done," as it were.

40. Searle, *Speech Acts*, p. 17.

41. On "language games," see Ludwig Wittgenstein, *Philosophical Investigations*, trans. G. E. M. Anscombe, 3rd ed. (New York: Prentice-Hall, 1999) §§23-43.

it seems to me that speech act theory resonates with a more incarnational ontology and anthropology that recognize that human beings are multi-faceted creatures, not just quasi-Cartesian "thinking things." And this res-onates with the elements of a pentecostal worldview that eschew the reductionism of rationalism and affirm the multifaceted aspects of com-munal embodiment. In other words, I think that the distinct pentecostal emphases on an affective epistemology and affirmation of embodiment (as seen in emphases on both physical healing and embodied worship, in-cluding tongues) should lead pentecostal theorists to find a helpful ally in speech act theory, insofar as it recognizes the multifaceted, embodied, communal, and performative elements of language.[42]

Speech act theory, then, provides an account of what language *does*. More specifically, Austin and Searle both distinguish three different kinds of linguistic acts:[43] (1) the *locutionary* act, which involves the vocal utter-ance of phonemes and/or sentences; (2) the *illocutionary* act, which is what one intends to "get done" in the utterance (e.g., promising, commanding, asserting, etc.); and (3) the *perlocutionary* act, which refers to the effect of the utterance (and illocutionary act) on the hearer(s).[44] These acts are of-ten overlaid in the same speech act; for instance, when I move my lips and tongue to utter the phoneme "Stop!" to my son, I am, in this one exclama-tion, uttering a word (a locutionary act), making a command (an illocu-tionary act), and (hopefully) effecting a change in my son's behavior (a perlocutionary act). But there is not a necessary identity between these three. For instance, the same phonematic utterance (e.g., "Sam smokes") can in fact be different illocutionary acts depending on the stance of the speaker. For instance, if I raise my voice at the end of the utterance, the illocutionary act will be a question: "Sam smokes?" If not, the illocution-ary act will be an assertion: "Sam smokes."[45] Furthermore, as Searle notes, "one can perform an utterance [a locutionary act] without performing a

42. Others have employed speech act theory in consideration of charismatic themes and communities. See, for instance, Matthias Wenk, *Community-Forming Power: The Socio-Ethical Role of the Spirit in Luke-Acts,* Journal of Pentecostal Theology Supplement 19 (Shef-field: Sheffield Academic Press, 2000), and Amos Yong, "The Truth of Tongues Speech: A Rejoinder to Frank Macchia," *Journal of Pentecostal Theology,* no. 13 (October 1998): 107-15.

43. Though Searle notes that he does not accept Austin's distinction between *locutionary* and *illocutionary* acts (Searle, *Speech Acts,* p. 23 n. 1).

44. For this threefold distinction, see Searle, *Speech Acts,* pp. 23-26, and Austin, *How to Do Things,* lectures 8-10.

45. Searle, *Speech Acts,* p. 24.

propositional or illocutionary act at all. (One can utter words without saying something.)"[46] Not every sound that comes out of a human mouth is a
speech act.

What is important to note here is that the perlocutionary effect of a
speech act might not be tied to the propositional content of an utterance at
all. What "gets done" by a locutionary act is not necessarily linked to what
is "said" in the act. Searle furnishes an interesting example:

> Suppose that I am an American soldier in the Second World War and
> that I am captured by Italian troops. And suppose also that I wish to get
> these troops to believe that I am a German soldier in order to get them to
> release me. What I would like to do is to tell them in German or Italian
> that I am a German soldier. But let us suppose I don't know enough Ger-
> man or Italian to do that. So I, as it were, attempt to put on a show of tell-
> ing them that I am a German soldier by reciting those few bits of German
> I know, trusting that they don't know enough German to see through my
> plan. Let us suppose I know only one line of German which I remember
> from a poem I had to memorize in a high school German course. There-
> fore, I, a captured American, address my Italian captors with the follow-
> ing sentence: *Kennst du las Land wo die Zitronen blühen?*[47]

As Searle notes, when I say, *Kennst du das Land . . .* , I do not intend to ask
whether the hearer "knows the land where the lemon trees bloom"; rather,
my intent is to *effect* something in the hearer, namely, the belief that I am a
German soldier. The content of the utterance in this case is completely irrelevant to that intended perlocutionary effect. In fact, what will be more
important are the guttural aspects of the actual phonemes that I utter,
which no doubt I will do with as much Germanic gusto as I can muster.
Speech act theory provides a unique account of the way language *works* —
or more specifically, that language is a realm of action that does work be-

---

46. Searle, *Speech Acts*, p. 24. Below, however, I will raise the question whether it is legitimate for Searle to confine speech acts, as he seems to do here, to *saying something.* Could it
not be the case that if speech is performative — that if speech *does* things — it might do
things beyond *saying?* Of course, I think we still need to distinguish speech acts from mere
noisemaking; I just think the distinction is harder to draw, and much that might seem like
noise (given speech act theory's sententional bias) might count as speech acts. But insofar as
speech act theory is interested in distinguishing noise from speech acts, it might also provide
a helpful critical framework for establishing the authentic practice of glossolalia for the
ecclesial community.

47. Searle, *Speech Acts*, p. 44.

yond the narrow task of conveying ideas from one mind to another. As such, it also does justice to the pluriform ways that language functions in different contexts and for different interests. As Kevin Vanhoozer summarizes, "Each sphere of life in which language is used develops its own relatively stable types of use."[48]

Now, how does speech act theory serve to illuminate a consideration of tongues-speech? In order to consider this, I want to bracket xenolalia, since clearly tongues-speech that involves the utterance of known languages (albeit without the prior knowledge of the utterer) would operate according to the given rules of that language and thus could be easily subsumed under standard speech act analysis. Instead, I want to take the "hard" case of ecstatic religious speech that is not identified as a known language and does not conform to the conventions of a given language.[49] To do so, I will consider a common scenario in contemporary pentecostal communities: prayers in tongues-speech uttered during an "altar call." Consider the following example:

> At the conclusion of a worship service focused on physical healing, the pastor invites the entire church to spend time at the front of the sanctuary — "at the altar" — in a time of prayer. Those with specific needs for physical healing are first invited to the altar, as a demonstration of faith and to seek healing from God. Others in the congregation are then invited to join them at the front, encircling each individual, laying hands on them, asking their specific prayer need, and then praying with them for healing. Seven people have gone to the altar for prayer, and gathered around each are five or six men and women interceding on their behalf. In a couple of the groups, intercessors begin to pray "in tongues" — in a kind of ecstatic speech that does not conform to a known language: "hack shukuna ash tuu kononai; mee upsukuna shill adonai; etc."[50]

48. Vanhoozer, *Is There a Meaning?* p. 210.

49. It should be noted, however, that even ecstatic tongues-speech has been shown to conform to a certain kind of convention or habit of phonematic formulation. See E. M. Pattison, "Behavioral Science Research on the Nature of Glossolalia," *Journal of the American Scientific Affiliation* (September 1968). To identify a mode of tongues-speech as "ecstatic" is not to deny that it is conventional, but only to deny that it conforms to the conventions of a given, known language. Indeed, if ecstatic tongues-speech were not conventional in some way, it could not count as a speech act, since the definition of a speech act is an utterance governed by (some kind of) rules.

50. I will also bracket normative theological considerations about whether such practices are warranted by the New Testament.

Does speech act theory help us to understand what is happening here? I think so. The question we should ask is *not*, "What does this prayer *mean?*" but rather, "What does this prayer *do?*" What is the illocutionary stance of the one praying, and what is the perlocutionary effect on the hearers, especially the person seeking healing? The intention of the prayer is less about *saying* something and more about *doing* something. Let us first consider the illocutionary stance of the person praying. What does the pray-er mean to do? I think we could suggest at least two linguistic acts that accompany such an utterance in this context.[51] First, an *illocutionary* act of *praying* or *beseeching:*[52] the person praying in tongues is, first and foremost, doing just that — *praying,* and praying *to God,* and thus seeking to express a desire to God "in groans too deep for words" (Rom. 8:26). Such a prayer is not intended to communicate propositional content, but rather to express the depth of a desire when "we do not know how to pray as we should" (Rom. 8:26). Such a glossolalic prayer expresses a depth of dependency upon God, and thus a humility before the divine. It also indicates a dependence upon the Holy Spirit in particular since the Spirit is thought to be the one who "intercedes" through such groans (Rom. 8:26) that do not conform to the conventions of a given language. One might say that such a prayer in such a context is a kind of sacramental practice of emptying, recognizing the failure of even language to measure up to such an exchange. Glossolalic prayer is a means of making oneself both receptive to and a conduit of the Spirit's work.

Second, the glossolalic prayer utterance has a *perlocutionary* dimension on the hearers, and in a twofold sense: (1) as a prayer, one of the hearers is God, and the *desired* perlocutionary effect is for God to act in healing; but also (2) the other hearers of the utterance include the person seeking healing and others who are interceding for her. It seems to me that

51. Context is a central feature of speech act theory; what a speech act does or effects shifts with context. The same is true for the utterance of the phonematic string "hack shukuna ash tuu kononai; mee upsukuna shill adonai." In fact, it might be the case that in the sacramental context of the prayer service, this phonematic string "counts" as a speech act, but if something similar were uttered by a toddler it would not. (However, not even the latter is a given, since — as Augustine suggested in book 1 of the *Confessions* — sometimes the garbled phonematic strings and grunts of a baby are intended to have perlocutionary effects (the provision of a bottle, the retrieval of a toy, etc.).

52. Among the illocutionary acts that Searle cites as examples are the English verbs "request" and "demand" (Searle, *Speech Acts,* p. 23). Prayer is clearly a mode of requesting (or even demanding).

the glossolalic utterance also has the perlocutionary effect of encouraging faith in the (human) hearers and encouraging them to open themselves up to the miraculous. In other words, precisely by uttering a speech act that does not conform to "normal" or natural speech, the person who utters the speech act effects on a lingual level what is being sought on a physical or bodily level: a certain "interruption" of the "normal" in order to effect healing. The prayer, then, often has the perlocutionary effect of encouraging openness to such interruptions.[53]

It must be noted that both these illocutionary and perlocutionary acts are produced by utterances whose content is basically irrelevant. Like the American who utters *Kennst du das Land . . .* in order to effect his identification as a German soldier, so the one who prays in tongues utters phonemes that do not have any essential connection to the illocutionary or perlocutionary acts. Indeed, the utterances are not propositions of any sort.

So tongues-speech is a kind of speech act that can be illuminated by the categories of speech act theory, but at the same time it resists one of speech act theory's fundamental assumptions and thus calls for a revision. In fact, for tongues-speech to even "count" as a speech act will require a certain retooling of some basic assumptions in Austin and Searle. As noted above, one of the baseline axioms of speech act theory is that *sentences* are the basic units of language; in other words, for an utterance to "count" as a speech act for Austin, it needs to conform to the rules of what counts as a *sentence*.[54] On that account, the prayer in tongues does not count. But our speech act analysis of a glossolalic utterance above has already yielded philosophical fruit. So why should we assume, as Searle does, that only sentences *do* something when uttered? To get at this differently: Searle offers a basic hypothesis, which is eventually "substantiated": "[A] speaking a language is engaging in a rule-governed form of behavior. To put it more briskly, [A'] talking is performing acts according to rules." Searle takes A' to simply be a (more

53. Of course, there could be a whole host of perlocutionary effects of glossolalic prayer, not all of which are good. For instance, the one uttering such a prayer may do so to bring about the perlocutionary effect of securing a superior status in the religious community, or to "appear spiritual" to those gathered around. These perlocutionary effects are probably as common as (or more common than) those I have described above.

54. "Illocutionary and propositional acts consist characteristically in uttering words in sentences in certain contexts, under certain conditions and with certain intentions" (Searle, *Speech Acts*, pp. 24-25). I will take his qualifier "characteristically" as an open door for suggesting that it could be otherwise, even if we might concede that *for the most part* this is true.

"brisk") restatement of A. But this is not necessarily true. Could there not be a mode of "talking" (speech) that is governed by rules but such rules are not identifiable as the rules of a discernible *language?* It seems that one could affirm A′ but reject A. If one were to properly restate, backwards as it were, A′ in the terms of A, one should say simply that "speaking is engaging in a rule-governed form of behavior"; the stipulation that one must be speaking *a language* (by which Searle seems to mean an identifiable natural language) is unwarranted.[55] Admittedly, Searle's concern is to distinguish vocal utterances that count as speech acts from verbalizations that are simply "noise." What distinguishes the two is precisely the rule-governed character of the former. But it is not at all clear that the only way to secure rule-governed utterances is to require that they submit to the rules of given languages.[56] One could easily imagine utterances being governed by rules, but ones that cannot be mapped onto a given language. For instance, hunters or soldiers on a reconnaissance mission might create a system of "calls" — vocal utterances — that communicate a change in direction, approaching danger, etc. As such, they must be said to count as illocutionary and perlocutionary acts. The case of tongues-speech analyzed above suggests the same and indicates yet another way that glossolalia's resistance to given philosophical categories is nevertheless constructive.

The Politics of Tongues-Speech: A Language of Resistance

In the first sections of this chapter we considered the way in which tongues-speech could be illuminated by three strains in philosophy of

55. This raises fascinating questions that cannot be fully pursued here. But immediately after the above hypothesis, Searle says his goal is to "state some of the rules according to which *we* talk" (*Speech Acts*, p. 22, italics added). But who is this "we"? A later discussion indicates that Searle is a kind of deep structuralist on this score. When discussing the relation of languages to speech acts, he says: "Different human languages, to the extent they are inter-translatable, can be regarded as different conventional realizations of the same underlying rules" (p. 39). So the speech act, in French, *je promets,* and the English speech act, "I promise," are different according to the conventions of utterance but the same according to the supposedly universal "rules" of promising. So while Searle speaks of convention, convention does not go "all the way down" for him. Searle's "we" seems to denote some universal lingual community — a notion I think could be legitimately questioned.

56. Of course, with respect to tongues-speech, if glossolalia is understood as xenolalia, then this stipulation is easily met. But if there is to remain legitimate space for glossolalia as ecstatic speech not hooked to known languages, then the speech act account must be revised.

language, as well as how its resistance to given categories pointed a way forward for philosophy of language. As a kind of vocal utterance on the margins of language, tongues-speech functions as an instructive "limit case" for the philosophy of language. But philosophy of language is not the only mode of philosophical analysis that should find tongues-speech a topic of interest. In this final section I want to consider yet another way in which tongues-speech is a language of resistance that illuminates and is illuminated by another sector of philosophy, namely, social and political philosophy. Speech act theory provides a transition to our second consideration of tongues as a discourse of resistance. As an *action,* one of the things that speaking in tongues *does* is to effect a kind of social resistance to the powers-that-be. Or perhaps we should say that tongues-speech is the language of faith communities that are marginalized by the powers-that-be, and such speech can be indicative of a kind of eschatological resistance to the powers.[57] We might say that the proletariat speaks in tongues.

This account could be substantiated historically (see, e.g., Steve Land and others on early Pentecostal community),[58] but I want to consider this from a contemporary perspective enlisting some insights from the social sciences coupled with the critical theory of Herbert Marcuse and the neo-Marxism of Michael Hardt and Antonio Negri. What we will find, I suggest, is a certain confluence between "Marx and the Holy Ghost."[59]

In his recent analysis of the almost exponential growth of urban poverty, concentrated in slums that parasitically grow on the world's megacities, Mike Davis documents the way in which this is a result of the globalization of capitalism. What we are seeing, he suggests, is the "late capitalist triage of humanity," a "global residuum lacking the strategic economic power of socialized labor, but massively concentrated in a shanty-

57. On "powers," see John Howard Yoder, *The Politics of Jesus,* 2nd ed. (Grand Rapids: Eerdmans, 1994), chapter 8, and Marva Dawn, *Powers, Weakness, and the Tabernacling of God* (Grand Rapids: Eerdmans, 2001).

58. More recently, see Gary B. McGee, " 'The New World of Realities in Which We Live': How Speaking in Tongues Empowered Early Pentecostals," *Pneuma: Journal of the Society for Pentecostal Studies* 30 (2008): 108-35. Robert Beckford, following Michael Dyson, has suggested that for black pentecostals, "speaking in tongues can be experienced as speaking a radical language of equality." Robert Beckford, "Back to My Roots: Speaking in Tongues for a New *Ecclesia," The Bible in Transmission* (Summer 2000): 1. Cp. Beckford, *Dread and Pentecostal: A Political Theology for the Black Church in Britain* (London: SPCK, 2000), pp. 171-73.

59. This is the title of the final section of Mike Davis's essay "Planet of the Slums: Urban Involution and the Informal Proletariat," *New Left Review* 26 (2004): 5-34.

town world encircling the fortified enclaves of the urban rich."[60] But the extent of disempowerment prevents the urban poor from even constituting "a meaningful 'class in itself,' much less a potentially activist 'class for itself.'"[61] Marxist talk of "historical agency" seems misplaced and illusionary.

But here Davis notes a significant shift: "Marx has yielded the historical stage to . . . the Holy Ghost."[62] More specifically, he suggests that Pentecostal Christianity, especially in Latin America and sub-Saharan Africa, now occupies "a social space analogous to that of early twentieth-century socialism and anarchism."[63] In this respect, he draws on the earlier (albeit contested) analysis of Robert Mapes Anderson, who claimed that the "unconscious intent" of Pentecostalism was "revolutionary."[64] Described as "the first major world religion to have grown up almost entirely in the soil of the modern urban slum," pentecostalism "has been growing into what is arguably the largest self-organized movement of urban poor people on the planet."[65] Thus quite contrary to what one might have expected on Marxist terms, Davis sees in pentecostalism a revolutionary streak of radical resistance: "with the Left still largely missing from the slum, the eschatology of Pentecostalism admirably refuses the inhuman destiny of the Third World city that *Slums* [the UN Report] warns about."[66]

But what does this have to do with tongues-speech? While glossolalia is only one of several distinctives of Pentecostal faith and practice, it is a central and particularly symbolic one. I would like to suggest that, at least on a certain level or from a certain angle, tongues-speech could be seen as

60. Davis, "Planet of the Slums," p. 27. Davis's essay considers the findings of the report from UN Habitat, *The Challenge of Slums: Global Report on Human Settlements, 2003* (London: UN-HABITAT, 2003).

61. Davis, "Planet of the Slums," p. 28. He notes that "because uprooted rural migrants and informal workers have been largely dispossessed of fungible labour-power, or reduced to domestic service in the houses of the rich," they "have little access to the culture of collective labour or large-scale class struggle" (p. 28).

62. Davis, "Planet of the Slums," p. 30. Throughout he also suggests a parallel role for "populist Islam," which I will not consider here.

63. Davis, "Planet of the Slums," p. 30.

64. Robert Mapes Anderson, *Vision of the Disinherited: The Making of American Pentecostalism* (Oxford: Oxford University Press, 1979), p. 222. See also Jean Comaroff, *Body of Power, Spirit of Resistance* (Chicago: University of Chicago Press, 1985). For helpful cautions about avoiding Anderson's reductionism, see A. G. Miller, "Pentecostalism as a Social Movement: Beyond the Theory of Deprivation," *Journal of Pentecostal Theology* 9 (1996): 97-114.

65. Davis, "Planet of the Slums," pp. 31, 32.

66. Davis, "Planet of the Slums," p. 34.

the language of the dispossessed — or the language of the "multitude"[67] — precisely because it is a mode of speech that can be an expression that resists the powers and structures of global capitalism and its unjust distribution of wealth. In other words, tongues-speech is a discourse that is symbolic of a deeper and broader desire to resist and call into question the existing economic and political structures. It is the language of a counter-cultural "exilic" community.[68]

I think Marcuse once again provides categories for us to think about this. In his account of late capitalist society (now globalized), Marcuse describes the way in which "the reality principle" — and the corresponding rules of rationality — takes form as the "performance principle": "under its rule society is stratified according to the competitive economic performances of its members."[69] As a result, humans are instrumentalized and alienated from their labor (the negation of the pleasure principle).[70] Even leisure time, supposedly for pleasure, is colonized by work and gives birth to an entertainment industry.[71] What counts as "rational," then, is governed by the material interests of industrial, capitalist society; indeed, this performance principle is what constitutes what counts as "real." But as we noted in chapter 3, Marcuse also points to a chink in the armor of the reality principle: the role of imagination or "phantasy" and its ability to resist the strictures of the performance principle (the late capitalist instantiation of the reality principle). The "mental forces" of imagination and fantasy "remain essentially free from the reality principle" and thus are free to envision the world otherwise.[72] Because this was expressed by the imagination, we noted, Marcuse saw such resistance and revolutionary intimations

67. The "multitude" is Hardt and Negri's term for "the set of all the exploited and the subjugated, a multitude that is directly opposed to Empire" (Michael Hardt and Antonio Negri, *Empire* [Cambridge, MA: Harvard University Press, 2000], p. 393). Cf. their expanded and more recent discussion in *Multitude: War and Democracy in the Age of Empire* (New York: Penguin, 2004).

68. Davis, "Planet of the Slums," p. 33.

69. Herbert Marcuse, *Eros and Civilization: A Philosophical Inquiry into Freud* (Boston: Beacon Press, 1966), p. 44.

70. Marcuse, *Eros and Civilization*, p. 45. Marcuse does suggest the possibility of "libidinal work" that would accord with the pleasure principle (p. 47 n. 45).

71. Marcuse, *Eros and Civilization*, pp. 47-48.

72. Marcuse, *Eros and Civilization*, p. 139. As in Marx, we find in Marcuse a kind of quasi eschatology that envisions (and hopes for) a "nonrepressive civilization." This is decidedly *not* "utopian." In fact, he criticized the reality principle for pushing this hope off into an impossible utopia (p. 143).

in the realm of *art,* and more specifically, in surrealism.[73] But could we not also envision tongues-speech as a kind of linguistic surrealism? If, globally, pentecostalism is the religion of the urban poor (the "multitude"), Davis suggests, this is because it resists the unjust structures of global capitalism, and glossolalia is the language of such resistance — a mode of speech that remains "essentially free from the reality principle" of late capitalist logic (and for that very reason is castigated as "mad").[74] It is the language of an eschatological imagination that imagines the future otherwise — the foreign speech of a coming kingdom.

73. Marcuse, *Eros and Civilization,* pp. 144-45.
74. I would venture a hypothesis that is admittedly anecdotal: as Pentecostal denominations (such as the Assemblies of God in the United States) climb the ladder of social class (John Ashcroft, former attorney general in the Bush administration, is an A/G member), the practice of tongues-speech in congregational worship contexts decreases. This, I would suggest, is precisely because such a "strange" practice does not conform to the rationality (reality principle) of capitalist logic; and insofar as such upwardly mobile congregations are seeking to advance *by* capitalist logic, they eschew the language of resistance.

Pentecostal Contributions
to Christian Philosophy

The cartoon outline has been sketched, inviting the work of other creators to attend to the details, add color from their own rich palettes, even revise the image. In the spirit (Spirit?) of Plantinga's "Advice to Christian Philosophers," my goal has been to encourage and embolden pentecostal philosophers to articulate the unique understanding implicit in pentecostal practice. Working in the space carved out by Reformed epistemologists and other Christian philosophers, pentecostals can make their own unique contributions to current philosophical discussions, working unapologetically *as* pentecostals whose imaginations have been informed by the embodied rhythms of pentecostal worship and spirituality. But while I hope pentecostals can take a seat at the wider philosophical table, I hope they won't forget the simple, humble tables "back home." And if, *mirabile dictu*, pentecostal philosophers come to regularly wander among the dreaming spires, or at least in the vicinity of the Golden Dome and Touchdown Jesus, I hope they will still remain philosophers who also serve their pentecostal sisters and brothers — saints who don't have much time for ontology or epistemology but are nonetheless empowered by the Spirit for mission. May we see wise, faithful philosophy as an expression of that ministry, may our philosophical reflection serve that mission, and may the kingdom even be glimpsed in those thinking in tongues.

Name Index

Subject Index

Aesthetic, pentecostal, 80-85
Affections, xix, 25n.13, 26, 30, 36, 58, 59, 62, 77-78n.72
Affective prefocusing, 80
Assemblies of God, 6n.13, 41n.67, 150n.74
Azusa Street revival, xv, 45, 46, 61, 63, 87

Bethel Pentecostal Tabernacle, xi, xxii

Canadian Theological Society, xi
Canonical theism, 117-20
Charismatic movement, xvi-xvii, 32, 39n.60
Classical Pentecostalism, xv-xvi
Church of God (Cleveland, Tenn.), xv
Cleveland school, the, 6n.13
Cognitive fundamentalism, 75
Cognitive science, 114n.16
Cognitive unconscious, 75
Cognitivism, 52, 56, 59, 74n.62, 119
Concepts, 5-6
Conflict of interpretations, 23-24
Correlationism, 94
Cosmology, 40n.65, 41, 94

Divine action, 104-5

Dualism, 12n.25, 42, 60-61, 91, 93, 96, 99n.29

Eastern Orthodoxy, 88n.1
Embodiment, 41-43, 54-61, 66, 76, 81-82, 101, 114n.16, 141
Emotion, 26, 56n.19, 58, 65-80, 82; and film, 72-80
Emotionalism, 26n.15, 58
Eschatology, 44-46
Experience, xx, xxi, xxii, 12, 13, 16n.33, 25n.11, 25n.13, 30, 43, 71-80, 88, 110-15

Feminist philosophy, xxiiin.33, 13n.27, 26n.15, 57n.21, 63n.29, 64-65n.37

Glossolalia, xxi, 45, 123-50; manual, 134n.20. *See also* Xenolalia

Healing, 12, 13, 41-43, 46, 47, 61, 86, 104, 133, 141, 143, 144-45
Hermeneutics, 22-24, 135-39. *See also* Legitimate sectarian hermeneutic

Imagination, 28, 30, 44, 47, 52, 83-85, 120, 149-50. *See also* Pneumatological imagination

154

Laws of nature, 103-4
Legitimate sectarian hermeneutic, 24-25
Liminality, xx-xxii, 64, 107, 123
Liturgy. *See* Worship

Miracles, 12, 13n.27, 15, 92, 96, 97, 104-5
Music, 77n.72

Narrative. *See* Story
Narrative causality, 70
Naturalism, 34-35, 37, 59, 86-105, 139; en-
    chanted, 89, 97, 102n.38; metaphysical,
    86, 88; methodological, 87, 90, 94n.15,
    104; varieties of, 90-97. *See also* Super-
    naturalism

Pacifism, 46
Participatory ontology, 88-89, 99-101
Pauline epistemology, 68-70
pentecostal (small-*p*), defined, xvii
Perspectivalism, 59
Phenomenology, 126-34
Philosophical anthropology, 13, 43-44,
    54, 57, 59, 62, 72, 76, 111-13; cognitivist,
    113
Philosophical theology, 108, 111
Philosophy, history of, 14-15
Pneumatological imagination, 30-31
Pragmatism, 67-68
Primitivism, 12n.23, 38n.59
Prophecy, 12, 31n.36, 38, 39, 86, 93n.13,
    137, 138
Prosperity gospel, 43
Psychoanalysis, 76-78

Rationalism, critique of, 52-62, 110-14
Reformed epistemology, xviii-xix,
    10n.20, 14n.31, 108-9, 121n.33

Saul's armor, xiv
Semiotics, 126-27
Social imaginary, xviii, 11, 29-32, 81, 84,
    88, 90, 98, 100, 103, 120n.31. *See also*
    Worldview
Society for Pentecostal Studies, xiiin.3,
    1n.1

Society of Christian Philosophers, 1n.1,
    2n.3, 7
Speaking in tongues. *See* Glossolalia
Speech act theory, 139-46
Spirits, 41
Spiritual gifts, 39
Spiritual warfare, 12, 41
Spirituality, pentecostal, xviii, xix-xx,
    xxii, xxiii, 26, 30, 31n.36, 81; carried in
    practices, 11, 15-16; as a form of life
    (Wittgenstein), xx, 112; as interpreta-
    tion, 25-26; and pentecostal
    worldview, 30; relation to pentecostal
    philosophy, 27; relation to theology, 4,
    26-27; relation to worldview, 31-37; as
    sacramental, 76n.67
Story, xxiiin.32, 43-44, 51, 62-71; as narra-
    tive knowledge, 64-65, 69
Supernaturalism, 81n.83, 87, 89-98; anti-,
    92; hyper-, 87, 104; interventionist, 93;
    naive, 87; noninterventionist, 96, 98

Testimony, xxii-xxiv, 9, 13, 48-53, 62-71,
    133, 140
Theology, 3-6, 25-27; as grammar, 3-4;
    relation to philosophy, 3-5
Third Wave, xvi-xvii

Verstehen (understanding), 29, 30,
    58n.24, 64n.35
Virtue epistemology, 69n.52

Wesleyan tradition, xv-xvi
Worldview, 27-29; pentecostal, xviii-xix,
    4, 11-12, 15, 17-47, 52, 81, 82, 86, 87, 103,
    104. *See also* Social imaginary
World Christianity, 31n.36, 33
Worship, xxii, xxiv, 3n.5, 15, 17-22, 30-33,
    39, 43, 51, 59, 76-77, 80, 81-82, 99, 110-
    13, 118-19, 150n.74; body essential to,
    61-62; philosophical anthropology im-
    plicit in, 72; relation to thinking, 25-27

Xenolalia, 124, 132, 143, 146n.56. *See also*
    Glossolalia